UnAfrican
Americans

UnAfrican Americans

Nineteenth-Century
Black Nationalists
and the
Civilizing Mission

Tunde Adeleke

THE UNIVERSITY PRESS OF KENTUCKY

Publication of this volume was made possible in part
by a grant from the National Endowment for the Humanities.

Scholarly publisher for the Commonwealth,
serving Bellarmine College, Berea College, Centre
College of Kentucky, Eastern Kentucky University,
The Filson Club Historical Society, Georgetown College,
Kentucky Historical Society, Kentucky State University,
Morehead State University, Murray State University,
Northern Kentucky University, Transylvania University,
University of Kentucky, University of Louisville,
and Western Kentucky University.

Editorial and Sales Offices: The University Press of Kentucky
663 South Limestone Street, Lexington, Kentucky 40508-4008

98 99 00 01 02   5 4 3 2 1

Library of Congress Cataloging-in-Publication Data

Adeleke, Tunde.
    UnAfrican Americans : nineteenth-century Black nationalists and
the civilizing mission / Tunde Adeleke.
        p.   cm.
    Includes bibliographical references and index.
    ISBN 0–8131–2056–X (cloth : alk. paper)
    1. Black nationalism—United States—History—19th century.
2. Afro-Americans—Relations with Africans—History—19th century.
3. Pan-Africanism—History—19th century.   4. Imperialism—United
States—History—19th century.   I. Title.
E185.625.A34   1998
973´.0496—dc21   97–50430

This book is printed on acid-free recycled paper meeting
the requirements of the American National Standard
for Permanence of Paper for Printed Library Materials.

Manufactured in the United States of America

DEDICATION

This book is dedicated to the memory of three extraordinary human beings. First, my father, Liasu Ajani Adeleke ("Special Ade"), who instilled in me a deep appreciation of the importance of education. Second, Mama Hadiza, who nurtured and raised me. Third, a dear and wonderful friend, Dr. Ernest D. Mason of North Carolina Central University in Durham ("Ernesto," as I fondly called him). The book is also dedicated to "Larai," whose timely intervention saved a naive six-year-old from being swept away by the currents of the River Niger in Ashaka, Midwestern Nigeria, in the early 1950s. I am eternally grateful.

CONTENTS

ACKNOWLEDGMENTS

A project of this magnitude could not have been accomplished without the assistance and contributions, directly and indirectly, of many people. The book grew out of a paper I coauthored with my former teacher, Dr. Johnson Adefila of Bennett College, Greensboro, North Carolina. Dr. Adefila taught me black American history at the University of Ife, Nigeria (now Obafemi Awolowo University), in the late 1970s. He is responsible for kindling my interest in black American history. After a hiatus, we reestablished contact during my one-year visit to North Carolina State University in 1994-95. We decided to mark our reunion with a joint presentation and chose the topic "The Imperial Factor in Late Nineteenth Century Black American Nationalism." The paper was presented to the annual meeting of the Southern Conference on Afro-American Studies, in Baton Rouge, Louisiana, in February of 1995. After the conference, I assumed sole responsibility for revising the paper for publication. Attempting to shorten a forty-page article on such a topic proved difficult, as I continually confronted the challenge of further explaining and contextualizing complex issues. It quickly became obvious that the subject deserved much broader coverage and study. The result is this book. My sincere gratitude to Dr. Adefila for being a part of the gestation process and, above all else, for inspiring my interest in black diaspora studies.

In North Carolina, I was also reunited with Onaiwu Wilson Ogbomo, my former student at the University of Maiduguri, Nigeria, who was then with North Carolina Central University and who has since moved to Allegheny College, where he remains a very close friend and colleague. Special thanks to Wilson for his insightful comments on the article. Several of his suggestions for improvement have been incorporated into the book. My sojourn in North Carolina would most certainly have been difficult were it not for Wilson and his lovely wife, Queen. Two other individuals made my North Carolina experience intellectually nourishing and rewarding. First, the late Dr. Ernest D. Mason, to whose memory this book is dedicated. Always ready and willing to assist, generous with his time and resources, "Ernesto" was quintessentially African. He epitomized the true African personality that many black Americans theorize about but hardly emulate. The ideas developed in this book in fact took shape in the course of the intellectual discourses we had during our occasional "boxing" vigils in his home in Chapel Hill. He did not always agree with my contentions. Second, Dr. Joyce Russell, now of Fayetteville State University, whom I met through "Ernesto." Joyce has been steadfastly friendly and intellectually engaging and supportive.

I must acknowledge my intellectual indebtedness to two other scholars who have been instrumental in shaping my academic career, and whose accomplishments remain a shining example of intellectual excellence: Professors Ian Steele and Craig Simpson, my teachers and wonderful friends at the University of Western Ontario, London, Canada. They not only guided my intellectual travail at Western, but also have been steadfastly supportive of my academic endeavors and pursuits. I could never repay their generosity and efforts in the support and furtherance of my intellectual and professional advancement. They inspired this book in ways they could not have imagined. Their intellectual accomplishments have always served as a source of pride and inspiration, reinforcing in me the notion of academia as a place for productive scholarship. Over the years I have benefited immensely from the generosity and friendship of Winston and Sheila Husbands of Toronto, Ontario, Canada. Our relationship began in the early 1980s on the intellectual terrain of "purple and proud WESTERN." It is indeed a testimony to the depth of the love and mutual respect binding us that distance has not separated us. We have remained close, and our relationship has strengthened. The two anonymous readers of the University Press of Kentucky deserve credit for critical comments and insights that undoubtedly improved the quality of this work. Davina McClain and Wilfred Major, both of the Department of Classics, Loyola University, deserve my gratitude for being always willing and ready to provide assistance when I encountered the many computer glitches that arose during the preparation of this book. My colleagues and friends of the History Department at Loyola deserve recognition for their support and encouragement: David Moore, Maurice Brungard, Bernard Cook, Nancy Anderson, Sister Grace Swift, Robert Gerlich, Leo Nichol and Mark Fernandez. The History Department of Loyola University remains indisputably the quintessence of congeniality and collegiality. Although all of the aforementioned scholars have thus been a part of this project, I bear sole responsibility for the ideas and theses advanced in the book, for their implications, and for any and all errors associated with them.

This book could not have been completed without the love, support, and sacrifices of my wonderful and loving family—my wife and friend, Gloria, and our children, Tosin, Toyin, and, the gem of the family, Chinyere. Finally, I must acknowledge the deep and abiding love and support of my mother, brothers, and sisters in Nigeria: Hajiya Aminatu, Raufu, Ganiyu, Mosudi, Muritala, Fausa, Mukaila, Isiaka, Idaya, Morili, Dauda and Lati. This book is for you all. My self-imposed exile has been both emotionally and psychologically painful and unsettling. Through it all, God and the spirits of our ancestors have sustained us. Distance could never obliterate the love and bond we share.

PREFACE

This study attempts to bridge an intellectual lacuna. Black American nationalism has been a particularly engaging subject since it attracted scholarly and popular interest in consequence of the Civil Rights upsurge of the 1960s. The outpouring of scholarly books and articles, especially in the last two decades, has tremendously enriched our understanding of the subject. There are critical studies of the careers of leading black nationalists; of their ideas, ideologies, and schemes; of the internal and external dynamics of their nationalism; and of the response and relationship of black American nationalism to the broader Euro-American culture and nationalism. The phenomenon of black nationalism has historically been depicted as a radical movement directed against enslavement, domination, and oppression. This view of black nationalism as based in conflict, or as countercultural and "militant," has been the most emphasized and, consequently, seems to have shaped the general conception of the subject. It has become conventional to presume a certain militancy in all black nationalists. This tendency remains perhaps one of the most enduring legacies of the Civil Rights context that ignited scholarly interest in the subject. It took a while before scholars began to broaden the perspective of analysis, and acknowledge the nuances and complexity of black American nationalism.

The thoughts of black American nationalists encapsulate a complex mix of ideologies and programs—accommodation, integration, separatism, and cultural pluralism. The "militant" dimension, often associated with separatism and emigrationism, especially in considerations of the second half of the nineteenth century, has received wider coverage, and its complexity and nuances widely recognized. Several studies focus more attention on the reactive and contradictory character of black American nationalism, underscoring two critical factors: first, that it developed in reaction to, and against, the policies and experiences emanating from the Euro-American contact, and second, that it harbored a curious paradox reflected in adaptations of elements of the Euro-American worldview against which it was contrived. There is, however, a third and equally critical perspective that has curiously been ignored. The paradox/contradiction eventuated in a compromise or synthesis designed to harmonize two previously discordant elements—black American and Euro-American nationalism. The contradiction that many scholars acknowledge and perhaps even lament is therefore not as critical, if examined from an African perspective, as the compromise and synthesis that eventually developed. Although black American nationalists initially rejected and criticized Euro-American influences and their hegemonic disposition, even while imbibing Euro-American values, there was a far greater degree of compromise between the two. Black American nationalists not only imbibed Anglo-Saxon values, but also articulated and forcefully defended the imperial ambitions of Anglo-Saxon nationalism.

There was, therefore, a "marriage" between black American nationalism and European nationalism. Emerging from contradictory backgrounds, the two eventually harmonized, a development that bore ominous consequences for Africa's territorial integrity and sovereignty. The facts of initial conflict and the appearance of contradiction between them notwithstanding, these traditions of nationalism laid a strong foundation for the European partitioning and occupation of Africa. Black American nationalism thus harbored a far deeper contradiction than has been acknowledged. It seems pertinent, therefore, to confront and critically analyze the contradiction from an African perspective. The objective is not to disparage or cast aspersion at any individual or group, but to highlight the dynamics and nuances of a historical contradiction with a view to broadening the perspective of analysis and enriching understanding of a historical phenomenon. Such factors as race, ethnicity, culture, and class shaped the articulation, formulation, and projection of black American nationalism in more complex ways than have been discerned.

What this study does is present black American nationalism from a perspective that traditional and prevailing paradigms and approaches have largely ignored: the African. This negligence has made it difficult to unravel the contradiction and paradoxes in black American nationalism to their fullest ramifications. The prevailing and popular tendency has been to portray black American nationalists as ideological combatants, struggling to defend African/black interests against Euro-American hegemonic drives. Although factual to a considerable degree, this perspective fails to explore the convergence of black American and Euro-American nationalisms and, *ipso facto*, the underlying contradiction between black American nationalism and African interests and nationalism. This study suggests that indigenous Africans probably did not see black American nationalists as combatants in defense and furtherance of Africa's interests.

Black American Nationalism: Definition, Background, Concepts

In his *Nations and Nationalism,* Ernest Gellner defines nationalism as "primarily a political principle, which holds that the political and the national unit should be congruent."[1] Nationalist sentiments and movements have historically evolved in response to the lack of this congruence. The existence of national harmony or disharmony is often influenced and sustained by an assortment of economic, social, political, and cultural factors. The lack of a correspondence between a political unit and its constituent nations is unmistakably the defining character of an oppressive and dysfunctional polity. Wherever one confronts this disharmonious and oppressive context, one is most likely to witness the generation and evolution of nationalist consciousness. The nonexistence of such correspondence or compatibility has consequently been the underlying dynamic of black American nationalism from time immemorial. The glaring contradiction between the historical profession of a liberal, open, and democratic American society/culture and the reality of slavery, racism, and segregation aroused black American national consciousness.

The denial to a people of basic human dignity and freedom often induces alienation and protest. In its protest mode, therefore, nationalism expresses desires, goals, and visions that are often encapsulated in such values as equality, freedom, and sovereignty. The quest for these ideals is usually associated with affirmations of the need for unity and common identity. People are drawn together by the accompaniments of group identity: shared experiences or cultural attributes. John Hutchinson and Anthony Smith provide the following summation of the dynamics and essential elements of nationalism:

Nationalism was, first of all, a doctrine of popular freedom and sovereignty. The people must be liberated—that is, free from any external constraint; they must determine their own destiny and be masters of their own house; they must control their own resources; they must obey their own "inner" voice. But that entailed fraternity. They must be united; they must dissolve all internal divisions; they must be gathered together in a single historic territory, a homeland; and they must have legal equality and share a single public culture. But which culture and what territory? Only a homeland that was "theirs" by historic right, the land of their forebears; only a culture that was "theirs" as a heritage, passed down the generations, and therefore an expression of their authentic identity.[2]

Nigerian scholar E.U. Essien-Udom, a leading authority on black American nationalism, underscores essentially the same factors in his widely quoted definition. According to him, nationalism expresses "the belief of a group that it possesses, or ought to possess, a country; that it shares, or ought to share, a common heritage of language, culture and religion; that its heritage, way of life, and ethnic identity are distinct from those of other groups."[3] The two definitions rightly identify autonomy, identity, and unity as crucial components of nationalism.

Although significant to the nationalist aspirations of black Americans in the nineteenth century, the quest for autonomy, identified with an independent nation or homeland, was the least desirable and most fragile of the elements. Among black Americans, the desire for a homeland shaped both the emigration culture of the nineteenth century and the Pan-African and protest movement later spearheaded by Marcus Garvey in the early twentieth century. The desire for autonomy also surfaced in the anti-establishment and religious nationalism of the Black Muslims (about whom Essien-Udom wrote), and in many of the other anti-establishment and countercultural groups of the militant 1960s.[4] For much of its history, however, black American nationalism expressed deep-rooted American consciousness. Black Americans generally longed to be identified and accepted as Americans. This explains why, for much of the eighteenth and nineteenth centuries, black American nationalists, and indeed, black American leaders in general, regardless of ideological disposition, espoused integrationist aspirations and values. They all combined feelings of alienation and deprivation with faith in classic American middle-class values of industry, thrift, and economy. This faith informed the universalist ethos of the early Negro Conventions and the moral suasionist ideology that shaped them. It also shaped the integrationist values and aspirations of Frederick Douglass and the accommodationist ethics of Booker T. Washington. There is, therefore, a certain truth to Alphonso Pinckney's poignant assertion that "in any discussion of nationalism among black people in the United States, one must somehow contend with what appears to be a complex of contradictions."[5]

The inception of slavery and oppression set in motion, albeit imperceptibly to the eyes of slavocrats, the processes that eventually nurtured nationalist consciousness in blacks. The cruel paradox of American history—that is, the juxtaposition of two visibly contradictory experiences, freedom and slavery— sustained black nationalist consciousness. Although enslaved, brutalized, and dehumanized, blacks were exposed to the lure of the life-affirming, life-sustaining, and elevating qualities of freedom. Rather than succumb to the fatalism and self-abnegating culture of slavery, they opted for the freedom to be themselves and to control their destinies and resources. Confronted by a society and nation bent on keeping them down, they endeavored to unify their consciousness and resources for mutual elevation.

This unifying consciousness assumed different forms and did not always yield positive results. It shaped the insurrectionary traditions of Nat Turner, Gabriel Prosser, and Denmark Vesey, the numerous self-help and cooperative activities of northern free blacks, and black abolitionist efforts in general. The drive for unity of purpose and direction also conditioned the emigrationist and nationalist platforms and movements of the mid-nineteenth century and beyond. In all these cases, segments of an oppressed and marginalized group organized to more effectively advance the cause of freedom and justice. The quest for a homeland, often associated with emigration and the Pan-African movements, assumed preeminence in the second half of the nineteenth century and resulted from frustrations over the intractable and elusive American nationality. Feeling rejected and alienated, blacks turned toward Africa, the land of their ancestors. Africa offered solace and hope. Above all else, it offered the basis of an identity, inspired a sense of worthiness, and awoke a consciousness of a rich and significant history. In essence, Africa instilled hope and confidence in possibilities beyond the range of the limited and gloomy horizon of enslavement.

The study of black American nationalism, like the study of nationalism in general, is a relatively recent phenomenon. As an ideology and movement, nationalism did not become a contentious force in black American history until the second half of the nineteenth century, and it did not become a subject of serious scholarly inquiry until almost a century later. The civil rights movement and the black militant resurgence of the 1960s thrust black American nationalism into prominence, making it a field of serious scholarly research. A potent force in the evolution and development of nations, nationalism continues to energize contemporary international relations. It is at the root of some of the major crises in Asia, Ireland, the Middle East, Africa, and Eastern Europe.

A product of cross-cultural interactions, nationalism can be traced to the very beginning of human contacts. Similarly, the root of black American nationalism has been traced to the institution of slavery. Black Americans were forcibly brought to the New World and subjected to the shock of a new experience. They were enslaved and socialized to acknowledge the morality and legitimacy of slavery. Contrary to the designs and expectations of the slavocrats, however, enslavement nurtured and shaped black nationalist consciousness. Most experts conceive of black American nationalist consciousness as a product of shared experiences—both negative and positive— that led to the construction of group identity, an identity that is often premised on experiential and historical compatibility. In other words, contrary to the ideology of slavery, which propagated a gloomy and psychologically destructive conception of black history, contrived to induce in the enslaved a fatalistic and complacent disposition, slaves actually developed complex responses that bolstered emancipatory consciousness. The development of this consciousness represents one of the unintended consequences of slavery. Blacks were supposed to be docile slaves, with their visions defined by and limited to the horizon of the master class. The ideology of slavery offered blacks no vision of a credible past and no hope of a bright future outside the plantation. Enslavement was deemed the beginning of history and civilized existence, the formative agent that would transform blacks into civilized beings, its brutality and inhumanity notwithstanding. Instead of developing a viable historical and cultural consciousness, slaves were expected to have a bleak image of themselves and their past. Paradoxically, out of the brutalities, contradictions, and challenges of slavery, blacks evolved different reactions that challenged and negated the vision and values of the master class. Africa was central to the formation and sustenance of this protest culture. Blacks found solace and transcended the limitations imposed by slavery in residual African cultural values and norms. The world of the slave was thus not totally controlled by, and shaped according to the will of, the masters. Slaves created a "primary environment" separated from the purview of the "secondary environment" of the master's domain. Within this primary environment, they assumed roles that contradicted the expectations of the plantation, roles that nurtured emancipatory vision and consciousness.[6] Central to this self-enhancing and elevating consciousness was a strong sense of identity with Africa. In the eighteenth and nineteenth centuries, blacks in Philadelphia, New York, Boston, Chicago, Detroit, and other northern cities formed African societies and institutions. Africa was the centerpoint of their struggle. Subjected to the most inhumane experiences, many blacks, slave and free, sought emotional relief by arming themselves with the only positive cultural experience they retained consciousness of: Africa.

By the late eighteenth century, with the process of Afro-Americanization or acculturation at an advanced stage, and African consciousness growing distant and fuzzy, black American consciousness became increasingly reflective of the complex cultural experiences of the New World. The consciousness of shared historical, cultural, and even ethnic identity, as blacks of African ancestry, began to compete with a growing integrative consciousness emanating from the reality of New World acculturation. As Africa became remote, black American national consciousness projected aspirations that were quintessentially American. The reality and experience of being born in America, coupled with contributions to the development of the nation, bolstered black Americans in affirming and proclaiming their American identity. Their aspirations betrayed a strong integrative tendency, even as many continued to embrace Africa. This integrative mind-set propelled the abolitionist crusade. The quest for this American nationality, however, shaped both integrative and emigrative orientations. Integrationists evinced a more optimistic attitude toward the possibility of achieving American nationality.

Emigrationists took a more pessimistic view of America and sought a new life in a predominantly black/African setting abroad. Denied rights and privileges, constantly frustrated and marginalized, these blacks turned to Africa, which became the solution to the problem of American nationality. The turn to Africa notwithstanding, emigrationists harbored very deep integrationist ambitions. Critics have often de-emphasized or outrightly ignored the integrative essence of emigration. Emigration was not aimed solely at building an external state. Equally critical to emigrationism was the objective of positively transforming the American context, that is, bringing an end to oppression (slavery and racism) and winning meaningful freedom, equality, and the benefits of American nationality for the millions of blacks, slave and free, who were left behind. Infused with a strong consciousness of being part of the American nation, black Americans, regardless of ideological disposition, boldly staked their claim to American identity and all the accompanying rights and privileges. Although Africa remained alive in their consciousness, they evinced a deep sense of affinity to the United States. In essence, black Americans combined a strong affection for Africa with an equally strong, perhaps even stronger, commitment to becoming fully and beneficially American. Black American nationalism was thus characterized by a dual national consciousness, by ambivalence on the question of identity. America was never completely out of the equation, even in the calculations of those who embraced Africa. There were frequent shifts between demands for American and African nationalities. This dual character or ambivalence has provoked controversy among scholars on the true nature of black American nationalism.

Numerous studies of black American nationalism have addressed its contents, theoretical underpinnings, and historical development. The last twenty years, in fact, have witnessed the publication of largely revisionist studies that deal critically with some of its theoretical, axiological, pragmatic, and cultural nuances. Three distinct historical traditions of black American nationalism have been identified as predominant. The first category encompasses the nationalist aspirations and values of those who either contemplated or used violence to attain American nationality. Driven by the brutalities of slavery, some individuals or groups adopted extreme and violent strategies. To this category also belong those who simply theorized on the nationality problem. Examples are the insurrectionary ethics of Nat

Turner, Gabriel Prosser, and Denmark Vesey and the revolutionary and apocalyptic visions of David Walker. The second category encompasses essentially the moderate, optimistic aspirations and visions of those who sought the rights and privileges of American nationality peacefully. Black abolitionism, especially the moral suasion imperative that shaped black American protest thought in the first half of the nineteenth century, belongs in this group. The third category is the Pan-African tradition, composed mainly of emigrationists who had given up on the country and who sought an alternative nationality in Africa.

The emigration/Pan-African alternative, however, is a complex category that has been the subject of gross ideological simplification, resulting in a blurring and misunderstanding of its inner dynamics and contradictions. There has been a tendency to ascribe Pan-Africanism to anyone who advocates cooperation between blacks in the diaspora and Africa. This presumption emanated from the ideological climate of the militant 1960s. Scholarly interest in black American nationalism, which gathered momentum in the aftermath of the civil rights movement, perforce embraced the instrumentalist and militant slant of the historiography of the epoch. The consequence has been a narrow and skewed interpretation of black American nationalism, often leaving unexplored the broader, complex, and very often ambivalent socioeconomic and cultural dynamics of the relationships between black Americans and Africa. The construction of black American nationalism within an instrumentalist mold fostered the mistaken perception of it as an inherently radical phenomenon. The prominence of militant nationalist movements and groups in the 1960s, such as the Black Power, Black Panther, and Black Muslim movements, informed the perception of black American nationalism as inherently and historically anti-establishment and anti-American. Recent studies, however, show that, as radical as the nationalism of the 1960s seemed, its character was complex and that movements and leaders often displayed complex, fluid, and dynamic idiosyncrasies. This fluidity was not peculiar to the 1960s, but it has been a consistent feature of black nationalism and black American leadership. Depending on circumstances, the same person often switched between pro- and anti-establishment positions. Such flexibility characterized black leadership styles in the nineteenth century.[7] In essence, there was a greater degree of pragmatism to black

American nationalism than has hitherto been acknowledged. This nationalism exhibited a kaleidoscopic character, embracing various economic, political, cultural, religious, and intellectual visions, including aspirations and strategies that were sometimes radical, sometimes conservative, sometimes revolutionary, and sometimes accommodationist.

Regardless of the particular vision, black American nationalism expressed a people's desire for self-determination, for progress, and for the essential and indispensable rights and privileges of free humanity. Thus, nationalism was at times racially constructed and ideological. But its contradictory nature can be traced to the fact that often it was also pragmatic and complex. This pragmatism demands a serious reconsideration of the monolithic paradigms (the conception of a simple black American/African mutuality, for example) that contemporary radical cultural and political nationalists apply to black American history, to black nationalism, and to the relationship between Africa and the black diaspora. In other words, there has been a tendency to overemphasize doctrinaire and ideological posturing and rhetoric at the expense of the more realistic, and perhaps even more crucial, paradoxes and ambivalence. Blacks who espoused nationalist and Pan-African ideas and ideals have been deemed militant and radical. This reductionist perception beclouds the complexity of nationalism. It is only in the last two decades that scholars have begun to move away from the radical perspective and that revisionist accounts of the black American experience have begun to illuminate its cosmopolitanism and complexity. The scholarship of Wilson J. Moses, Sterling Stuckey, August Meier, Elliott Rudwick, Ottey Scruggs, Bill McAdoo, and Gregory Rigsby, to name a few, underscores the ambivalent and complex nature of black American nationalism: the profession of identity with Africa was matched by an abiding interest and faith in cultural affinity with Euro-America.

This work is conceived in the revisionist mold, and it delves into the intricacies and complexities of black American nationalism in the second half of the nineteenth century. It is not a historical survey of the origin and development of black nationalism, however, but a critique of the values and orientation of some of its notable proponents: Martin Delany, Alexander Crummell, and Henry McNeal Turner. Several scholars, including those identified above, have enriched our knowledge of the history and development of black American nationalism, and some have even undertaken critical studies of its values, goals, and visions, thus illuminating its flexibility, fluidity, and changing dynamics through history. This complexity was often graphically displayed in the lives, careers, and ideological idiosyncracies of leading nationalists.

The theoretical anchor of this study is the European imperial concept of the "civilizing mission" (*mission civilisatrice*). Europeans depicted their intrusion into Africa as a humanitarian endeavor, inspired by a disinterested commitment to the universalization of the benefits of "superior" European civilization. They supposedly embarked on a mission to extend the frontiers of civilization to Africa. Backed by a strong nationalist ideology, European imperialists gravitated toward Africa, occupying the entire continent (with the exception of Liberia and Ethiopia) by the second decade of the twentieth century. Although revisionist studies discern a strong ideological linkage between black American nationalism and the civilizing mission, little work has been done beyond acknowledging this relationship. This study therefore seeks to fill this gap by moving beyond acknowledging cultural and ideological linkages to probing their practical and imperialist ramifications. In other words, if both Europeans and black American nationalists embraced and shared a worldview ensconced in the concept of a civilizing mission, it seems appropriate to, first, examine the extent to which black American nationalists defended, sustained, and strengthened this relationship and, second, determine the implications of their actions for both normative Victorian assumptions about, and traditional paradigms for studying, Africa and the black diaspora nexus. Consequently, this study is a critical analysis of the implications of the imperialist values and orientations of late-nineteenth-century black American nationalism. The theoretical framework benefits from recent scholarship on the relationship between race and the ideological construction of imperialism. The works of J.M. Blaut, Paul Gordon Lauren, Audrey Smedley, and Jan Nederveen Pieterse, among others, have opened up new perspectives on the imperialist ramifications of race and racism. Although utilizing different perspectives and contexts, these scholars deal extensively with the relationship between race and the construction of a hegemonic worldview, facilitating a broader and deeper analysis of the relationship between black American nationalism and Euro-American civilization.[8]

There was a certain duality to black American nationalism in the era covered in this study. It embraced a complex mix of values that at times simultaneously projected anti- and pro-establishment agendas, both within the United States and abroad. It often combined racially exclusive and racially inclusive, anti- and pro-imperialist strategies and agendas. Leading advocates erased the racial boundaries as often as they drew them, staking paradoxical positions. Unfortunately, the pro-imperialist dimension has not been explored in greater depth, despite the acknowledgment of its existence. On the contrary, radical nationalist historiography tends to perceive a certain consistency in the ideological and practical schemes of black nationalists. Delany, Turner, and (to a certain degree) Crummell have all been depicted as inspired by deep nationalist and Pan-Africanist aspirations and consciousness in their schemes for the freedom and elevation of fellow blacks and Africans. In furthering their schemes, however, these nationalists displayed ideological ambivalence by embracing the ideals of the dominant Euro-American culture against which they (especially Delany and Turner) professed to be struggling. The bond between black American nationalism and European nationalism extended beyond ideological compatibility to a shared imperialistic vision. The appearance of conflict between the two, highlighted by many scholars, is indeed deceptive. Black American nationalists played an activist role in shaping and legitimizing European imperialism in Africa. Although European statesmen, politicians, missionaries, explorers, and traders were highly visible and vocal in articulating, projecting, and legitimizing imperialistic ideas and schemes in Africa, black American nationalists remained active in the background, strongly prodding and encouraging the Europeans with much needed moral support. By engaging this intriguing and neglected subject, I hope not only to illuminate the pragmatic and complex nature of black American nationalism but also to broaden understanding of the dynamics and nuances of the historical relationship between Africa and the black diaspora.

It is important at this juncture to define and clarify my understanding of certain key words and phrases that recur throughout the pages of this book. A *nationalist* is anyone who articulates the core ideas and values in the definitions of nationalism by Hutchinson and Smith and Essien-Udom—the desire for freedom and liberation from oppressive conditions, emphasis on black people acquiring greater control over their destinies and resources, a conviction that blacks, regardless of geographical location, share identity, cultural and historical experiences, and emphasis on a distinct black worldview, culture, and heritage. The articulation of these ideals and convictions in itself does not make one a nationalist. What distinguishes a nationalist is the ability to translate those convictions into concrete actions aimed at the realization or defense of the ideals. In other words, any black person who actively participates in effecting a convergence or congruence between the professed ideals and values of the American polity and the aspirations and interests of blacks is a black nationalist. Very few outstanding individuals have manifested this quality. A racist and oppressive context such as blacks confronted, and still confront, in America breeds feelings of alienation in many, inducing aspirations for positive and meaningful changes. Historically, however, few have been willing and able to seek change. Those who are able to transcend alienation and engage actively in the practical exigencies of change are the true nationalists. In attempting to spearhead change, they often mobilize and invoke national consciousness.

National consciousness refers to the conviction that blacks as a group share certain unique and unifying experiences, which form the basis of confraternity and confer a defining character on the group. The concept "black American nation" and the characterization of black Americans as "a nation within a nation" represent manifestations or expressions of national consciousness. Black Americans have historically laid claim to American nationality. Many have boldly asserted and defended this claim and have sought recognition and acceptance through the conferment of the rights and privileges of American citizenry. Others who have become frustrated by the elusive character of American nationality have turned their searchlights abroad for an alternative and independent black or African nationality that would serve as the geographical base that confers legitimacy and international recognition to the struggles and aspirations of blacks, while solidifying their national consciousness.

Those individuals whose national consciousness betrays enduring faith in the American nationality are referred to in this study as *integrationists.* Their ideological opponents are the *emigrationists,* who sought an independent nationality abroad. *Pan-Africanism* represents the highest expression of black nationalism. It developed out

of the conviction that Africans and blacks in diaspora share historical, cultural experiences and worldview and that these should constitute the bedrock for solidarity in the face of enthralling and compelling adversity. This consciousness and the movement it engendered
originated among blacks in the diaspora. Most scholars identify the
subjects of this study—Delany, Crummell, and Turner—among the
pioneers of Pan-Africanism.

The Cultural Context of Black Nationalism: Racist Ideology and the Civilizing Mission

An informed and holistic study of black American nationalism in the second half of the nineteenth century has to begin with an understanding of the ideological and cultural context that both inspired and shaped its core ideas and programs. This nationalism developed within the broader Euro-American cultural nationalism, flowering contemporaneously with the latter, albeit in reaction and opposition to it. Black nationalism evolved out of the context and ramifications of the historic encounter between Europe and Africa. Over time, black American nationalists appropriated the values and idiosyncrasies that distinguished Euro-American nationalism and expansionism. In spite of this intimate connection, scholars have yet to subject the expansionist and imperialist character of black American nationalism to critical analysis and exposition.

The second half of the nineteenth century has gone down in history as the age of the *mission civilisatrice*. Driven by a combination of factors on which scholarly opinions remain sharply divided— economic, diplomatic, psychological, political, and social—Europeans embarked on a historic drive to occupy the lands of, and to impose their rule on, the weaker and less developed societies of the world, under the guise of extending the frontiers of civilization. Motivated and energized by an expansionist and holier-than-thou worldview, Europeans proceeded to intervene in the course of developments in other parts of the world. This imperial extroversion was disguised as an impulsive and disinterested humanitarian calling to extend the benefits of "superior" European values and civilization to the "primitive" societies of the non-European parts of the globe. The "civilizing mission" was thus stamped with the mark of divinity and historical inevitability. Scientific, historical, and ideological postulations legitimized the "civilizing mission" and defended a Manichaean construction of the world. The world was perceived as consisting of an advanced, civilized European sector and a primitive, backward, non-European sector.

Europeans viewed the world through culturally and ideologically skewed and tinted lenses. Through these lenses, they saw a vast external world of fundamental difference defined by "primitivism" and "absences" (that is, absence of the "superior values" and cultural and material accomplishments of Europeans).[1] The ethnological and cultural divergences of the two spheres were deemed sufficient justifications for the preeminence of one sphere over the other. In other words, the "inherently backward" and "primitive" non-European sector had perforce to defer to the hegemony of the advanced European sector. Imperialism was consequently balanced on this bipolar global construct: two culturally and ethnologically distinct but unilaterally interactive sectors—a dynamic and innovative center and a sterile and ahistorical periphery.

Imperialism remains a subject of controversy, and its students must confront conflicting definitions and conceptions. We can assume, however, that during what J.M. Blaut calls its "classical age" (the nineteenth century), diffusionist values, reflective of the ethnocentric and cultural biases that informed Europe's "tunnel vision" of the world, propelled imperialism along its course. Imperialists dichotomized reality into an Inside (Europe) and an Outside (non-Europe). The Outside was perceived from the vantage point of the Inside. According to Blaut, "World history thus far has been, basically, the history of the Inside. Outside has been, basically, irrelevant. History and historical geography as it was taught, written, and thought by Europeans down to the time of World War II, and still . . . in most respects today, lies as it were in a tunnel of time. The walls of this tunnel are, figuratively, the spatial boundaries of Greater Europe. History is a matter of looking back or down in this European tunnel of time and trying to decide what happened where, when, and why."[2]

This tunnel vision bore and sustained Europe's assertive power and force. It legitimized self-exaltation and self-glorification at the expense of the diminished and devalued Outside. Herein lies the legitimizing factor of imperialism. Christine Bolt's concise definition of imperialism as "sustained assertion of power over others, and the development of justification for its assertion," underlines two of the cardinal elements of European imperialism as it relates to Africa—the assertion of power over Africa, and the development of ideological justification for the exercise of that power.[3] Power and its ideological underpinning radiated from two potent and idiosyncratic European concepts: Eurocentrism, the proclamation of Europe's superiority over non-Europe, and diffusionism, the attribution of cultural change and innovations to external interventions, i.e., to the diffusion of ideas and values from elsewhere. Eurocentric diffusionism, therefore, negated the theory of independent invention or parallel development, projecting "development," "change," and "civilization" as products of the infusion/diffusion of superior European ideas and institutions. This became the springboard for the third and final assumption of imperialism: the occupation of Africa. The relationship between Europe and Africa in the late nineteenth century can be simplified to the following formula: POWER + IDEOLOGY = OCCUPATION.

Europe's assertion of power and authority over Africa evolved in the context of the broader development of European intellectual history—a history that, in virulently ethnocentric terms, declared Europeans to be the most advanced and civilized of the human race. The liberal ideals of the Enlightenment—liberty and equality—were ascribed not universally but solely to Europeans. In fact, the Enlightenment was itself riddled with contradictions. In the words of Jan Nederveen Pieterse, the Enlightenment was "a far more heterogeneous period than the image of 'enlightenment' allows for."[4] The Age of Reason, of empirical and scientific reasoning, also rationalized old prejudices. To sustain Europe's exaltation and resolve the problematic of a glaring contradiction between the appropriation of the liberal and libertarian tradition, on the one hand, and a growing propensity to demean, objectify, and dehumanize "outsiders," on the other, Europeans advanced intellectual and philosophical rationalizations of the world order they were constructing.

Imbued with cultural arrogance and ethnocentrism, Enlightenment thought justified European expansionism. In his *Histoire Naturelle*, Comte de Buffon, an eminent Enlightenment scholar, referred to black Africans as "crude, superstitious and stupid."[5] A crosscurrent of ideologies and theories upheld the unequal separation of human groups. Proponents of geographical determinism ascribed people's unique physical and cultural attributes to ecological and climatic factors, and they justified slavery and racism. Polygenesis, the theory of separate creations, taught that God created true humans (i.e., Caucasians) in the garden of Eden and other races, including blacks, in other places and times. Polygenesists insisted on racial distinctiveness and segregation. Josiah Nott, a physician and ethnologist, strongly defended polygenesis in his *Types of Mankind*, published in 1854. Nott described Caucasians as the most superior of humankind and blacks as the most inferior.[6]

Although several Enlightenment thinkers rejected polygenesis, most embraced climatic determinism. Montesquieu, for instance, opposed slavery yet affirmed that "there are countries where the heat so exhausts the human body and undermines morale that people can be brought to undertake heavy physical labor only through bodily punishment."[7] Arthur Gobineau's *Essay on the Inequality of the Human Races* (1853) became the standard text on race theories. In his schema, Europeans occupied the top rung of the racial ladder, and blacks sat on the lowest. Gobineau equated civilization with racial purity. He condemned miscegenation, theorizing that it portended civilizational decline and decay. Gobineau described race as a major force in the shaping of human history and, consequently, a key to an informed understanding of the human experience. He declared that races are biologically unequal and endowed with different qualities and capabilities.[8]

In a 1775 dissertation submitted to the University of Göttingen, Johann Friedrich Blumenbach pigeonholed humanity into "varieties": Caucasians, Ethiopians, Mongolians, and Americans. The Caucasians possessed positive qualities and constituted the most original of the human species. The Ethiopians, on the other hand, possessed negative qualities—black and ugly. Blumenbach espoused a theory of monogenesis in consonance with the biblical notion of one humanity. However, his belief in monogenesis did not negate his racial compartmentalizations; people remained distinguished by innate capacities and attributes. Blumenbach attributed differences in capacities and intelligence to geographical and cultural factors. He proposed what was essentially a geocultural determinism. The food, climate, and living conditions of a locale, in Blumenbach's submission, account for the visible differences among human beings.[9] Blumenbach was just one among the many racial classifiers of the epoch, all of whom were inspired by ethnocentrism to vilify and objectify non-Europeans. By the opening decade of the nineteenth century, however, Blumenbach's position had changed slightly. He became more "sympathetic" to the interests of Negroes. Paradoxically, as this study demonstrates, leading black American nationalists and "Pan-Africanists" embraced the latter Blumenbach and quoted him copiously, while also incorporating his works into theirs.

Voltaire, a leading advocate of free inquiry, equality, and the dignity of man, hypothesized that the physical appearance of Africans and Indians, and their "state of Civilization," suggested fundamental differences from Europeans. He portrayed blacks as animals.[10] Late in his life, G.W.F. Hegel described the Negro as the quintessence of "natural man in all his wild and untamed nature." "If you want to treat and understand him rightly," he continued, "*you must abstract all elements of respect and morality and sensitivity—there is nothing remotely humanized in the Negro's character*—Nothing confirms this judgement more than the reports of the missionaries." Hegel dismissed Africa as primitive and ahistorical. As he declared, Africa "shows neither movement nor development."[11]

Similarly, the Anthropological Institute of Great Britain rejected the Enlightenment stress on human similarities. Scottish philosopher David Hume amplified the ethnocentric bias of European thought in his *Essay and Treatise* (1768). Referring to Negroes, he affirmed, "I am apt to suspect the Negroes, and in general all the other species of men to be naturally inferior to the whites. There never was a civilized nation of any other complexion than white, nor even any individual eminent either in action or speculation. No ingenious manufactures among them, no arts, no sciences."[12] The renowned Jamaican planter and administrator Edward Long, who was also considered by many to be an authority on African slaves, advanced a theory of racial classification that underscored both the superiority of Europeans and the subhuman character of blacks. The two broad categories of his racial schema are Europeans and other humans, blacks and orangutans. Long elaborated on the bestial nature of blacks in his *History of Jamaica* (1774). According to him, "[The Negro's] faculties of smell are truly bestial, nor less their commerce with the other sexes; in these acts they are libidinous and shameless as monkeys, or baboons. . . . [The orangutan] has in form a much nearer resemblance to the Negro race than the latter bear to white men."[13]

The proclamation of the superiority and preeminence of European civilization imposed a responsibility of immense magnitude on Europeans: to export rudiments of their "superior" civilization to "backward" groups beyond Europe. This is the birth of two epic concepts: the "white man's burden," i.e., Europe's responsibility for eradicating the ignorance and barbarism that supposedly engulfed the rest of the world; and Manifest Destiny, a mandate to civilize and dominate the rest of humanity, including, of course, the "African barbarian." The colonization of Africa consequently acquired the seal of historical inevitability and the appearance of a humanitarian venture.

To further strengthen and legitimize Europe's claims, European intellectuals and pseudointellectuals of various disciplines—anatomy, anthropology, craniology, history, religion, sociology—worked diligently to legitimize what Hannah Arendt called "race-thinking." They identified race as the substructural context for cognitive and epistemological development. The assertion of white superiority became a pervasive and ubiquitous trait of Western socialization and intellectualism. In France, Britain, Germany, and Italy, scholars, administrators, politicians, and the ordinary people all shared a common faith in the superiority of white over black. Goaded by this self-exaltation, Europeans embarked on the conquest and occupation of "primitive and backward" Africa.[14]

"Race-thinking" was, however, one among the many contending trends that distinguished European thought before the epochal scramble for Africa. On the eve of this scramble, two ideologies had become dominant, based on their capture of European public opinion and their power of persuasion: the first, otherwise called historical materialism, interpreted history as an economic struggle of classes; the second, imbued with a Darwinist twist, explained history as a natural fight among races and postulated a hierarchical order of humanity based on racial features, with "primitive Africa" appropriately positioned at the base of the racial pyramid.[15]

The relegation of Africa was indeed the logical ramification of the social Darwinist construct. Social Darwinists explained inequality as a logical and necessary consequence of a social competition in which inherent racial traits determined performance. The Darwinist paradigm enabled the rich and super-rich to attribute their accomplishments to racially determined factors. By the same token, the condition of the poor and downtrodden was ascribed to presumed innate racial deficiencies. Social Darwinism both explained and justified the racial and economic gaps between blacks and whites. As Bernard Magubane suggests, "Darwinism was especially strengthened by the fact that it followed the path of the old might-is-right doctrine. It was generally believed that history would reveal the gradual emergence of the white race as the victor in the struggle for survival since it seemed to be obviously so much better equipped to subjugate peoples of other colors. This in itself was considered an indication of inherent superiority and thus a mandate for domination."[16] In fact, many believed that history had already demonstrated Europe's preeminence. Industrialization and technological and economic advancement confirmed the inherent superiority of Europe. Culture was consequently linked to race in a rigid, ahistorical manner. Nations that were yet to industrialize or that had underdeveloped economies were quickly tagged inferior and, in consonance with the dictates of Manifest Destiny, became perfect candidates for the "civilizing" function of the "superior" European culture. Positioned on the apex of the human pyramid, the British, French, and Germans prepared to descend on societies at the base.

Nowhere was Eurocentric diffusionism more pronounced than in Victorian England. Leonard Liggio traces the origin of English ethnocentric consciousness to England's handling of the Irish. Throughout the sixteenth and seventeenth centuries, particularly during the reign of Elizabeth I, English hostility toward the Irish reached new heights. The British invaded Ireland on many occasions and displayed contempt for Irish culture, people, and lifestyles. By the seventeenth century, the English had grown accustomed to regarding the Irish as savages.[17]

Demeaning and objectifying the Irish, Liggio argues, ultimately conditioned the English to perceive and treat every outsider in like manner. The conception of the alien as savage bolstered English cultural chauvinism and narcissism. The Victorians considered themselves the quintessence of civilization, pioneers of industry and progress. The authentic Victorian outlook, according to Ronald Robinson and John Gallagher, was "diffused with a vivid sense of superiority and self-righteousness." The Victorians constructed a hierarchical world order, with the races positioned according to "proven capacity for freedom and enterprise." The British occupied the top of this hierarchy, followed in descending order by the Americans, the Latins, the "orientals" of Asia and North Africa, and the "aborigines" (black Africans included here).[18]

Industrialization constituted a major dynamic of Victorian self-exaltation and, *ipso facto*, imperialism. Industrial power induced an "expansive spirit," as the Victorians became convinced of their responsibility and capacity to intervene and influence human conditions elsewhere. Expansion became a moral duty. In the words of Cecil Rhodes, a prominent Victorian imperialist, "Expansion is everything." Expansion was understood to be "preordained and irreproachably right." Industrialists, manufacturers, and colonists quickly unleashed an expansionist crusade. The English were, however, not alone in this development. The European worldview was imbued with ethnological biases against the "savage," who perforce had to be transformed through cultural contact and diffusion. Expansionism was thus a European phenomenon.[19] According to historians Adu Boahen, Jacob Ade Ajayi, and Michael Tiddy, the expansion of Europe toward Africa was also energized by one of "the greatest of the operating political forces" of the time, nationalism. This was particularly evident in the 1870s, with the attainment of nationhood by Germany and Italy. European nations desperately sought to partition Africa because colonies had become symbols of national greatness.[20]

On the eve of the conquest of Africa, Europeans' self-conception as "naturally superior" was, according to Peter Worsley, "a standard article of faith," and the word *primitive* was applied indiscriminately to colored peoples of the world. The European perception of reality, especially of alien cultures, assumed a racial overtone. The European was viewed as human and civilized, whereas the non-European was savage and primitive. What distinguished the nineteenth-century "savage" was, as Jan Nederveen Pieterse explains, what he/she lacked; that is, the "savage" was distinguished by absences—the absence or scarcity of clothing, possessions, and, perhaps most significantly, the attributes of civilization. Negative qualities and objectification delineated the icon of the savage, and no "savage" was as maligned and objectified as the African, who possessed several negative qualities: immorality, heathenism, cannibalism, thievery, indolence, murderousness, and the *absence* of civilization, culture, and history. The African "savage" lacked both a history and positive cultural values.[21]

European self-righteousness and self-exaltation, combined with a Eurocentric intellectual tradition, sustained a worldview that projected Caucasians as generally superior to all other races and, in consequence, obliged Caucasians to assist and even force "less civilized" peoples to adopt and adapt to "civilized" modes of thought, behavior, and living. Eurocentric diffusionism articulated a unilinear cultural relationship. Cultural values were to flow out of the advanced European world into the backward non-European world, with no movement whatsoever in the opposite direction. This unilinear interaction, according to J.M. Blaut, was considered the "natural, normal, logical and ethical flow of culture, of innovation, of human causality—Europe was the source of most diffusions, non-Europe was the recipient."

Advocates of the diffusionist theory constructed a dependency framework of the world, establishing a relationship of dependence between a center and periphery, or an *inside* and *outside*—a permanent and dynamic center of ideas and innovations, and an Outside that was to change in response to the influence of the Inside. The diffusionist paradigm was based on two significant presuppositions: first, that most human societies were lethargic, static, and traditional; second, that a few cultures were inventive and constituted the nerve centers of progress and change. Blaut identifies seven fundamental tenets of the diffusionist theory as it pertains to the relationship between Europe and non-Europe. Six of them are worth outlining:

1. Europe naturally progresses and modernizes. That is, the natural inclination of the European is to invent, innovate, and change. Europe is historical.
2. Non-Europe is stagnant and traditional. Innovation is alien to this sector. Non-Europe, the outside, is therefore ahistorical.
3. Europe's progress is the result of unique qualities inherent to the European mind.
4. The non-European lack of those unique qualities results in a static condition.
5. The only way for progress to occur in the non-European sector is through the diffusion of innovation and progressive values from Europe.
6. The compensation for the diffusion of civilized ideas from Europe to non-Europe is a counterdiffusion of material

wealth: minerals, agricultural products, labor, and so forth. Nothing, however, can fully compensate for the gift of civilization. Colonial economic exploitation was thus morally justified. In the diffusionist philosophy, colonialism gives more than it receives.[22]

All six tenets of Eurocentric diffusionism identify progress, modernity, and innovation with Europe. The diffusion of European cultural influence through colonialism became identified as Africa's medium for overcoming poverty and historical inertia. Resource exploitation and loss of sovereignty became the prices to be paid by Africans—indeed, became the compensation to Europeans—for the gift of civilization. Black American nationalists adopted a similarly mercenary view of Africa's resources. This was precisely the reason why, as this study demonstrates, leading black American nationalists such as Martin Delany, Alexander Crummell, and Henry McNeal Turner had no qualms about advocating European exploitation of Africa's economic resources.

The six principles of Eurocentric diffusionism functioned collectively to fire the engine of European imperialism. Energized and propelled by this tunnel-vision grasp of reality, Europeans moved to subdue most parts of Asia and North America while inching toward Africa. Since Africa belonged to the non-European Outside, no consideration was given to the possibility that anything civilized or of cultural value already existed there. By the first decade of the twentieth century, Europeans had occupied virtually the entire continent of Africa (with the exception of Ethiopia and Liberia). Africans consequently felt the brunt of Europe's ethnocentric extroversion much more than any other groups in history. Paul Lauren, for example, identifies the "most striking and significant feature of the second half of the nineteenth century" as the outburst of imperialist activities, the *intensity of which was felt most in Africa.*[23]

The decision by the Europeans to invade and partition Africa in the closing years of the nineteenth century was preceded and facilitated by decades of preparations by explorers and missionaries, who "discovered" and exposed the material and natural resources of Africa. Their activities provided the practical grounding for the sustenance of Eurocentrism. Their negative and pejorative depictions of the cultures they encountered reinforced "race-thinking." Exploration opened up the continent and was presented as expediting the processes of "pushing back the frontiers of ignorance" and "adding to the store of knowledge." However, the addition to knowledge was more in the field of mythmaking designed to authenticate colonialism. The "discovery" of Africa and the information that European missionaries and explorers provided about African peoples and cultures strengthened the diffusionist view. Europeans were reluctant to probe beneath the surface and acquire a better understanding of the cultures they encountered. Misunderstood, misrepresented, and vilified, Africa became the perfect candidate for an extension of Europe's "superior civilization."

European explorers and missionaries approached Africa with ingrained prejudices and preconceptions. Such terms as *monsters, barbaric, primitive,* and *heathens* were featured prominently in their diaries, memoirs, and reports. David Livingstone, T.J. Bowen, the brothers John and Richard Lander, Mungo Park, Hugh Clapperton, and Henry Morton Stanley, to name a few, provided both the practical leverage for Eurocentrism and the magnetic force that strengthened Europe's resolve to conquer Africa. Essentially, the magnet was Africa's immense material and natural resources. The practical leverage was found in the alleged "backward and primitive" character of African societies, which accorded legitimacy to the "civilizing mission."

David Livingstone's reports about Africa made him the folk hero of Victorian society. Like other explorers, he juxtaposed the wealth and resources of the interior of Africa with the alleged backwardness, inferiority, and lack of intelligence of the indigenes. This appealed favorably to the Victorian sense of mission by establishing the need to "redeem" Africans from social and cultural evils, poverty, ignorance, and tribal warfare. Livingstone found "nothing interesting in a heathen town." He entrusted the Anglo-American race with responsibility for the liberty and progress of the rest of humanity. Instructing an assistant on the Zambezi, Livingstone declared unequivocally, "We come among them as members of a superior race and servants of a government that desires to elevate the more degraded portion of the human family."[24]

Inability to understand and relate to African societies and cultures compelled European explorers and missionaries to label Africans "barbaric and backward." Race, as Hannah Arendt has aptly surmised, became the "emergency explanation for shattering experiences," for explaining the unknown and the strange.[25] Confronted by Africa and its exotic customs and traditions, and overwhelmed by the complexity and "strange" character of African societies and peoples, the Europeans conveniently invoked race. The explorers' reports excited the European public and inspired dreams of a vast, virgin continent, richly endowed but inhabited by a people lacking in the intelligence and capacities necessary to exploit and develop those resources. These inhabitants also appeared desperately in need of spiritual and secular salvation. The "discoveries" of the explorers and missionaries were widely publicized, and they generated and energized self-conceited Victorian views, reinforcing a Manichaean conception of the world as the arena of conflict between a "superior" Caucasian civilization and a "backward and barbaric" Africa.

The "horrors" and excesses of African cultural and behavioral tendencies that the explorers uncovered supposedly touched the hearts of Europeans and unleashed their humanitarian energies. Rescuing Africans from barbarism and cultural decadence consumed the attention of Europeans, with missionaries and explorers recommending two different but complementary strategies. The missionaries opted for evangelism. They presented Christianity as the key to Africa's salvation and civilization. The explorers advocated the infusion of intelligent and industrious skills to develop untapped resources, a solution that can also be summarized in one word: commerce. The missionaries and explorers of the various European nations then appealed to their respective governments and sponsors to provide the framework necessary for the success of the two strategies: colonization. This appeal bolstered the existing and developing expansionist impulse that had engineered the explorations and "discoveries" in the first place. Here, then, is the origin of the famous three C's: Christianity, commerce, and colonization.

Stereotypical conceptions of Africa and of blacks in general intensified during the late nineteenth century and became the justification for imperialism. The exaltation of Europeans and whites as the bearers of civilization had far-reaching consequences for black Americans. Essentially, it denied them a positive frame of reference. Being black and of African ancestry rendered them susceptible to all the negative and demeaning attributions associated with Africa. Many of them felt a desperate need to become integrated into the new framework or world order conceived by Europeans.

The works of Eurocentric and diffusionist scholars and the reports of the explorers and missionaries were widely read by educated Americans. In fact, white supremacist scholarship, sometimes respectfully referred to as "aristocratic scholarship," evolved and flourished in the United States, where it sustained a culture of "race-thinking" that was similar to, and accomplished precisely the same objectives as, the broader Eurocentric scholarship: the objectification, subordination, and dehumanization of blacks/Africans. "Race-thinking" soon developed and maintained a consensus on the character of the American Negro and the causes of inequality. George Fredrickson's writings clearly outline the crystallization and dominance of racist and racialist values among American intellectuals by the second half of the nineteenth century.[26] Scientists, pseudoscientists, historians, ethnographers, anthropologists—all propounded theories on the superiority of the Caucasian and the inferiority of the Negro. The concept of white superiority and a narrow perception of reality underpinned the evolution of Manifest Destiny, which in turn unleashed American expansionism. Americans defined themselves as a "chosen people" destined to influence and dominate others. Despite this assertion, the United States did not participate in the partitioning of Africa. Manifest Destiny was directed at Asia, the Pacific, and the Caribbean, where the racial ideology was used to justify the conquest and despoliation of indigenous populations, including Cubans, Filipinos, Hawaiians, Puerto Ricans, and inhabitants of Guam.[27] The irony is that, in the second half of the nineteenth century, it was black Americans who staunchly advocated the application and extension of Manifest Destiny to Africa and lamented American isolation from the partitioning of the continent.

This review of the theoretical basis of European imperialism is necessary if we are to understand the dynamics of the imperialist elements in the thoughts and programs of late-nineteenth-century black American nationalists. The development and propagation of imperialist ideology has traditionally been identified with the activities and pronouncements of European scholars, explorers, missionaries, and statesmen. Because of this emphasis on the European factor, the purview of research has not extended to the contributions of black American nationalists, especially those of Martin Delany, Alexander Crummell, and Henry McNeal Turner, who supposedly exemplified the very best of the black nationalist tradition. Although several scholars acknowledge the Anglo-Saxon and Victorian character of black American nationalism, very few attempts have been made at in-depth study of the imperialistic implications of this connection.[28] The depth of black American nationalist subscription to Eurocentric diffusionist ideals and cultural narcissism, along with the implications of this for black American conceptions of nationality and identity, especially in the context of the diaspora, have not been adequately explored. Put differently, scholars have yet to fully explore how the imperialist inclinations of black American nationalists compelled identification with and support for policies that resulted in what many characterize as the second enslavement of Africans: colonialism. Traditionally, most scholars simply mention the theoretical fact of adaptation to—and adoption of—Eurocentric and Anglo-Saxon values and ideas, without probing the practical and logical ramifications.

The hegemonic character of Eurocentric diffusionism significantly influenced black American political thought. Just as Eurocentrism worked to justify the subordination and exploitation of colored peoples elsewhere, particularly in Africa, Jim Crow culture, with its appurtenances of legislation and "scholarship," rationalized and secured the marginalization and impoverishment of black Americans. In an increasingly gloomy and miserable environment, black Americans responded with postulations and solutions aimed ostensibly at rolling back the progress of Jim Crow and at establishing a solid foundation for the survival and elevation of all blacks—an African nationality. In other words, they invoked what they perceived as their racial and ethnic essence as blacks and descendants of Africa. However, as black American nationalists turned toward Africa ideologically, psychologically, philosophically, and physically, with the apparent intention of reclaiming an identity that had long been denied and maligned in the United States, they borrowed copiously from Eurocentric nationalism. Reflecting the prevailing Eurocentric mind-set, they accepted and projected a narrow view of reality, accepting and deferring to the European depiction of Africa as primitive. Unfortunately, they also had to deal with the troubling quandary of being black and of having African ancestry, while living in an environment and cultural context they had been socialized to recognize as the quintessence of civilization. This is not to suggest that black American nationalists embraced Eurocentric tunnel vision uncritically. They were critical of Eurocentrism and did recognize certain inherent qualities in African societies, cultures, and values that, in their estimation, equally and incontrovertibly established Africa's claim to civilization. However, the full force of black American nationalism weighed in heavily on the side of European nationalism.

Black American nationalism consequently exhibited the dual character of European nationalism: an intellectual (theoretical) tradition distinguished by ethnocentrism and negative evaluation and objectification of Africans; and a practical component contrived to rationalize the *mission civilisatrice,* that is, colonialism. Black American nationalists did much more than imbibe Anglo-Saxon cultural and nationalist values. They contributed to strengthening the ideological and practical rationale for European colonization of Africa. What has not been explored exhaustively is the convergence on Africa of two traditions of nationalism and two imperial schemes in the second half of the nineteenth century: European and black American. The implication and complicity of black American nationalists in the European economic and imperial designs on Africa deserve closer scrutiny. The historical significance of this complicity lay not so much in black American nationalism's theoretical adaptations from Eurocentrism as in the practical ramifications. In this respect, it constituted a vital arm of Eurocentric nationalism. In fact, it seems plausible to venture a depiction of the two as obverse sides of the same coin—a curious juxtaposition, given the appearance of conflict.

Generally, critiques of black American nationalism rarely move beyond acknowledging its Anglo-Saxon character. In *The Golden Age of Black Nationalism,* Wilson J. Moses highlights the ambivalence in the nationalist thoughts of Delany, Blyden, and Crummell, particularly their affection for European values and their disdain for African societies and indigenous African traditions and norms. He also reveals their support for the subjugation of African states under the pretense of civilization and modernization. Unfortunately, Moses devotes just a small section of a chapter to this important but neglected dimension of black nationalism. The ambivalence displayed toward Africa by black American nationalists, their subscription to Eurocentrism, and their support for European hegemony remain perhaps the most critical developments resulting from "the context of Western civilization" within which black American nationalist thought evolved in the eighteenth and nineteenth centuries.[29]

If the black American value and belief system was significantly shaped by this very same dynamic context, it seems reasonable to investigate the extent of black Americans' internalization and reflection of the hegemonic essence of that context. In fact, black American nationalism, conceived as a "reaction to attitudes of white supremacy," evolved an ambivalent relationship to white supremacy that included both rejection and adaptation. That is, black American nationalists combined a condemnatory reaction to Euro-American domination and exploitation of blacks in the United States with an adaptive and accommodative response to European hegemony abroad (i.e., in Africa). This ambivalence, especially the self-abnegating dimension of adaptation, deserves detailed study and critical reevaluation. It is perhaps even more pertinent that this reevaluation be undertaken from an African perspective. It seems important to consider how indigenous Africans must have perceived and felt about the ideas and schemes of black American nationalists. Emphasizing this African perspective has serious implications for normative assumptions about the African and black diaspora nexus.

In his sharp and poignant critique of Edward Wilmot Blyden, Valentin Y. Mudimbe convincingly establishes the ideological connection between the ideas of Blyden, the highly respected and acclaimed black nationalist and Pan-Africanist, and the colonization schemes of the European powers.[30] Blyden combined two contradictory elements in his thought: a strong defense of African civilization and an equally strong endorsement of European occupation of the continent. He envisioned colonization as an effective means of transforming Africa. Despite his Pan-African convictions, Blyden expressed strong admiration for British, French, and Belgian imperial policies. In what is essentially a *tour de force,* the historian Clarence Walker challenges and debunks the conceptual paradigms that have traditionally informed interpretations of the black American experience. He calls for "deromanticizing" black history. His collection of critical essays challenges the ideological biases of black American historiography. One nationalist at whom Walker directs a stinging critique is Marcus Garvey. Walker describes Garvey as a colonizationist, a Zionist, and an imperialist who appropriated European symbols and values to propagate an exploitative nationalist agenda. Garvey in effect hoodwinked many blacks into embracing what Walker characterizes as an essentially self-serving, elitist, and narrow-minded nationalist program.[31] Blyden and Garvey both exemplified the paradoxes and nuances of black nationalism that have hitherto been suppressed or, more appropriately, sacrificed on the altar of a monolithic, global black experiential construct.

Of equal relevance is the work of Anthony Appiah. In his book *In My Father's House: Africa in the Philosophy of Culture,* Appiah methodically dissects Alexander Crummell's ideas, underlining their debt to the Victorian and Anglo-American *Weltanschauung.* Crummell venerated Anglo-Saxon values and castigated and scorned indigenous Africans.[32] Like his contemporaries and predecessors, Crummell utilized conceptual tools derived from Eurocentric epistemology, thus stunting his vision and enabling him to perceive only the Africa that had been invented by Europeans. Appiah, unfortunately and perhaps understandably, does not focus sufficient attention on the imperialist ramifications of Crummell's ambivalence. Nevertheless, his and other revisionist studies serve as signposts, brightly illuminating the paths for more detailed revisionism. Acknowledging that black Americans connived with and encouraged Europeans in their quest for hegemony over Africa is understandably unsavory, given the cultural-nationalist slant of contemporary black American thought. Yet it is a historical reality, and it deserves to be confronted if the phenomenon of black nationalism is to be appreciated in its complexity.

This study is by no means a sweeping indictment of black American leadership throughout history. Numerous scholars, including Wilson J. Moses, Sterling Stuckey, Elliott Skinner, and Sylvia Jacobs, have demonstrated that black American leaders genuinely sympathized and empathized with Africans and that on numerous occasions prominent individuals and groups attempted to transcend empathy and assume a more active role in defending African causes.[33]

Elliott Skinner's work is particularly illuminating in this respect. Focusing on the careers of those he identifies as "early African Americans," Skinner shows how black Americans in the diplomatic service fought to influence U.S. policy toward Africa. J. Milton Turner, John H. Smyth, Henry H. Garnet, Moses A. Hopkins, and Charles H. James, who served as U.S. envoys to Liberia from the 1870s until the establishment of colonialism in Africa, used their "limited political power in the interest of Africa . . . in the hope that their activities would protect Africa and aid African peoples the world over."[34] Along with other prominent black Americans including George Washington

Williams, the Reverend William Henry Sheppard, John L. Walter, and William H. Ellis, they were alarmed by the onslaught of imperialism in Africa and often appealed to U.S. national interest, campaigning vigorously for greater American attention to the threats of imperialism, particularly in Liberia, the Congo, Madagascar, and Ethiopia.

As diplomats, black envoys had to function within the confines of, and in consonance with, the rules laid down by the State Department. Skinner does show that, as concerned as these blacks were with protecting Africa's interests, they were Americans whose primary functions were shaped by American national interests. Although the envoys often cooperated "with powerful whites in order to help Africa," their objective, Skinner argues, "was not to bolster white power but rather to help Ethiopia stretch forth its hand and rid itself of the burden and shame of white domination."[35] Those working within the confines of diplomacy often have a very limited range for independent initiatives, especially on critical issues of international relations. Consequently, any semblance of contradiction in the work of these government envoys is excusable, albeit regrettable. This does not apply to independents and avowed nationalists, particularly the likes of Delany and Turner (only marginally discussed in Skinner's book), who boldly and unambiguously proclaimed a commitment to opposing the United States and its values. They possessed a greater degree of independence, and their ideas, strategies, activities, accomplishments, and limitations deserve greater scrutiny.

In combination, the three nationalists chosen for this study—Delany, Turner, and Crummell—defined the ideological framework and the tone of black American nationalism in the second half of the nineteenth century, when the European powers began to redefine their relationship with Africa. During this period, Britain, France, Portugal, Holland, Belgium, and Germany jettisoned their hitherto low-key presence along the West African coastline in favor of expanding into the African interior. To institutionalize and rationalize a new relationship mandated by industrialism and the changing European political economy, the European powers marshaled the entire Eurocentric diffusionist ideology against Africa. Surprisingly, instead of opposition and stiff resistance from black Americans, who had been alienated and affected as much as Africans by the negative and racist postulations of Eurocentrism, the Europeans received (often unsolicited) encouragement and support.

★ 2 ★

The Historical Context of Black Nationalism: The Quest for American Nationality

B lack American national consciousness, Bill McAdoo contends, "has deep roots in the historical existence of the black masses in this country."[1] Few will disagree with McAdoo's contention. In fact, many critics trace this deep-rooted historical consciousness back to slavery. In the words of one leading authority, "Slavery was, in a sense, the cause of black nationalism."[2] The traumatic and dehumanizing experience of slavery, even with the denial and negation of the history, culture, and nationality of blacks, failed to completely "denationalize" the consciousness of blacks. Paradoxically, the more blacks were demeaned and alienated, the stronger their national consciousness grew. Regardless of status—free or slave—blacks developed a vision of nationality. The expressions of this national consciousness assumed different forms. Some were violent, manifested in slave plots and revolts. These revolts were often attempts to claim equal rights and privileges as citizens of a given nation.[3] At other times, national consciousness took mediatory shapes, designed to socialize blacks and introduce values that would facilitate their acceptance and integration into an existing nationality. The latter is exemplified in the multifarious self-help, benevolent, and cooperative societies founded by free blacks in Philadelphia, New York, Boston, and other northern cities during the eighteenth and nineteenth centuries.[4] Finally, the antislavery crusade and the struggle to end oppression and marginalization represented forceful exhibitions of national consciousness.[5] In other words, the quest for integration in the United States constituted a strong expression of black American national consciousness.

Historian Herbert Aptheker finds ample expressions of the nationalism ingrained in the consciousness of prerevolutionary blacks.

During the early phase of their ordeal in America, blacks experimented with schemes and strategies—radical, moderate, and conservative—all aimed at ameliorating their condition and ending oppression. A few relatively educated free blacks reflected on the dynamics of national consciousness and offered suggestions on how best to strengthen it. One such writer was David Walker, whose famous *Appeal to the Colored Citizens of the World* was published in 1829. Walker sharply criticized slavery, insisting not only that blacks deserved better treatment but also that they were American citizens who deserved all the benefits of American nationality. In fact, Walker rejected colonization, that is, the scheme to relocate free blacks outside the country, arguing that blacks possessed even greater qualification for American citizenship than whites. As he contended, "This country is as much ours as it is the whites, whether they will admit it now or not, they will see and believe it by and by. . . . We have enriched it with our blood and tears. The greatest riches in all America have arisen from our blood and tears."[6] His claim to American nationality was forceful and unambiguous. He envisioned divine retribution for the ill-treatment of blacks, a doom that could only be averted if black enslavement and alienation ended. Walker did not just proclaim the citizenship of blacks. He also underscored the importance of unity and cooperation among blacks and emphasized the linkage in the destinies of Africans and blacks in the diaspora.[7] Aptheker acclaimed the *Appeal* as "the first sustained written assault upon slavery and racism to come from a black man in the United States." Sterling Stuckey credits the *Appeal* with creating "the rationale for Pan-Africanism," the central theme in the book being "the indispensability of a unified struggle by blacks for them to be free and to defend their freedom."[8]

The Pan-African consciousness, a deep awareness and consciousness of this more extended sense of nationality, was equally evident in the thoughts of Paul Cuffe and Lott Cary, two contemporaries and nationalists who preceded Walker. The two evinced strong desires for American nationality, but at the same time insisted that the destinies of black Americans and Africans were inextricably joined. Both implored black Americans to contribute to the development of Africa, a contribution that, they argued, would have a salutary impact on the experience and condition of blacks in the diaspora. Cuffe and Cary espoused values and strategies that future generations of black American nationalists embraced. They sought to mobilize black American resources and consciousness toward building a strong foundation in Africa.[9]

Another early expression of nationalism was Henry H. Garnet's "Address to the Slaves of the United States of America," delivered at the 1843 Negro National Convention in Buffalo, New York. In his address, Garnet reminded slaves not to forget that "you are native-born American citizens, and as such, you are justly entitled to all the rights that are granted to the freest." He urged them to "arise, arise, strike for your lives and liberty."[10] Many critics view the "Address to the Slaves" as the quintessence of militant black nationalism.[11] Garnet's nationalist consciousness blossomed, and as the years progressed he grew increasingly critical of black alienation and forcefully proclaimed and defended the American nationality of blacks. As he once inquired rhetorically, "Sir, if the privilege of American citizenship is granted in return for services done in contributing to the agricultural prosperity of the country, what class of Americans stand above the colored inhabitants of the soil?"[13] His Pan-African consciousness also developed as he lost hope in integration. Garnet became a champion of African colonization and the creation of an African nationality.[14]

A deeply felt black national consciousness also molded the dominant values of the Negro national and state convention movement that spanned the decades from 1830 to 1860.[15] Nevertheless, these values were complex and diverse, often changing with time and circumstances. At times the values supported integrationist objectives— a rejection of colonization, or any scheme of expatriation, and a strong affirmation of American identity. According to James Oliver Horton, "At the national black conventions held throughout the antebellum period, resolutions expressed black identity and commitment—both racial and American. Blacks were both African and American. They were, in fact, special Americans, dedicated to the spirit of American liberty as few others were. They were not alienated Americans, even though for them American society was alienating. They were not discouraged Americans, even though the racial restrictions were discouraging. They were committed Americans determined to improve the country's treatment of its peoples."[16] They invoked both the Constitution and Declaration of Independence in support of their claim to American identity and nationality. They persistently reminded the nation that it had yet to live up to its proclaimed ideals. Black Americans expressed deep love for the United States, while resenting slavery and segregation. Their protests thus represented a strong affirmation, not repudiation, of national identity. Integrationists were determined to fight for and realize a nationality within the United States, either as a constituent part of American nationality, with all the accompanying rights and privileges, or as an independent nationality within its boundaries, a kind of "state within a state." With a few possible exceptions (most notably, the 1854 emigration convention), the conventions represented a movement for the realization of American nationality. Throughout these meetings, blacks affirmed their American nationality and discussed means of obtaining its full range of privileges. Regardless of the context of the conventions, state or national, the overriding objective was integration. Even as national conventions gave place to state conventions in the 1840s, and as militant and immediatist strategies displaced moral suasion, the majority of blacks remained optimistic about the possibility of ultimately becoming full-fledged American citizens.

At other times, however, black American nationalism manifested a deeper consciousness of alienation, seeking the creation of an independent nationality outside the United States. This emigrationist ethics was particularly strong in the 1850s, with the passage of the infamous Fugitive Slave Law, which, *inter alia*, pledged federal support for the pursuit, apprehension, and reenslavement of fugitives. Many black Americans perceived the law as a threat to the freedom of all blacks regardless of status. Perhaps the most critical implication of the law was the federal government's support of strengthening slavery. This heightened the apprehension of many free blacks, convincing them that slavery was about to become a national institution.[17] Two other developments in the 1850s reinforced this fear. First, Congress passed the Kansas-Nebraska Act of 1854, which reopened the slavery question and conferred on territorial governments the right to decide whether to permit slavery. This act opened up to slavery an area from which it had been banned by the earlier Missouri Compromise—territories north of the 36°30' parallel. Second, the Dred Scott Decision of 1857 stripped blacks of all semblances of rights, privileges, and protection by denying them citizenship. According to the verdict, blacks had no rights that whites were obliged to respect.[18] This declaration rendered all blacks vulnerable to reenslavement, leaving them completely at the mercy of all whites, particularly the slavocrats. Never had blacks, particularly the so-called free blacks, felt so besieged by oppressive legislation and judicial decisions. Many discerned a hardening of racial lines and a growing antiblack sentiment. Convinced that slavery was about to spread nationwide, some leading blacks advocated emigration and looked abroad for a new nationality. The rising interest in expatriation reflected the depth of black alienation. Martin Robison Delany (1812-85) led the emigrationist and nationalist crusade from 1850 until the outbreak of the Civil War, providing ideological justification for emigration in a myriad of publications and lectures and by actively participating in the search for a new nationality.[19]

Emigration momentum engulfed the 1850s and reached a climax in the early 1860s, only to be temporarily halted by the outbreak of the Civil War, as blacks, enlivened by the prospect of destroying slavery, refocused on domestic politics and became optimistically integrative. Blacks responded enthusiastically to the opportunity presented by the war. Regardless of the convictions and assertions of national politicians, for blacks the Civil War was fundamentally a conflict between two major forces—freedom and slavery—and there was no doubt on which side they belonged. They offered their services to the Union cause and fought gallantly and heroically in defense of national unity, but also in the service of freedom, convinced that this time, unlike in past national conflicts, they would be rewarded with lasting benefits.[20] There was no doubt that blacks expected the war to result in the realization of the elusive American nationality; that is, they expected that finally they would be acknowledged as equal citizens of the American polity, deserving of all the attendant rights and privileges. National policies in the immediate aftermath of the war strengthened black optimism. The Emancipation Proclamation, which came into effect in January 1863, and the Thirteenth Amendment of 1865 freed the slaves of the rebellious states and outlawed slavery, respectively. The subsequent Fourteenth and Fifteenth Amendments, passed in 1868 and 1870, conferred citizenship and the franchise on blacks, respectively. Not only were blacks acknowledged as citizens of the United States but they were also guaranteed the equal protection of the law and promised that their rights would never be abridged on account of race or previous condition. These reforms associated with the phase of radical Reconstruction

(1866-76) opened up a wide political playing field for blacks. They could now vote and run for office. In consequence, blacks were suddenly entrusted with immense political responsibilities. In several southern states—South Carolina, Georgia, Virginia, Tennessee, Louisiana, Mississippi, Texas, Alabama, Florida—blacks functioned as legislators, attorneys, state treasurers, trial justices, deputy governors, and so on. They performed remarkably well, given their inexperience and legacy of political subordination and alienation.[21]

The dramatic turn of events notwithstanding, it was obvious to perceptive black leaders and politicians that the gains of the Civil War and Reconstruction were enforced and policed by the power of the Republican-controlled federal government. The entire nation had not endorsed black emancipation and political elevation. Former slave owners remained resentful of radical Reconstruction, and it was clear that they would stop at nothing to overturn it. Black political elevation seemed fragile and ephemeral. President Andrew Johnson, who assumed office after the assassination of Abraham Lincoln, adopted a pro-Southern policy. He pardoned former confederates and restored the lands they had forfeited to the government, thus creating a solid foundation for their economic recuperation. It would be wrong, however, to imply that Johnson's policies were solely responsible for undermining radical Reconstruction. As several studies have shown, radical Reconstruction failed to aggressively advance the interests of blacks. There was a certain reluctance on the part of the federal government to formulate and implement policies that would have solidified black freedom. By the mid-1870s, not only were conservative Democrats powerful and confident enough to begin a political comeback, but the Republican party was riddled with dissensions, as a constituency sympathetic to the South advocated jettisoning blacks in favor of a *rapprochement* with Southern white leaders. Democrats staged a successful return in the election of 1876. The epochal Compromise of 1877 restored to them full control of internal affairs in the South.[22]

The hope and optimism rekindled by the war dissipated in the aftermath of the overthrow of Reconstruction and the accompanying strengthening and consolidation of Jim Crow. Although the Thirteenth Amendment had abolished slavery, blacks were far from being completely emancipated and elevated. The demise of slavery opened a new phase in the "strange career" of Jim Crow, as blacks were subjected to experiences reminiscent of slavery. Racist ideologies developed and flowered to legitimize white supremacy and black subordination. Whites adopted a multiplicity of legal and extralegal measures—poll taxes, grandfather clauses, convict leases, intimidation, economic blackmail, and violence—designed to instill in blacks the knowledge of their assigned "place" and to impress on them the supreme importance of respecting racial boundaries.[23] It was obvious that the United States was to remain a "white only" land and that blacks would be accommodated solely as subordinates, in spite of their emancipation. In other words, though emancipated, blacks were held down and denied access to the rights and privileges of the elusive American nationality (and of the "American Dream"). Their capacity for growth and development thus circumscribed, blacks once again embraced nationalism, exhibiting a strong emigrationist character.[24] Again, some emigrants, or "Exodusters," as one authority refers to them, sought refuge in the American West and Midwest, settling in Oklahoma, Kansas, and Ohio.[25] Others looked abroad, especially in the direction of Africa. Delany played a relatively marginal role during this post-Reconstruction phase of black American nationalism. Although a member of the Liberia Exodus Movement in South Carolina, Delany's nationalist career had already seen its heyday. Alexander Crummell and Henry McNeal Turner were much more active and successful in articulating nationalist ideas and strategies during this period.

It should be stressed, however, that nationalist consciousness among black Americans, whether domestically or internationally directed, was essentially contrived to effect the transformation of the American order, rendering it much more responsive to the needs of blacks. Put differently, this nationalism, regardless of the direction it took, had as its *raison d'être* the reform of the social and political contexts of the United States. It was essentially integrative. Black American national consciousness, therefore, symbolized a revolt against oppression and an attempt to address problems that undermined the prospects for integration. In its externally directed dimension, this national consciousness proffered an increase in awareness of Africa and a strengthening of racial identity. Attempts were made to instill in black Americans an awareness of kinship ties with Africa, a relationship supposedly built on shared historical experience and on racial identity. The burgeoning consciousness of mutuality was supposed to unify Africans and black Americans, peoples with a sense of shared destiny and obligatory responsibility for mutual development. According to August Meier, a leading authority on the subject, black American nationalism was distinguished by "loyalty to a group characterized by a common cultural experience which differentiates it from other groups, thus giving the members of said group a feeling that they belong together. Among the factors which frequently or usually serve to delimit national groups and form a basis of national feeling are language, religion, a glorious past of great achievement, a common past (and present) of suffering and tribulation, the idea of a national homeland, and a sense of mission for the future."[26]

By the second half of the nineteenth century, the state of nationalist consciousness among black Americans encapsulated the key features highlighted by Meier: group loyalty, emphasis on a unique historical, cultural, and social experience, a conception of identity sustained by cultural and racial factors, the quest for a nationality or homeland, and a missionary zeal for transforming that nationality into a foundation for survival. By 1850, in fact, the search for a nationality/homeland had assumed center stage in the thoughts of black Americans. Serious controversy, however, emerged over the definition of this nationality. A very vocal minority externalized the parameters for nationality. Frustrated at home, they turned their searchlights in the direction of the West Indies, Africa, and Central and South America. The majority, however, insisted on a domestic conception of nationality and were determined to work harder in pursuit of it.[27]

The search for a resolution of what Marxists call the "national question" thus shaped black American nationalist thought from time immemorial. The national question focuses on the critical issues of nationality and identity. Samir Amin writes, "The existence of nations raises the national question, and the process of unequal development makes this question particularly acute in the development of class struggle."[28] Although referring to a much broader historical context, Amin's analysis captures the reality of the black American struggle: black American ideologues posed the national question in reaction to the experience of "unequal development" within the American nation, seeking to compel a reassessment of the status of blacks. The ultimate objective of raising and projecting the national question was to establish the centrality of blacks to, and their compatibility with, the nation. Leading blacks such as Martin Delany, Frederick Douglass, Henry Garnet, David Walker, Nat Turner, George Washington Williams, William Wells Brown, and James W.C. Pennington staked their claim to American identity on a range of factors—patriotism, natural and legal rights, and the labor theory of nationality (i.e., contributions to national development as a basis of nationality).

They maintained that those slaves who were forcibly transplanted from Africa were black pioneers who had earned their citizenship rights at the same time and under the same conditions as European migrants—by contributing to the development and transformation of the wilderness into a livable and productive environment. Those born in America also earned citizenship through a combination of factors: birth, patriotism, labor, and natural right.[29]

There were few blacks who doubted their American nationality and identity, even while acknowledging African ancestry and heritage. Slavery and racism, the twin evils that defined the status of blacks, however, challenged and denied black nationality and humanity, proclaiming America a "white-only" land. It is no exaggeration to contend that the whole black antislavery struggle was waged primarily to resolve the national question and firmly establish black entitlement to the rights and privileges of U.S. nationality. It is therefore no coincidence that the intellectual endeavors of the black "intelligentsia" stressed black contributions to the United States—a powerful argument for inclusion.

The difficulties of the national question were compounded by the racist character of the dominant culture and the restrictive contexts of black existence. Black Americans were completely written out of the American nation and at the same time were denied any viable and credible alternative nationality with which to identify themselves. They were told that they had no history to invoke. Africa, their ancestral homeland, was represented as a dark, backward, primitive, and barbaric place, an environment from which they should consider themselves lucky to have been rescued. The dominant intellectual conception of the "Negro" and his heritage is well articulated in an article published in the summer of 1856:

> [The Negroes] have invented no writing, not even the rude picture-writing of the lowest tribes. They have no gods and no heroes, no epic

poems and no legend, not even simple traditions. There never existed among them an organized government. . . . Might alone is right. They have never known the arts, they are ignorant even of agriculture. The cities of Africa are vast accumulations of huts and hovels, clay walls or thorny hedges surround them, and pools of blood and rows of skulls adorn their best houses. *The few evidences of splendor or civilization are all borrowed from Europe* . . . all knowledge, all custom, all progress has come to them from abroad. The Negro has no history—he makes no history.[30]

This quotation encapsulates the Eurocentric worldview. It postulates a *tabula rasa* conception of Africa—as an environment distinguished by the absence of law and order, knowledge, culture, and history, a ghastly and horror-ridden place. Blacks were denied not only American nationality but also a credible ancestry. They were in effect suspended in a stateless space, doomed to perpetual servitude and subordination. By the middle of the nineteenth century, according to Cedric Robinson, "Western civilization, both at the strata of intellectual and scientific thought and that of popular opinion and mythology, had effectively sealed the African past. The undercurrent which gave some recognition to the African's and the Black slave's humanity, and which had been used to nurture much of the earliest antislavery sentiments and literature, had been overwhelmed by the more constant and morally profound tradition of racism." The construct "Negro," Robinson continues, "suggested no situatedness in time, that is, history, or space, that is, ethno- or politico-geography. The Negro had no civilization, no cultures, no religions, no history, no place, and finally no humanity which might command consideration."[31] This objectification of the black self and negation and nullification of black culture and history was designed to erase any positive imprint of Africa from black consciousness. The objective was to totally de-Africanize black consciousness or, failing in this, to implant only negative memories that would permanently confirm blacks in a state of alienation from the self and from African ancestry.

The attempt to de-Africanize, robotize, and control the consciousness of American blacks failed, however. Rather than becoming fatalistic and nonreflective, and acknowledging the reality given and defined by whites, many blacks affirmed their humanity by assuming a persistently critical disposition. This critical reflection, along with a subconscious rejection of the world as defined by the ruling class, shaped resistance to slavery, racism, and subordination, as well as the intellectual response of the nationalists. Resistance became an expression of a national consciousness that both negated the notion of a static, ahistorical, and backward Africa and strengthened claims to American nationality. Black American nationalists articulated positive ideas and values meant not only to rehabilitate and elevate Africa as a countercultural alternative but also to reverse or arrest the debilitating and destructive effects of Eurocentrism on the consciousness of blacks. More significantly, these same values and ideas were propagated to instill in blacks both the desire for, and a commitment to, change. This ethos of self-enhancement undergirded black American nationalist thought.

At critical moments in American history, therefore, blacks seized every opportunity to restate their claims to the nation. During the Revolution and the Civil War, blacks came forward courageously and risked their lives in the service of the nation to underline their American identity and nationality. Both periods generated rising expectations. Many blacks had hoped that freedom would ultimately resolve the intractable national question. But neither war satisfactorily resolved the problem. In fact, it was largely because the Revolution failed to resolve the question that slavery continued and developed in strength, creating further friction that resulted in the Civil War. The failure of the Revolution in this regard also explains the preeminence of the national question in the black abolitionist crusade in particular and in abolitionism in general. This failure also bolstered colonizationist and emigrationist consciousness. The outbreak of the Civil War rekindled hopes of finally resolving the question of black nationality. The enthusiasm with which blacks offered their services and sacrificed their lives in defense of the Union underlined the expectation that here, finally, was an opportunity to realize the elusive American nationality. This optimism quickly dissipated as the joys of the Reconstruction era gave place to the dark, gloomy, and bloody realities of the Jim Crow era. The ascendance of Jim Crow compelled blacks to revive the nationality issue in the closing decades of the nineteenth century. The search for a black or African nationality again assumed preeminence.

By 1880, therefore, when European powers intensified the pace of their activities in Africa, black America was at a crossroads. Betrayed by the national Compromise, denied the equal protection of the law, left vulnerable to the whims and caprices of their longtime oppressors, black Americans sought desperately for succor. Although the majority remained hopeful that ultimately America would become an open and free society, resulting in full citizenship rights and privileges for all, a vocal minority insisted that the national question was unresolvable within the United States and that blacks should abandon their expectations of ever being acknowledged as Americans. This minority, the emigrationists, urged blacks to seriously consider reactivating and regenerating thoughts of their ancestral homeland as the foundation of a Negro nationality.

It became immediately obvious to many that the failure to resolve the nationality question was racially conditioned—the consequence of a reluctance by whites to acknowledge the humanity and nationality of blacks. The racial factor was not confined to the United States, however. It was a global condition, or conspiracy, as some blacks perceived it, organized by Anglo-Americans and their Anglo-Saxon cousins to keep blacks in perpetual subordination.[32] The pertinence and pervasiveness of race and the conviction of a global conspiracy profoundly shaped black American nationalism during the second half of the nineteenth century. The nationalists enthusiastically proclaimed their African identity and theorized on the need for a strong African and black diaspora nexus, built on a foundation of shared culture and problems. Although compelled to identify with and embrace Africa, these nationalists harbored strong reservations. Socialized in a Eurocentric environment, where they were imbued with negative conceptions of Africa, they approached Africa with the same paternalism and condescension that the Europeans had adopted. Quick to affirm the validity of the myth of the "dark continent," they pledged to assist Europeans in rescuing Africa. Ridding Africa of barbarism became the foundation of a black nationality. Out of the ashes of the "dark continent" would emerge the black man's "city on a hill." Delany, Crummell, and Turner were among the leading advocates of this black nationality. Martin Delany dominated the epoch from 1850 to 1862. Alexander Crummell and Henry McNeal Turner, working independently, shaped the contours of black American nationalism from the 1870s to the first decade of the twentieth century.

Martin Robison Delany:
The Economic and Cultural
Contexts of Imperialism

The ideal personality to begin this study with is Martin Delany (1812-85), described as "the father of black American nationalism," the ideological godfather of black radicalism, one who unequivocally and uncompromisingly stood in defense of black American and African interests.[1] To his nineteenth-century peers, Delany embodied the quintessence of black nationalist thought. Frederick Douglass once described him as "the intensest embodiment of black nationality to be met with outside of the valley of the Niger."[2] Indeed, few black American nationalists of the epoch articulated black nationalist and Pan-African ideologies as forcefully and as effectively as Delany. Little wonder then that few disputed his characterization as "the Father of black nationalism." Delany undoubtedly deserved the accolades showered on him. Few nineteenth-century nationalists matched the vehemence and conviction with which he pursued the realization of his nationalist convictions.

But Delany did not begin his career as a black nationalist. A firm believer in the "American Dream," Delany spent the early, and, in fact, the greater, part of his career in the pursuit of integration. He was born to a free mother in 1812 in Charlestown, Virginia (now in West Virginia), and consequently inherited the free status of his mother. Freedom, however, made fundamentally little difference for Delany, and early in life he discerned the ubiquitous character of racism. Growing up a free black in Jeffersonian Virginia was quite an enlightening experience. He saw the deep cut on his father's face, inflicted by slaveholders bent on destroying the father's sense of manhood. He could not have missed the fright and horror in his mother's face as she spirited him and his brothers to safety in Chambersburg, Pennsylvania, to secure them from the clutches of

Virginian authorities who were determined to persecute her for no other cause than that her children had somehow attained literacy. It was a crime in Virginia, as in other slaveholding states, for blacks to be educated. Perhaps most painfully, he was denied opportunities for education in Chambersburg and had to move to Pittsburgh in the early 1830s.

Delany thus witnessed and shared in the depraved, oppressed, and humiliating lifestyles of his parents, grandparents, and blacks in general. He consequently embraced the black struggle and "registered his vows against the enemies of his race."[3] Convinced that blacks were Americans, and therefore deserving of all the rights and privileges due to every American citizen, Delany committed himself to liberalizing American society. His faith in the Protestant work ethic and normative middle-class values led him to spearhead the crusade for the economic and moral improvement of black Americans in the 1830s and 1840s. He was, in essence, a moral suasionist who believed that black fortunes would change as blacks improved themselves.[4] Success in self-improvement, many moral suasionists hoped, would unleash the reform impulse of the nation. This was the underlying principle of the philosophy of moral suasion that shaped abolitionist movements in the first half of the nineteenth century. Black as well as white abolitionists faithfully and optimistically preached the gospel that self-improvement would lead to elevation and equality. A greater responsibility for change was thus placed squarely on the shoulders of the victims, rather than the victimizers. Blacks were told that their *condition* (i.e., situational deficiency), rather than *racism,* was responsible for their negative experience and the dysfunctional state of society.[5]

None was more convinced of the validity of the situational deficiency thesis than Delany. He spent the greater part of two years, 1847-49, preaching the gospel of moral suasion to northern free black communities. He implored fellow blacks to cultivate the habits of industry, economy, and temperance. A radical transformation in the character and condition of blacks through the cultivation of these values, he believed, would appeal favorably to the moral conscience and reform instincts of whites.

> You can scarcely imagine the effect it would have over the pro-slavery feeling in this slave holding country, if, in addition to the few business

Martin Robison Delany. Courtesy of Moorland-Spingarn Research Center, Howard University

men we have, there were in New York city, Philadelphia, Boston, even in Baltimore, Richmond, Norfolk, Washington city, and all other ports of entry where colored men are permitted to trade, and Buffalo (which has one colored mercantile house), Cleveland, Detroit (which has another), Milwaukee, Chicago, Cincinnati and Pittsburgh, and many other places, but one shipping house, wholesale or retail store, the proprietor or proprietors of which are colored men, and one extensive mechanic of any description of trade. Such indisputable evidence as this of the enterprise and industry of the colored man, compared with that of the white, would not admit of controversy. It would bear with it truths as evident as self-existence—truths placed beyond the shadow of a doubt.[6]

Unfortunately, moral suasion failed. Work as hard as they could, blacks failed to convince whites that they deserved an extension of citizenship rights, privileges, and equality. By the late 1840s moral suasion was rapidly losing ground, giving way to immediatist and political strategies. Delegates to the state convention of Pennsylvania blacks spoke for other blacks when they observed in a petition to the voters of the commonwealth,

The barriers that deprive us of the rights which you enjoy finds no palliative in merit—no consolation in piety—no hope in intellectual and moral pursuits—no reward in industry and enterprise. Our ships may fill every port—our commerce floats on every sea—we may exhaust our midnight lamps in the prosecution of study, and be denied the privileges of the forum—we may be embellishing the nation's literature by our pursuits in science—yet with all these exalted virtues we could not possess the privileges you enjoy in Pennsylvania, because we are not "white."[7]

This declaration sounded the death knell of moral suasion. Delany was in attendance and fully endorsed the declaration. However, nothing convinced him of the futility of self-help and the ubiquity and virulence of racism as much as the Fugitive Law of 1850. Delany described the law as a clear evidence of the irredeemably racist character of American society. In Delany's estimation, the law sentenced all blacks to a life of perpetual subservience. Underscoring this point, he declared, "By the provisions of this bill, the Colored people of the United States are positively degraded beneath the level of the Whites . . . are made liable at any time, in any place, under all circumstances, to be arrested . . . and upon the claim of any White person, without the privilege, even of making a defense, sent into endless bondage." Black Americans were indeed "slaves in the midst of freedom, waiting patiently, and unconcernedly . . . indifferently, and stupidly, for masters to come and lay claim" to them. The development of the black American experience was not an isolated occurrence, however. Delany situated the black American predicament in a global context and likened it to that of colonized and marginalized nationalities elsewhere—"the Poles in Russia, the Hungarians in Austria, the Welsh, Irish and Scotch in the British dominions." He referred to blacks as a "nation within a nation"—a marginalized nationality, an oppressed minority, stripped of all semblances of humanity, denied the opportunities to develop. Like many oppressed minorities, therefore, blacks had no choice but to emigrate and establish an independent nationality—their own nation, free from the hegemony of whites.[8]

Underscoring the linkage between freedom and participatory democracy, Delany wrote that "no person can be free who themselves do not constitute an essential part of the *ruling element* of the country in which they live." Delany insisted that blacks had no choice but to emigrate if they were to attain meaningful freedom and elevate their status. Emigration became the key to the national independence of black America. He offered emigration as a realistic and realizable option, given the vast resources and opportunities in Africa. Africa possessed all the prerequisites, what Delany called the "essential ingredients" for a great nationality: landmass, natural resources, and an industrious population. Africa had everything, he emphasized, except the requisite level of intelligence and enterprise for the development of a nationality. This is where black Americans of intelligence, wealth, and enterprise, those he fondly referred to as men of "sterling worth," came in.[9] He specially appealed to wealthy black Americans to commit themselves to the idea of an independent nationality. Delany represented emigration as a historical necessity, indispensable to the survival and elevation of black Americans, and the ultimate expression of sovereignty. As he put it, emigration is "choosing one's own rulers, seeking self-government, aiding our self-emancipated brethren to sustain a black nationality."[10]

Delany predicted despair and perpetual misery for blacks in America. In a poignant review of the prevailing condition, he debunked the myth of a liberal North. Regardless of where blacks resided, North or South, they shared experiences of rejection and dehumanization and confronted a white population determined to subordinate them *ad infinitum.* "The only successful remedy for the evils we endure," he informed blacks, "is to place ourselves in a position of potency, independent of our oppressors."[11] A virulent cancer of racism ate deep into the moral fiber of the nation. Delany was especially distrustful of white liberals and abolitionists. Regardless of their professed sympathy for, and commitment to, the interest of blacks, white liberals generally shared the prevailing and normative assumptions about black inferiority. Delany harbored a very cynical view of white Americans in general. He described whites as patriotic and fanatically law-abiding citizens who respected the laws of the land regardless of their hateful intent and character. According to Delany, the Fugitive Slave Law, which portended doom for blacks, betrayed a white consensus on black inferiority and subordination and was further evidence of the imminent nationalization of slavery. Consequently, he deemed any expectation of assistance from whites the height of self-delusion. As he surmised, "Their country is their Heaven . . . their Laws their Scriptures . . . and the decrees of their Magistrates obeyed as the fiat of God. It is the most consummate delusion and misdirected confidence to depend upon them for protection; and for a moment suppose even our children safe while walking in the streets among them. A people capable of originating and sustaining such a law as this, are not the people to whom we are willing to entrust our liberty at discretion."[12]

Delany identified racism as perhaps the single most significant factor in U.S. race relations. He portrayed America as a society sharply and perpetually divided along racial lines. Underlining the significance of race, he wrote, "It would be duplicity longer to disguise the fact that the great issue, sooner or later, upon which must be disputed the world's destiny, will be a question of black and white, and every individual will be called upon for his identity with one or the other."[13] This statement remains perhaps the strongest expression made in the nineteenth century of the centrality of race in black-white relations.

The pervasive and endemic character of racism rendered the pursuit of integration unrealistic. Since whites seemed disinclined to relate to blacks in contexts other than that of master-servant, Delany sought to discourage integrationist aspirations. Even if successful, integration, according to Delany, harbored the dangerous and destructive potentiality of blacks losing their racial and cultural identity. He believed that it was impossible for blacks to integrate into America and at the same time retain their distinct identity and culture. Although Delany affirmed and strongly defended black American claims to American nationality, he envisioned the United States as a culturally pluralistic nation, one that recognized and respected both the rights and privileges of blacks as citizens and their cultural and racial distinctiveness. Although initially optimistic on the possibility of blacks acquiring American nationality and retaining a distinct identity, the depth and virulence of racism soon convinced him that such a scenario was inconceivable. Anglo-Americans, he finally acknowledged, would never accommodate blacks as distinct and equal members of the same nationality. The price for integration, in Delany's judgment, was complete acculturation, that is, the loss by blacks of their distinctiveness, and their total immersion in Anglo-Saxon culture. He deemed this too high a price, further underscoring the inevitability of emigration. To strengthen the case for emigration and an independent black nationality, he stressed the global magnitude of the threat against blacks. Just as Anglo-Americans oppressed blacks in America, their cousins, Anglo-Saxons, unfurled the banner of white supremacy abroad. He was particularly apprehensive of the imperialist ramifications of the globalization of racism. In fact, he discerned in the "conspiracy" of Anglo-Saxons and Anglo-Americans a sinister scheme for global dominance, and he warned blacks of the dire consequences of complacency and indifference.[14]

Delany's observations on racism and imperialism proved perceptive and prophetic. As already indicated, by the second half of the nineteenth century, "race-thinking" and its concomitant, the ideology of Eurocentrism, propelled European expansionism. Delany associated this expansionism with one goal: the subordination and exploitation of blacks. As he argued, "One of the most prominent features in the present conflicts, struggles, and political movements among the nations of the world seems to be: which can reduce us to a condition the best adapted to promote their luxury, wealth and aggrandizement[?]"[15] The global ambitions of Europe threatened the survival and independence of blacks, portending impoverishment and disaster.

Delany's doomsday philosophy, however, won few converts. Although he addressed issues that were central and pertinent to the experience of blacks, the solution he proffered appealed to very few. The majority of blacks remained integration-minded and optimistic that eventually American society would change for the better, the ubiquity and virulence of racism notwithstanding. This integration-ist *Weltanschauung* shaped the Negro convention movement, which began in the 1830s and reached its climax at the Rochester National Negro Convention in 1853. The gathering in Rochester was summoned by Frederick Douglass primarily to reaffirm the black commitment to integration and to claiming all the rights and privileges of American citizenship.[16] Emigration was an unpopular minority option among blacks. Many likened it to the obnoxious, proslavery colonization scheme and harshly criticized Delany for spearheading such a movement. At a state convention of Illinois blacks, delegates resolved to "regard all schemes of colonizing the free Colored people of the United States in Africa, or any other foreign land, originating in whatever motive, as directly calculated to increase pro-slavery prejudice, to depress our moral energies, to unsettle all our plans for improvement, and finally to perpetuate the wicked and horrible system of slavery." They affirmed their strong opposition "to the call for a National Emigration Convention, as put forth by Martin R. Delany and others, and discover in it a spirit of disunion which, if encouraged, will prove fatal to our hopes and aspirations as a people."[17] Delegates accused Delany of peddling a scheme that was destructive to the hopes and aspirations of blacks. This failure on the part of the majority of blacks to appreciate the enormity and global character of "white conspiracy" disturbed Delany. From his perspective, other blacks seemed oblivious to the threat of Eurocentrism and resigned to perpetual subordination. "Is subordination our normal condition? Is it true that we are not to be permitted anywhere to govern ourselves, but must have white rulers? Have we no other destiny?" Delany inquired, with a tinge of desperation and lamentation.[18]

By strengthening the linkage with Africa, Delany sought to make blacks free of both Anglo-American and Anglo-Saxon domination and exploitation. Africa represented the last hope—in fact, the new frontier—for building and solidifying black American nationality. There is, however, a political-economy consideration to Delany's construction of the global push of European imperialism. Although induced and sustained by deep-rooted racism, Europe's global advance was also the product of materialist dynamics: commerce. Delany identified commerce as the glue that bound and harmonized American and European interests. Commerce functioned as a unifying and dynamic force among whites, indeed, as the force that conferred power and authority and facilitated hegemony. Through the acquisition of commercial wealth, Europeans became economically powerful enough to exercise authority over other nations.[19] Commerce thus possessed ennobling and empowering qualities because it constituted the bedrock of political power. Delany located four centers of global economic power: New York, Boston, Liverpool, and London. Here the major political policies of the day were formulated and implemented. In Delany's analysis, therefore, the exploitative and racist disposition of whites resulted from the economic power they exercised. He thus displays a keen awareness of the economic character of European power and dominance.

Commerce, however, seemed like a double-edged sword, simultaneously producing wealth/affluence (the appurtenance of power) and aggressive hegemonic inclination (the root of domination and exploitation). The positive dimension of wealth, power, and affluence was then counterbalanced by a negative dispensation to dominate and exploit. Commerce thus embodied both negative and positive consequences, rendering it difficult for Delany to assume a consistent oppositional posture. He attributed Anglo-American global dominance to the transatlantic economic/commercial solidarity between Britain and the United States (represented by the dominance of the merchant exchanges of Boston, New York, London, and Liverpool), and black American marginalization to the lack of sufficient awareness of and attention to the utility of commerce. The commercial opulence of Europeans and white Americans enabled them to trample on the rights of other nations. To escape these unfortunate circumstances, Delany exhorted black Americans to emulate the Europeans by aggressively developing commercial ventures and thereby reaping the emancipatory, ennobling, and empowering benefits of commerce. He admonished black Americans to emigrate to Africa to accomplish this, where, according to him, resources abounded for the development of a solid economic and commercial power base.[20] The preeminence of commerce in Delany's nationalist thought probably explains one of his many contradictions: his solicitation of aid from the British and Europeans. This will become clear shortly.

Delany's advocacy of emigration and an African nationality suggests a total rejection of Eurocentric values and a commitment to stemming the tide of European hegemonic drives. His criticisms of slavery and racism, and his depiction of the United States as a racist society, coupled with his earlier glorification and exaltation of African civilization, embody the kernel of black nationalism and Pan-Africanism. Little wonder then that many of his contemporaries, as well as modern scholars, distinguished his thought as the quintessence of the struggle for black independence and nationality. His ideas profoundly influenced black American nationalism from the appearance of the Fugitive Slave Law to the outbreak of the Civil War. The Fugitive Slave Law reinforced Delany's growing concern over the possible nationalization of slavery. It confirmed his perception of America as a closed society and seemed to underscore the urgency of a new nationality.

From 1852 to the outbreak of the Civil War, Delany persistently hammered on the ubiquitous character of racism.[21] The American situation was clearly "a question of white against black." There was no middle ground, no compromise. His writings and speeches justified leaving America and directed the attention of black Americans to Central America, South America, the West Indies, and Africa. Of these places, he finally settled on Africa as the environment that possessed all the "necessary ingredients" for the development of a great nationality.

Delany spoke to the frustrations of black Americans at a crucial period of national despair. He offered ideological and practical alternatives—emigration in place of integration, and Africa in place of America. He built his emigration philosophy on the historical and cultural ties between black America and Africa. Delany conceived of emigration as a historical necessity, as the logical response of oppressed and outraged humanity, and as the first vital stage in the process of developing an independent nationality. The fact of African origin conferred legitimacy on the African aspirations of black Americans, making Africa a viable foundation on which to develop a nationality.

As Delany focused his attention on Africa, he had to deal with the regnant images of Africa popularized by Europeans, images that seemed to influence black American perception of and reactions to Africa. In European thought, Africa was the "dark continent," a jungle inhabited by beastlike creatures who lacked civilization, history, and culture. Delany struck back with a strong intellectual defense of indigenous Africa, pointing out that it had not always been what the Europeans portrayed. In fact, he blamed the Europeans for much of Africa's predicament, portraying Europe's first contact with Africa as an encounter that derailed and destroyed the glories and accomplishments of indigenous African civilizations—civilizations that not only preceded those of Europe but were also far more advanced in their accomplishments in the arts, the sciences, architecture, literature, and technology. Setting the intellectual tone for twentieth-century Afrocentric scholarship, Delany wrote, "It is simply ridiculous for ethnologists to claim the few Berbers who are found in and about Egypt, as the remnants of the ancient Africans, and erectors of the mighty pyramids, and authors of the hieroglyphics. The present Berbers of Egypt are none other than mixed bloods of the ancient Egyptians who once inhabited it,—who were pure black."[22] He praised the morals, character, industry, and accomplishments of the ancient Egyptians, whom he characterized as a scrupulous and conscientious people, a "people or race possessing in a high degree the great principles of pure ethics and true religion, [and] a just conception of God."[23] Delany identified the essential ingredients of civilization in the ethics, moral, and behavior of Africans. He proclaimed Egypt the "cradle of the earliest civilization," where the arts and sciences progressed at a time when the Greeks were "uncivilized." Negroes, according to Delany, were "foremost in the progress of time; first who developed the highest type of civilization. National civil government and the philosophy of religion were borrowed by the white races from the Negro" (319, 324). He blamed the lack of knowledge of ancient African civilization and accomplishments on the destruction of the famous Alexandrian library, which was then a repository of "the earliest germs of social, civil, political and national progress" (325).

Delany's adulation of Africa induced in black Americans a sense of importance, a positive self-conception, a reversal of the demeaning and denigrating historical and cultural perspective implanted by slavery and Eurocentric propaganda. It was heartening for many blacks to learn of the antiquity of civilization in Africa and of its influence on European civilization. Delany expressed hope that before long Africa would be regenerated "by her own legitimate children."[24] In 1854, he summoned a National Emigration Convention in Cleveland, Ohio, to establish modalities that, the delegates hoped, would result in the creation of a black nationality outside the United States.[25] The convention created a National Board of Commissioners charged with exploring emigration possibilities. Delany was appointed its first president. Although a minority movement, emigration attracted quite a few notable blacks willing to stake their fortune on the prospect of a new black nationality. In 1858, the board commissioned Delany to undertake an exploratory trip to the Niger Valley of West Africa.[26] The turn to Africa in fact reflected a global reality. Just as black Americans were turning to Africa, other nationalities, most prominently Europeans, were becoming aggressively interested in the continent.

For decades European missionaries and explorers had pioneered the exploration and "discovery" of the interior of Africa and fabricated the myth of the "dark continent," a process that gave birth to the "civilizing mission." What is often hidden behind the humanitarian mask of these interventions is the reality of industrialization and the critical search for raw materials. The industrial revolution compelled a change in the prevailing relationship between Europe and Africa. Slave labor had produced the resources that launched the industrial revolution. This revolution, as the late Eric Williams persuasively argued, in turn transformed European demands and rendered slavery obsolete. Instead of slaves, the Europeans now wanted tropical products—cotton, rubber, palm oil and kernel, and groundnut.[27]

The publication of Reverend T.J. Bowen's *Central Africa* and David Livingstone's *Missionary Travels and Researches in Southern Africa* in 1857 ignited black American interest in Africa. Many began to debate seriously the fate of black Americans, the future of Africa, and the necessity and prospect of emigration. A group of Wisconsin blacks, led by Jonathan J. Myers, a grocer, conferred with Delany on the possibility of a black American response to the new literature. Prof. M.H. Freeman, principal of Avery College in Allegheny City, Pennsylvania, also read the works of Bowen and Livingstone; he became convinced of the strategic importance of Africa to the future of black America and shared his conviction with Delany. Until the late 1850s, Delany's knowledge of Africa came from books he had read and stories he had heard. But, as he prepared to go to Africa, he could not help but be influenced by the interest generated by the "discoveries" of the Europeans, even though they were a race he had come to suspect and detest. Delany quickly purchased and perused the writings of Livingstone and Bowen; he was particularly impressed by the latter's description of the economic potentialities of central Africa, especially the industry and wealth of the Egbas, an ethnic group in the southwestern part of what later became Nigeria.[28]

Although inspired by the "discoveries" of European explorers, Delany deplored the expanding range of European activities on the West African coast. He described the European influence as negative and destructive, accusing the Europeans of sowing the seeds of discord among Africans. He reaffirmed his theory of an Anglo-Saxon and Anglo-American conspiracy to subordinate and destroy blacks.

Delany implored black Americans to challenge the worldwide imperial push of Europe, an imperialism that threatened to engulf the entire world, including territories that rightly belonged to blacks. He likened European imperialism to a hydra-headed monster that thrived on the subordination and exploitation of others. Unless black Americans became equally imperialistic and contrived an aggressive economic agenda premised on the development of a cotton economy in Africa, Delany warned, the chances of effectively neutralizing the European conspiracy were slim. The successful cultivation of cotton would sound the death knell of the American cotton economy and, by extension, slavery.[29]

The future of black Americans, therefore, depended on their adoption of economic and commercial schemes similar to those of whites. The establishment of trading ventures to Africa and the cultivation of cotton would accelerate the pace of black elevation. He advised that blacks should "enter into the more elevated and profitable industrial pursuits, and become contributors to the social and commercial relations of society and the world, as well as become recipients of the benefits arising from the relations."[30] Delany's economic agenda envisaged the colonization of Africa by black Americans. His choice of cotton was dictated by a determination to destroy slavery. Since American slavery thrived on the profitability of cotton on the international market, Delany sought to initiate a competitive source that would undermine the sale of American cotton, thus rendering slavery unprofitable.

Since few black Americans embraced emigration, Delany sought a wider audience. He chose religion, a choice dictated by his understanding of the preeminence of religion in the black American worldview. Juxtaposing emigration and religion was supposed to render the former more attractive. Delany consequently clothed emigration in religious robes. By relocating to Africa and taking advantage of her abundant economic resources, black Americans would simply be fulfilling God's plan, taking control of what he had reserved for them.[31] Essentially, Delany used providentialism to legitimize emigration and the accumulation and appropriation of wealth. He reasoned that, since the Lord created the earth and its resources primarily for human exploitation, black Americans' reluctance to take advantage of Africa contravened God's plan. Not only had God set Africa aside for black Americans, but slavery itself seemed to bear the imprint of the "finger of God"! Although an involuntary episode, slavery was nonetheless a progressive experience. It bred enlightened black Americans who "studiously *increased* in numbers, *regenerated* in character, and have grown mentally and physically vigorous and active, developing every function of their manhood, and are now, in their elementary character, decidedly superior to the white race." Black Americans seemed destined for a greater purpose: the inheritance of Africa.[32] "The land is ours. . . . [T]here it lies with inexhaustible resources," he affirmed. "Let us go and *possess* it."[33] This divine rationalization of slavery is a theme that recurs in the thought of Crummell and Turner: the institution of slavery (an evil) nurtured the future and salvation of Africa (a good end).

Spearheaded by several Wisconsin blacks, an organization called the Mercantile Line of the Free Colored People of North America emerged in the late 1850s. Members approached the Royal Geographical Society in London through a British professor of history at Wisconsin State University. In 1858, Delany and two others, J.J. Myers and Ambrose Dudley, wrote a letter on behalf of the Mercantile Line to the Geographical Society, requesting information on the best place to locate a colony in Africa. The letter was delivered to Thomas Clegg, a prominent Manchester cotton spinner who had been promoting cotton cultivation in Africa since 1850.[34] The turn to London at this crucial early stage is significant. Even as Delany discerned a global conspiracy against blacks and Africans, he had no qualms about soliciting assistance from the alleged perpetrators of the conspiracy.

In fact, as soon as the Emigration Convention of 1854 approved an exploration venture to Africa, its leading explorers, Delany and the West Indian Robert Campbell, turned immediately to the British for financial and logistical support. Campbell went ahead to London in April 1859 and in May publicly appealed for support from British abolitionists and industrialists, particularly those dependent on American cotton: manufacturers in Lancashire and Manchester. He reminded them of the precarious condition of the American cotton market, given the growing sectional tension, and stressed the need for an alternative source of cotton. His appeal struck a responsive chord, for British industrialists were already becoming jittery over the increasing tension in the United States. Campbell won the support of leading manufacturers, including Thomas Clegg. He also secured the endorsement of the British Foreign Anti-Slavery Society and met with several members of the Manchester Cotton Supply Association. He was able to garner both moral and financial supports. In fact, his passage from Liverpool, to Lagos on the West African coast, was financed with contributions from British industrialists.

Delany's nationalist/emigration scheme, his search for an independent black nationality in Africa, and his plan for an economically powerful and politically independent black state appeared compromised almost from the start by his contact with, and request for aid and support from, a segment of the very group of people whom he had blamed for the unfortunate predicament of blacks and whose policies appeared aimed at perfecting a world order of black subordination. The activities of Delany and Campbell, therefore, compromised their capacity for independent action. While Delany and his emigration cohorts thought in terms of securing an economic and political power base for blacks, the British, in line with the developing European imperialism, thought more in terms of a secure and viable economic base that would continue to service the industrial revolution.

Delany left for Africa in May 1859 to investigate Africa's economic resources and other considerations pertinent to the projected relocation of black Americans. Robert Campbell joined him a few months later. Both men visited Liberia, established in 1822 by the American Colonization Society as a colony for the resettlement of free blacks. They were warmly received by the political and ideological leaders of the black settler community, among them Edward Blyden and Alexander Crummell. Delany delivered a series of lectures on the black American condition, focusing on the trajectories of the struggle for freedom and equality.[35] He and Campbell traveled extensively in Liberia and Sierra Leone. They found evidence of industry and an abundance of economic resources, particularly tropical products, such as palm oil and kernel, groundnuts, cotton, rubber, and cocoa. Delany particularly noted the fertility of the soil and its suitability for the cultivation of cotton of the highest quality. After several days in Liberia, the party moved to Lagos. They traveled extensively through several communities in what later became southwestern Nigeria. In the town of Abeokuta, the local chiefs responded positively to Delany's request for land on which to resettle black Americans, agreeing to cede a portion of their territory. From this settlement, the migrants hoped to launch the projected cotton revolution.[36] The observations and findings of Delany and Campbell confirmed the reputation of Africa as a treasure house of economic resources.

Despite the Manichaean worldview that Delany had earlier espoused, he was quick to associate his African scheme closely with the developing European ideology and program. His thoughts changed dramatically with respect to both the condition of Africans, whose values and customs he had praised (and would continue to praise), and European activities and influence. Delany's travels and observations in Africa revealed dimensions of Africa and Europe that he had not reckoned with. This changed the entire complexion of his nationalist thought. He developed a much more positive attitude toward the activities of the Europeans, especially the missionaries, and shifted from a position of criticism and rejection to one of commendation and exaltation. He glorified the efforts of the missionaries, especially the Protestant missions. Wherever they set their feet, he declared, there you find evidence of "purer and higher civilization" among indigenous Africans. Although Christianity constituted a positive force, Delany cautioned against overemphasizing religion and suggested that equal attention be devoted to improving the temporal and secular condition of Africans. He applauded missionaries' contributions to educating Africans and spreading "civilized" manners and customs among them. He was particularly impressed by the introduction of the English language, which he described as an effective civilizing medium. In these assessments of European influence one confronts one of Delany's paradoxical positions. He found several African customs abhorrent and demeaning, and he exhorted the missionaries to obliterate as many of these customs as possible. Indigenous Africa was in dire need of improved acts of civilized life, and he admonished external agents, preferably the African-descended people of the diaspora and particularly those of moral integrity, intelligence, and financial means, to assume this task.[37]

What Delany found objectionable among indigenous Africans touched at the very essence of their lives—for example, the practice of eating on the floor in the open compound, rather than at a table inside a house. He equally despised the customs of eating with the fingers, sleeping on mats, and wearing light clothing that covered only parts of the body. He enjoined the missionaries to train Africans in the use of knives, spoons, and forks, and to instill in them the habits of wearing clothes that covered the whole body, sleeping in beds, and eating at a table inside a house. Delany focused on precisely those same "barbaric" practices that the European missionaries and explorers had similarly deemed abominable. He thus strengthened the case for the *mission civilisatrice*, the underlying rationale for European imperialism. He also argued forcefully for the extension of European influence into the heart of the continent and for the imposition of European practices (105-6). It is not clear whether he realized the contradiction or disjunction between his earlier condemnation of European values and his later support for the imposition of those same values on Africa. This imperialistic aspect of Delany's character, indeed, his reconciliation with European imperialism, was powerfully illuminated as he explored the economic prospects of his nationalism in Africa.

Unfortunately, Delany did not provide any explanation for his sudden change of mind about Africa. It is difficult to fathom or speculate on the reasons for the dramatic shift in his consciousness. The transformation of Delany from a radical nationalist and advocate of black American and African freedom and elevation into a defender of imperialism in Africa, who espoused values that compromised his earlier position, remains intriguing. A possible explanation lies in the discrepancy between the conceptual Africa that Delany had heard about and grown up to admire and defend, on the one hand, and the real Africa that he finally confronted, on the other. The transformation could also have been the result of "culture shock," or a manifestation of Delany's Euro-American acculturation, a reality that he shared with black Americans in general. It is an undeniable fact that years of acculturation in the New World had significantly altered the cultural values of peoples of African descent. Although geographically and historically of African origin, and racially black, New World blacks were far from being culturally and ethnically African. The African identity had merged with a greater and "complex pattern" of identity that led to an equally complex and often conflicting self-consciousness.[38]

This is a provocative thesis to advance in the context of a resurgence of Pan-Africanism and the ascendance of Afrocentricity, an intellectual paradigm that situates black American cosmology and epistemology in Africa and insists on an African definition of identity.[39] The reality and complexity of the diasporic transformation is, however, beclouded by this reductionist theoretical construct, which erroneously postulates a monolithic diasporic and African identity. There is also an erroneous underlying presumption of a shallow and transient diasporic experience. It is largely because Afrocentrism perceives black Americans, and black diasporans generally, as culturally unchanged by the experience of transplantation that it places so great a premium on becoming intellectually centered in, and relocated in, the Afrocentric tradition. For Afrocentrists, focusing black American education on Africa and highlighting its positive dimensions became strategies for emancipation and development. Historically, however, attempts to project a monolithic African and black diasporan consciousness have often foundered on the rocks of diasporic complexity and contradictions. The experiences of some of the leading Pan-Africanists clearly establish the divergence and ambivalence inherent in the black diasporic experience and consciousness. Two examples are noteworthy: first, the opposition that Marcus Garvey confronted from fellow West Indians and black Americans and, second, the bitter conflict between the late Walter Rodney and the West Indian bourgeoisie (a struggle that ultimately took his life). The current debate between black American conservatives and radicals, a struggle that has its roots deeply buried in the past, presents similar issues.[40] The diaspora experience is real, complex, and culturally transformative. Most black diasporans confront an existential dilemma—awareness of a complex or, in the description of many, double identity. The ambivalence in Delany's nationalist thought, therefore, represents a manifestation of the inner tension and conflict resulting from his complex identities, a conflict that he perhaps subconsciously tried to suppress as he developed his nationalist and Pan-Africanist ideology. Delany unfurled the banner of his African identity as a response to the challenges of American life, but he knew relatively little about the nature, complexity, and nuances of Africa. When finally confronted with Africa and the compelling cultural and normative "discrepancies" it evoked, his submerged American identity surfaced and became predominant. Although still committed to the advancement of Africa, his American side became difficult to ignore. Perhaps without his realizing it, confronting Africa compelled Delany to speak as an American (or more appropriately, a foreigner). Consequently, though he did identify and sympathize with Africans, Delany's duality/complexity rendered absolute and unconditional identification with Africa inconceivable and problematic.

There was, however, an equally compelling economic explanation for Delany's change. Having determined that Africa had the resource and manpower base for the creation of an economically viable black nation, he confronted the difficult practical problem of procuring the financial wherewithal to bring it into existence. Although he had identified black Americans as the preferred, and indeed the legitimate, actors in the transformation of Africa, he was equally aware of the depth of black American opposition to emigration, especially among the middle class, whose cooperation he deemed fundamental. Given the paucity of support for emigration among black Americans, Delany was compelled to seek an alternative source of financial support for his scheme. It was in this search for funding that the racial and ethnic lines that demarcated his nationalism became blurry.

After a sojourn of about eleven months in Africa, Delany amassed a wealth of information and statistics about the economic potentialities of the continent. This, with the treaty he had signed with the traditional rulers of Abeokuta, clearly confirmed his optimism about the possibility of a black nationality in Africa. What was lacking were the financial resources and entrepreneurial skills. Remarkably, he turned to the British for assistance, arriving in London on May 16, 1860. This step is not as contradictory as it appears, however, for Delany had clearly suggested the inevitability and indispensability of cooperation between Europeans and black Americans. As he earlier declared, "To England and France, we should look for sustenance, and the people of those two nations—as they would have everything to gain from such an adventure and eventual settlement in the Eastern Coast of Africa."[41]

Two days after Delany's arrival in Britain, he and Campbell met with a group of British abolitionists and cotton manufacturers. Delany succeeded in obtaining recognition as sole and legitimate spokesman for black American interests.[42] The timing of his turn to Britain is significant. The British textile industry was in a state of panic over the increasingly volatile American cotton market. In fact, as the sectional conflict intensified in the late 1850s, British cotton manufacturers formed the Cotton Supply Association (CSA) primarily to explore alternative sources of cotton. The CSA turned to Lagos and Abeokuta. However, British interest in the development of a cotton economy in the Niger Valley predated the inauguration of Delany's exploration party. The British consul in Lagos, Benjamin Campbell, had long been experimenting with cotton production and was already exporting some cotton to Britain.[43] By 1860, Britain was importing an increasing amount of cotton from West Africa. Thomas Clegg, who operated cotton mills on the outskirts of Manchester, also owned production centers in West Africa—precisely, in Abeokuta, Onitsha, and Lokoja.

These ventures were represented as efforts to promote the "three C's." In reality, the economic activities of the British, both private and public, constituted the foundation for the British occupation of the region. Delany's arrival and the information he provided to British industrialists and cotton manufacturers bolstered British economic interest in Africa. Several of his lectures focused on the backwardness of Africa and appealed favorably to the "civilizing" impulse of the British. He provided detailed accounts of the interstate crises in the interior of Africa, particularly the civil wars among the Yorubas, and of the horrors of slavery in Dahomey.[44] He enjoined "philanthropic Englishmen who have some feeling for Africa" to convince the British government of the moral and material benefits that it would derive from assuming a much more prominent and assertive presence on the West African coast (133-34). The information he provided on the immensity of Africa's economic resources, coupled with negative portraits of African lifestyle, values, and religion, strengthened the case for the deployment of commerce and Christianity.

Delany offered Africa to the British as a land of vast economic resources, with rich soil conducive to the cultivation of cotton, and he pledged the services and partnership of black Americans in developing the resources of the continent. He gave British entrepreneurs, cotton manufacturers, and industrialists perhaps the most compelling reason to embrace his African scheme—the availability of cheap indigenous African labor. He proposed cooperation between British industrialists, black American middle-class workers, and African laborers (122-48). This was, indeed, the earliest manifestation of a strategy he would later propose as a solution to the problem of Reconstruction America—the "triple alliance."

In July 1860, prominent members of the CSA inaugurated yet another organization—the African Aid Society (AAS). Although depicted as a humanitarian organization inspired by a desire to abolish the slave trade, its underlying impulse was economic. The founders were mostly merchants and manufacturers associated with the textile industry. Their goal was to repatriate blacks to Africa for the purpose of cultivating cotton, silk, indigo, palm oil, and sugar (127). The society, therefore, had the larger interest of the British economy at heart, and it planned to sponsor further expeditions into the African interior. Delany and Campbell addressed and provided key members of the society with vital and timely logistical and statistical information. The society enthusiastically embraced Delany and Campbell and provided them with the much sought-after financial and moral support. Delany then met with "noblemen and gentlemen," representatives of the prestigious Royal Geographical Society—Lord Alfred S. Churchill, the Right Honorable Lord Carthage, the Honorable Mr. Ashley—all of whom had expressed interest in the "Condition and Prospect" of Africa (122-48).

Delaney spent about six months in Britain, shuttling between London and Glasgow. He emphasized the tremendous economic profit awaiting those who invested in Africa. Delany successfully forged commercial ties with several English and Scottish firms. He signed contracts with some of the greatest cotton dealers, among them Messrs. Crum, Graham, and Co., one of the largest of such firms in Glasgow. Several leading journals approved his mission. The *Newcastle Daily Chronicle*, in an article supportive of Delany, added that about three million Britons relied for employment on cotton being supplied by the United States, the disruption of which would result in a disaster of "unparalleled magnitude."[45] Perhaps apprehensive of Victorian self-exaltation, Delany insisted on an alliance based on equality between black Americans and British capitalists. What roles would be reserved for Africans in Anglo–black American economic cooperation? A closer examination of Delany's overall scheme points to one answer—subservient roles. The benefit of equality was not extended to Africans. They were to function as the providers of cheap labor, at the disposal of the two active and dominant partners of the so-called tripartite alliance.

Delany was undoubtedly naive to suppose that British industrialists would enter Africa as equal partners of black Americans, given the extent of ethnocentrism and racism, a condition of which he was fully conscious. This myopia resulted from an unwillingness to acknowledge and confront the reality of racism in Britain. Determined to court the goodwill and support of the British, Delany chose to ignore the globalization of racism he had earlier emphasized. However, to condemn racism and ethnocentrism in America, while completely ignoring these same evils in Britain, especially at a time when the evils were clearly in ascendance, betrays a selfish dimension of Delany's nationalist thought. His flirtation with British industrialists has to be examined in the context of the changing character of European interests in Africa. In 1851, the British government signaled the beginning of a new offensive toward Africa with its occupation of Lagos. Other European powers, notably France, Portugal, and Holland, were similarly committing greater attention and resources to Africa. It seemed quite obvious to Delany, and to other black American nationalists, that any scheme for a black nationality had to accommodate the expanding range of European interests and power. Fortunately for the promoters of such schemes, British industrialists and manufacturers appeared favorably disposed toward any suggestion that promised a steady supply of much-needed raw materials, such as rubber, palm oil and kernel, groundnut, cocoa, and, most critically, cotton.

Delany also presented his African discoveries to an International Statistical Congress in London and to various British organizations and societies, most notably those interested in tropical products. He repeatedly stressed the economic benefits that investing in Africa would bring. Africa possessed not only enormous economic resources but also excellent navigable rivers and port facilities—the Ogun, Ossa, the Niger, the Gambia, Senegambia, Orange, Zambesi, Lagos, Porto

Novo, Whydah—for the exportation of those resources (121-22). He couched his appeal in precisely the language that the imperialists understood: the development of trade and commerce in Africa would cripple the slave trade and extend the frontiers of civilization. In essence, Delany played the humanitarian card, appropriating the rationale of the imperialists, the one they adduced to justify their own schemes. The Europeans had consistently portrayed their encroachment on Africa as a humanitarian gesture aimed primarily at eradicating the inhuman practices associated with the "barbaric" customs of Africa, especially the slave trade. They pledged to replace slavery with trade in legitimate products.

Delany also displayed a keen awareness of the apprehensions of British industrialists and entrepreneurs, exploiting their fear of a possible decline, or total closure, of the American market for cotton—the lifeline of textile industries in Lancashire, Manchester, and Liverpool. He assured them that Africa possessed the right type of soil and climate and the plentiful supply of cheap labor needed to produce the highest quality cotton in the world (116-22). He stressed the fragility of the American cotton market, noting the probability of slave insurrections and the growing estrangement in the relationship between the North and South (the specter of civil war), all in a bid to focus British attention on Africa. He provided statistics to highlight the profitability of cotton cultivation in Africa: the average product per acre on the best Mississippi and Louisiana cotton plantations was 350 pounds; in Africa the average was 100 pounds. He presented more compelling statistical data on the importance of cotton to Britain: "Two-thirds of the population depends on cotton, directly or indirectly for their livelihood. About 25,000,000, or five-sixths of the population depend upon the article for subsistence" (118).

Private British citizens already engaged in the cultivation of cotton in Africa, and anxious for British involvement and support, were quick to embrace Delany and Campbell. In fact, a greater part of the pressure for a redefinition of Europe's relationship with Africa came from the merchants of the European nations, who requested national backing for their respective enterprises in Africa. Thomas Clegg joined forces with Delany and corroborated his claim of the superior quality of African cotton at a meeting in Manchester Town Hall (132-33). Ralph Clarence, a British cotton grower in Natal, South Africa, commended Delany's campaign. Clarence, who had been in

Natal for almost twenty-five years, was likely among the many British farmers who appropriated Khoisan lands and who had contributed to transforming the Khoisans into landless proletarians.[46] The Khoisans resisted, of course, rendering the labor situation in South Africa problematic and compelling the likes of Clarence to search desperately for alternative sources of labor and for greater British government support. In a letter to Delany, Clarence solicited his assistance in resolving the critical labor situation in Natal: "What we want is constant and reliable laborers."[47] He pleaded with Delany to encourage migration of laborers from West Africa to Natal.

Clarence visualized a future Africa "civilized" by foreigners entering the continent from two entry points—Delany's enterprise in the "West," and his in the "East," both dependent on the exploitation of cheap African labor (136-37). For Clarence, as for other imperialists, civilizing Africa meant essentially one thing: exploitation (of labor as well as material resources). Clarence's vision for the future of Africa was in consonance with Delany's emigration scheme: it necessitated the cooperation between two or more external agents in the exploitation of Africa's resources. It should be mentioned that these plans clearly conceived of indigenous Africans solely as objects—as primitives to be civilized and cheap laborers to be exploited. Indeed, they were treated as a people blessed with economic resources but miserably deficient in the intelligence and civilized disposition fundamental to progress.

To stabilize the African environment for imperial economic exploitation, Delany beseeched the British to apply force against the growing tide of interstate and intra- and interethnic conflicts in the interior of the continent (133-34). It should be remembered that the African interior in the second half of the nineteenth century was indeed a theater of conflicts, which were generated by an ongoing process of political realignment and integration, a process that, left alone, many scholars contend, would have resulted in the emergence of politically stable nation-states. Such states would undoubtedly have more effectively resisted the European imperialists.[48] Little wonder then that the imperialists exacerbated and exploited these crises, using them as excuses for invading the continent. Delany and other black American nationalists similarly depicted the internal crises in Africa as consequences and manifestations of barbarism, and they welcomed and encouraged European interventions.

Delany undoubtedly succeeded in bolstering British resolve to invade Africa. His reports on the economic resources of Africa provided the practical motive, while his depiction of certain African customs as barbaric boosted the humanitarian excuse. There is perhaps a pragmatic consideration to the contradiction inherent in Delany's turn to Britain for assistance. His knowledge and awareness of the role of economic power in politics has been discussed. Long before his British adventure, Delany had articulated the conviction that economic power was indispensable to the success of a black nationality. In fact, it is clear that economic power, what he referred to as "Political-Economy," ranked high in Delany's thought.[49] In his view, national greatness was inconceivable without economic power. This largely explains the preeminent role he assigned to the black American middle class. Unfortunately, the crusade for emigration, and indeed for a black nationality, failed to generate much support and commitment from the black middle class. This seriously circumscribed the domestic black American economic support base for an independent nationality, leaving Delany no choice but to turn to whites for assistance, just as Henry McNeal Turner and other black nationalists did later. Put differently, the only viable source of support for an African nationality, Delany found, was paradoxically the same force against whose power and influence that nationality was initially directed.

When Delany returned to the United States in early 1861, the Civil War had started. His mind was set on emigration, and he ignored the crisis. Instead, he embarked on a nationwide tour to generate public support for emigration. He presented black Americans with his findings on the prospects in Africa. To black Americans, however, Delany presented a much more positive picture of Africa. In a lecture on the "Moral and Social Aspects of Africa," he referred to Africans as a morally upright people who respected their women and were organized into stable political systems, with functional and impartial judicial systems governed by kings who respected the laws. He depicted African languages as melodious, civil, rich in vowels, and "capable of expressing a wide range of feelings and sentiments."[50] This portrait sharply contradicts that of the society of "barbarians" to which he had earlier justified the application of British force.

Less than eighteen months after he returned to the United States, however, Delany's African crusade came to a screeching halt. The quest for a black nationality and the need to develop and civilize African "barbarians" no longer seemed urgent. Overcome by his American desires and consciousness, Delany embraced the Civil War. With a renewed confidence in the "American Dream," he immersed himself in the struggle for a racially integrated America, and in 1863 he was commissioned the first black combat major in the Union army.[51] Meanwhile, the British, whom he had mobilized, went about the business of acquiring as much of a foothold in Africa as possible.

Delany's abandonment of Africa was induced, first, by the Civil War itself and, second, by the character and strength of the reforms that accompanied the Civil War and Reconstruction. It started in 1863, with the Thirteenth Amendment and the abolition of slavery. The subsequent Fourteenth and Fifteenth Amendments conferred citizenship and the franchise, respectively, on blacks. In addition, blacks were promised the equal protection of the law. The reforms of radical Reconstruction opened a wide spectrum of political space to blacks. Delany welcomed these changes. Had death struck him in the 1870s, Delany would most certainly have died a happy man. For him, it was as if the elusive "American Dream" had finally materialized. The nightmare was over.

Nothing expressed his elation and conviction so well as his declaration that blacks had become "an integral part and essential element in the body politic of the nation," and the vehemence with which he strove to prevent other blacks, especially the new political leadership, from upsetting and destabilizing the new order.[52] Throughout the ten-year radical Reconstruction period of 1866-76, Delany concentrated his efforts on creating and sustaining circumstances that, in his estimation, would strengthen the chances of blacks permanently realizing the elusive American nationality. He campaigned vigorously for compromise and reconciliation with southern whites, and he urged the federal government to grant unconditional pardon and amnesty to former rebels and slave owners. Such reconciliatory policy would, he averred, guarantee the complete integration of blacks, while equally enhancing the prospects for their economic advancement and that of the nation in general. Concern for the "primitive and heathenish" condition of Africa receded to the background. Black Americans no longer needed an African nationality.

Delany's optimism was, however, short-lived. The rights and privileges of blacks were soon eroded and obliterated in the wake of the decline and collapse of Reconstruction. In fact, by the early 1870s it was obvious to many that the days of Reconstruction were numbered. The Compromise of 1877, which officially terminated Reconstruction, also marked the resurgence of Jim Crow. In compensation to the South for acceding to a Republican administration in Washington, the federal government agreed to withdraw its troops from the region, effectively obliterating the force that had protected blacks in the exercise of their fragile freedom and its accompanying rights and privileges. This also paved the way for the political ascendance of the Democrats. In South Carolina, where Delany resided, the "Redeemers," as Democrats and former slavocrats fondly called themselves, assumed power with vengeance in mind, sworn and determined to undo the alleged damages, abuses, and mistakes of ten years of Reconstruction.

Betrayed, abandoned, despised, and threatened with the reimposition of forms of quasi slavery, black Americans once again turned to Africa. In South Carolina, they organized the Liberia Exodus Movement and appealed to the American Colonization Society for aid in relocating to Liberia. Delany joined the movement and became an active member. The quest for an African nationality again assumed center stage in his thought. He corresponded with several key society officials, requesting financial assistance for the resettlement of blacks in Africa.[53] Unfortunately, nothing concrete resulted from this latter phase of his nationalism. Its significance, however, lies in its further illumination of the utilitarian nature of Delany's African consciousness.

Alexander Crummell:
Religious, Moral, and Cultural
Legitimation of Imperialism

Alexander Crummell (1819-98) shared similar disillusionment with Delany over the deteriorating condition of black Americans, and he too developed a consuming desire to assist in effecting change. Born a free black in New York, young Alexander imbibed a strong African consciousness from his parents. His grandfather was a chief of the Tiammanee people, and his father was a prince. His father, Boston Crummell, was as proud of his American connection as he was of his African ancestry and vowed never to voluntarily relinquish his American identity. Young Alexander grew up in a circle of blacks who, like his father, grappled with what Crummell's biographer, Gregory Rigsby, has called "the black American dilemma," that is, the problem of identity and nationality.[1] The circle included Peter Williams, James McCune Smith, John Ruuswurm, and Samuel Cornish. Most black Americans confronted the problem of double consciousness—of being African and American. Although leading blacks extolled Africa and often professed a commitment to cooperating with Africans for mutual development, they were determined never to voluntarily mortgage their American nationality. For most of them, Africa was a memory, and America was the reality they knew. Like Boston Crummell, the members of his social circle sought the means of attaining and sustaining their American nationality. Their utterances and activities constituted the cultural artifacts in young Alexander's socialization.

Crummell also attained manhood under the shadows of the black convention movement. Although not old enough to participate in the early conventions of the 1830s, Crummell was certainly aware of the crises and conditions that prompted the conventions. As indicated in chapter 2, the conventions represented expressions of black American

Alexander Crummell. Courtesy of Moorland-Spingarn Research Center, Howard University

nationalism. The underlying impulse and the specific deliberations of the convention movement clearly establish that blacks were a people in search of acceptance and integration. They proclaimed their subscription to mainstream American values and boldly declared their American citizenship, rejecting any scheme of emigration or colonization. Crummell became active in the New York state conventions in the 1840s. He reached manhood in a world in which blacks acknowledged their African identity, while boldly and vehemently protesting attempts to circumscribe or deny their American nationality.

From his parents and society Crummell imbibed double consciousness, an awareness of African entity and a determination to strive for American identity. Regardless of the troubling nature of this predicament, there was no doubt that blacks accorded primacy to the American identity and nationality. Crummell developed a strong consciousness of Africa and fondly referred to himself as an African. Exposure to racism and violence emboldened him, and he immediately committed himself to the black American struggle. He professed a strong commitment to the defense and elevation of blacks and stressed the linkage between the plight of blacks in America and the experience of Africans. This Pan-African ethos remained a central component of his thought (1-53).

He also emphasized the importance of education to the success of any schemes for the elevation of blacks. He assigned the educated elite a leading responsibility in the struggle for black and African freedom, thus anticipating Du Bois's concept of the "talented tenth." He espoused a utilitarian conception of education, assigning it a higher and nobler purpose, beyond teaching students to read and write. Crummell defined the goal of education as the development of the intellect and the nurturing of the moral nature, both fundamental to the progress and improvement of society (42-46).

Like Delany, Crummell's quest for education further exposed him to the hostility and violence engendered by racism. There were few supports and provisions for black education beyond the elementary level. His search for higher education therefore took him to Noyes Academy in Canaan, New Hampshire, in 1835. At the school, which was operated for colored children by abolitionists, he met Henry H. Garnet and Thomas Sidney. His stay at Noyes was cut short, however, by antiabolitionist violence; mobs destroyed the school and attacked the black students (22-24). He returned to New

York and later entered the Oneida Institute, where he studied classics, Greek and Roman history, English history, language, and poetry, including such major English poets as Milton, Shakespeare, Coleridge, and Wordsworth. Crummell's training at Oneida had a profound impact, leaving him with a deep appreciation and admiration of English culture and civilization. It was also at Oneida that he decided to enter the priesthood. Education seemed to have instilled in him a sense of responsibility and a desire to serve humanity. It also nurtured his moral character, inspiring a commitment to truth and justice, and developed an emancipatory self-conception.

The attainment of an emancipatory self-understanding through education is crucial in the context of black marginalization. Despite a growing awareness of his historical and cultural heritage and a positive self-conception, Crummell was troubled by the inner conflicts of a complex identity—being both an African and an American. He responded with a philosophical reconciliation of the two identities. He espoused a Pan-African Christian ideology that underscored the historical and cultural connection between black Americans and Africans, as well as their mutual obligations and responsibilities for advancement (30-53). This philosophical response, according to Gregory Rigsby, was essentially metaphysical, and it left the existential problem of double identity unresolved (14).

This was, however, not unique to Crummell. Virtually all black American nationalists of the epoch responded to the problem of double consciousness philosophically and metaphysically at first, by asserting affinity with Africa and boldly proclaiming interest in strengthening the relationship through policies and programs of mutual elevation. The existential factor came into sharper focus after these blacks made contact with Africa. In fact, it is the convergence of the philosophical and existential perspectives that sharpens the contradiction in black American identification with Africa and that sheds more light on the imperialist dimensions of black American nationalism. Crummell's philosophical response, from the very beginning, bore the imprints of normative European assumptions about Africa. Consequently, his professed pride in being African was negated by both his proclamation of American identity and his later profession of alienation from Africa's barbarism. In a sermon in 1845, he referred to Africans as a heathen and superstitious people who needed to be redeemed through Christianity (49).

A unique feature of Crummell's early philosophical perspective was its Pan-African character. Crummell appealed for transatlantic black solidarity built on historical and cultural ties and sustained by strong Christian values. Within the prevailing context of cultural assumptions about Africa's "primitivism," however, this seemed inconceivable. Like Delany, Crummell assigned black Americans the task of "civilizing" Africa. A civilized Africa would in turn have a positive impact on black America, since the "primitive" state of Africa was used to justify the subordination of blacks in the diaspora.

Faith in the potency of religion as a weapon for the civilization of Africa probably propelled Crummell in the direction of the priesthood. After graduating from Oneida, he applied to the General Theological Seminary for admission, but was turned down. He later went to Boston, where he was ordained in 1844. Securing a parish was even more difficult: he failed in Providence, Philadelphia, Boston, and New York City. In desperation, he turned to Britain in 1848, primarily to raise funds for establishing a church. While engaged in fund-raising activities, Crummell enrolled in Cambridge University, from which he was graduated in 1853 with a bachelor of arts degree in divinity (54-70).[2] He undertook extensive lecture tours of Britain, visiting Birmingham, Liverpool, Manchester, and London. His lectures, focused on slavery and racism in the United States, succeeded in arousing public sentiments in favor of American abolition movements.[3] His lectures were equally infused with strong nationalist and strong Pan-African overtones. He stressed racial solidarity among blacks and the importance of Christianity as a foundation for the uplifting of the race. Africans and blacks in the diaspora shared "One Aim! One Goal! One Destiny!" (60-62). Abolition was no longer an end in itself; it was also a step toward the black solidarity for which Crummell called, toward the development of a strong linkage with Africa, and toward recognition of the reciprocity and mutuality between blacks in the diaspora and Africans. More than anything else, Crummell stressed the "duties" and "responsibilities" of "civilized" black diasporans toward Africa.[4]

Crummell set his eyes and mind on Africa. There was no better place to put his training in divinity into use. As he declared, "There is no spot, of all this wide world, to which my heart travels with more ardent affection than Africa. . . . [A]lthough born in the United States . . . I should think myself privileged . . . [to spend] the small measure of [my] ability . . . in efforts for the salvation of those to whom I am connected by descent in that benighted land" (61). He initially opposed colonization, believing solely in the potency of Christianity. He picked the gospel, rather than commerce and colonization, as the sole agency for the regeneration of Africa. He urged black Americans and Afro–West Indians, especially those motivated by missionary zeal, to assume full responsibility for propagating the gospel among heathen Africans. This group would elevate Africans from darkness and primitivism.[5] Once Christianity was effectively spread throughout Africa, everything else would follow.

Crummell's chance came when the African Mission, an arm of the Domestic and Foreign Missionary Society in America, appointed him a missionary to Liberia. This was Crummell's golden opportunity to contribute to the regeneration of Africa and the building of a Pan-African nationality. He arrived in 1853 to begin missionary activities, energized by the prospect of a Pan-African community unified by the Christian faith. The black American experience in America, despite its ugly and inhuman character, became in Crummell's estimation a valuable training experience in preparation for duty in Africa. He arrived in Africa with a curious sense of gratitude to Europeans and a positive perspective on his experience in the United States, despite the callous realities of enslavement.[6]

In the beginning Crummell seemed to propose a monolithic solution—everything hinged on the success of Christianity. The propagation of the gospel among Africans was sufficient to transform the entire continent. His faith in this solution was, however, short-lived. In Liberia, he quickly realized that Christianity would have to be supplemented with commerce, and he abandoned his opposition to colonization and threw his weight behind economic development. He spoke of the "elevating and civilizing" character of commerce. Commerce combined with Christianity became the perfect formula for the salvation of Africa, and black Americans remained the legitimate persons to apply this formula. He urged wealthy black Americans to purchase vessels and become more active in trade with Africa, just as the Europeans were doing. Like Delany, Crummell was critical of the standoffish posture of black Americans, who were handing Europeans a monopoly on the exploitation of Africa's economic resources—resources to which they, through ties of consanguinity, had prior claim.[7]

But how could Crummell justify to Europeans the role of black Americans as civilizing agents, given the universal assumptions of Eurocentrism? Put differently, since Europeans had lumped all blacks together as inferior and primitive, it became absolutely necessary that black Americans be distanced from Africans if their role as bearers of civilization to heathen Africa was to have a chance of being accepted by the Europeans. This was a problem that Crummell shared with other black American nationalists. Resolving it entailed rationalizing away what constituted, in European thought, an essential contradiction—one branch of a primitive race involved in the task of civilizing the rest of its own! Crummell found the solution in slavery.

He represented slavery as an experience that prepared and qualified black Americans to function as bearers of civilization to Africa. If Crummell's theory was right, slavery had implanted the seeds of black American imperialism. Although he denounced slavery, Crummell was nonetheless convinced that the institution had a divine seal of approval and that the experience of enslavement involved ennobling transformation. Slavery was consequently an elevating and civilizing experience, qualitatively superior to the "barbaric" and culturally inert African background. It was indeed "the fortunate fall," since it resulted in a positive experience and purpose (113). God sanctioned slavery precisely because he had a greater purpose in mind: that those who were enslaved, and who were ultimately elevated and civilized through contact with Western values, would return to change the heathens and barbarians left behind. Cleansed of their primitivism by slavery, black Americans were therefore qualified to function as bearers of civilization.[8] Of the three nationalists in this study, Crummell is perhaps the most vocal and forceful in the propagation of this thesis and in the negative depiction of traditional African societies. In Crummell's view black Americans had benefited immensely from enslavement, despite the pains and anguish of the experience. He acknowledged and promoted European civilization as inherently positive and superior, along with the notion that its values and influences deserved to be superimposed on Africans.

Commerce and Christianity became for Crummell, as for Delany and the Europeans, potent forces in the civilizing of Africa. However, Crummell's concept of commerce differed slightly from that of Delany. For Delany, commerce combined negative and positive qualities—it possessed the capacity both to enhance the fortune of a people and to destroy their freedom. Indeed, Delany viewed commerce as a double-edged sword: just as it elevated and modernized an enterprising Europe, it threatened other societies, especially the complacent and indifferent, with impoverishment and marginalization. Crummell, on the other hand, represented commerce as essentially a positive force, a potentially civilizing factor. Indeed, to him commerce constituted a yardstick for measuring the state of a people's civilization. A society shielded from commerce was prone to degeneration. Commerce is crucial to the well-being of the world, according to Crummell, because it "binds men and nations to each other . . . it promotes goodwill, and builds up sterling character." Underlining the utility of commerce, he declared, "There are few secular agencies so life-giving, so humane, and so civilizing, as is commerce. Let a nation sleep the sleep of a century's dullness, and then some propitious providence draw toward it the needs and desires of the nations; and up it starts to life and vigor."[9] Since Africa was blessed with enormous economic resources, commerce seemed the logical agency for the transformation of the continent.

Despite its significance, Crummell subordinated commerce to religion. Commerce alone could not save Africans from the depths of moral decadence. Africa was in the "moral desolation of the deepest, darkest ignorance." The whole continent "presents one broad, almost unbroken, unmitigated view of moral desolation and spiritual ruin." While others were engaged in building civilizations in Australia, Canada, and Europe, according to Crummell, Africa was locked in misery and darkness, "victim of her heterogeneous idolatries. . . . [T]hey are living without God. The cross has never met their gaze, and its consolations have never entered their hearts."[10] To reverse this moral desolation and decadence, he recommended a systematic "year to year push, more and more into the interior."[11] Although he assigned black Americans a key role in the development of Africa, he did not advocate the expulsion of Europeans. In fact, he welcomed their participation and applauded their activities. This was consistent with his subscription to the prevailing conception of European civilization as the ideal and standard against which to measure all others.

Against his positive assessment of the economic potential of Africa, Crummell juxtaposed perhaps the harshest and most negative critique of indigenous African societies and values by a black American. He characterized the Liberians as a deplorable, decadent, and barbaric people, desperately in need of the infusion of superior Western values. Referring to Africa in general, Crummell averred, "Africa lies low and is wretched. She is the maimed and crippled arm of humanity. Her great powers are wasted. Dislocation and anguish have reached every joint. Her condition in every point calls for succor— moral, social, domestic, political, commercial, and intellectual. . . . Great social evils universally prevail. Confidence and security are destroyed. Licentiousness abounds everywhere."[12] Africa, to Crummell, was blessed with treasures but inhabited by a people without skills or intelligence. Comparing Africa with India, he observed that Africa was as rich in resources as India, but "more unenlightened and has a less skillful population." These descriptions of Africa could well have come from the pen of a European missionary or explorer. Crummell undoubtedly meant to reveal to black Americans the deplorable state of Africa, perhaps to inspire their determination to participate in regenerating the continent.

In Crummell's thought, Europeans introduced sunlight to Africa "after years of darkness."[13] Although he extolled the operations of British and French firms there, Crummell lamented the poor representation of black America in the commercial exploitation of Africa. He deplored the monopoly enjoyed by foreign firms, and he entreated black Americans to organize trading companies similar to those of the British and the Dutch.[14] The complacent and nonchalant posture of black Americans disturbed Crummell the most and, like Delany, he appealed to religion to inspire greater involvement in the imperial cause:

> The Lord created the earth and its fullness . . . given to man irrespective of color or race. . . . [T]he main *condition of the obtainment* of it is *intelligence, forecast, skill,* and *enterprise.* If the black man, . . . civilized and enlightened, has lying before him a golden heritage, and fails to seize upon and to appropriate it, Providence none the less intends it to be seized upon and wills it to be used. And if the white man, with a keen eye, a cunning hand, and a wise practicalness, is enabled to appropriate it with skill and effort, it is his, God gives it to him, and he has a right to seek and to search for a multiplication of it.[15]

Crummell, Delany, and other black American nationalists viewed Africans as lacking the "condition of the obtainment"—intelligence, forecast, skill, and enterprise—of the resources of the continent.

Blacks in the diaspora, "civilized and enlightened" through the fortuitous experience of enslavement, consequently qualified to function alongside Europeans in Africa. This positive rendition of the transformative properties of acculturation in the New World was a pervasive theme in black American nationalism. Because they were qualified through acculturation and fitted with the requisite "condition of the obtainment" of the land and its resources, Crummell admonished black Americans to challenge European control of the African trade. Not only were black Americans qualified but they also had greater rights to the African trade. He was optimistic about the prospects "of an early *repossession* of Africa . . . by her now scattered children."[16] The call to "repossess" Africa is also a recurrent theme in black American nationalist thought. Africa was a vast, empty land at the disposal of Europeans and black Americans.

In his description of Africans, Crummell, more than Delany or any other nineteenth-century black American nationalist, appropriated the language and values of Eurocentrism. His strong devaluation of Africa helped no doubt to confirm the Victorians and other Europeans in their self-imposed responsibility of exporting "civilization." The characterization of Africans as a people blessed with economic resources, but devoid of intelligence and skills, only confirmed the Europeans in their racist views and bolstered their resolve to invade Africa. There is thus a fundamental convergence in European and black American conceptions of Africa, one that legitimized their designs on the resources of the continent. Crummell went as far as to deny any semblance of historical experience to Africans. "So far as western Africa is concerned," he wrote, "there is no history." Echoing Hegel's misconception, he denied the existence of intelligence in "the long, long centuries of human existence [in Africa]. Darkness covered the land, and gross darkness the people."[17]

Crummell attributed Africa's alleged backwardness and lack of history to centuries of isolation caused by the Sahara Desert (108). He thus pictured Africans as shielded from contacts with civilization and lacking in the intelligence necessary for independent invention. Civilization could only come to such a society through diffusion from outside. According to Crummell, Africa's isolation had bred paganism and superstition until the coming of slavery. European explorations, missionary activities, and slavery eventually ended this isolation and brought enslaved Africans in contact with the cultural influence of the West (109-29). Consequently, the redemption of those Africans unfortunate enough to have avoided enslavement and remain static and locked in primitivism had to come through the infusion of Western values.

Crummell portrayed the abolition of the slave trade, the coming of the missionaries, and the growth of legitimate commerce as mechanisms for the civilizing transformation that Africa desperately needed. He praised Mungo Park, Hugh Clapperton, brothers John and Richard Lander, and David Livingstone for bringing Africans in contact with civilization. He offered precisely the same "compelling" evidence as that adduced by European scholars to justify the myth of the "dark continent." He expressed enthusiasm over the "progress" he and other black American missionaries appeared to be making in Liberia. There were obvious signs, he said, that indigenous Liberians were receptive to, and benefiting from, Western education and the crusades for moral elevation and industry. He praised the missionaries of the Church of England and the Wesleyans for improving the educational and vocational skills of Liberians.[18]

The denial to Africans of a tradition and an experience of history was not new. This denial distinguished the corpus of scholarship that sustained the Eurocentric worldview and its sequels—slavery and colonialism. What is intriguing, however, is the espousal of Eurocentrism by black American nationalists. It is not clear whether Crummell and other black Americans who so curiously embraced Eurocentrism were aware of the self-abnegating implication of their action. The denial of an African historical tradition was applied to black America as well. In fact, this linkage had been forcefully defended from the earliest writings on the subject. Consequently, Crummell could not have been unaware of the fact that neither Africa nor black America was considered to possess a history. However, like many of his contemporaries, he seemed fooled by the assumption that the geographical and cultural distance between black America and Africa had rendered the inclusion of black Americans in the same category with Africans improbable.

Crummell's reinterpretation of the black experience in America is similarly remarkable in its apology for, and almost total rationalization of, oppression. A diffusionist to the core, Crummell ascribed "the universal prevalence of benightedness through all Africa" to isolation from "the mental and moral influences of superior and elevating forces." Contact with Europe, and the diffusion of "superior" European values, would redeem and civilize Africa.[19] Through contact with whites, black Americans, despite the past and continuing dehumanization of racism and segregation, were fortunate to have been exposed to such noble and immortal ideas as liberty and justice—values that, according to Crummell, were inherent to the English language and civilization. These ideas represented the mark of civility. As he put it, "It is only under the influence of Anglo-Saxon principle that the children of Africa, despite their wrongs and injustice, have been able to open their eyes to the full, clear, quiet heavens of freedom."[20] He invoked the intellectual authority of the German historian Barthold Georg Niebuhr in defense of diffusionism: "There is not in history the record of a single indigenous civilization; there is nowhere, in any reliable document, the report of any people lifting themselves up out of barbarism."[21]

Crummell thus permanently situated Africa's development and "civilization" within a diffusionist model. His application of the Niebuhrian thesis denied the possibility of indigenous African initiatives for change. Slavery was the connecting factor in Africa's contact with Europe and, *ipso facto,* the channel for the diffusion of superior European values! Crummell consequently de-emphasized the destructive and inhumane character of slavery. Regardless of its perpetration of "wrongs and injustice," Anglo-Saxon culture had been most beneficial to Africa. He likened the enslavement of Africans to the experience of the Israelites in Egypt. Such dehumanizing experience, however, harbored a deeper positive dimension. It represented a "process of painful preparation for a coming national and ecclesiastical responsibility." Slavery was indeed the "Babylonish captivity" of blacks, a captivity that was sanctioned by God in order to prepare them for a much higher and nobler undertaking. In fact, echoing classical Eurocentric conviction, Crummell clearly suggested that the benefits that accrued to blacks from their contacts with Anglo-Saxon culture and civilization far outweighed the evils, even slavery. This point echoes through several of his speeches and writings, including the "English Language in Liberia." As terrible as slavery was, Crummell contended, "It has not been the deadly hurricane portending death. During its long duration, although great cruelty and widespread death have been large features in the history of the Negro, nevertheless, they have been overshadowed by the merciful facts

of great natural increase, much intellectual progress—and generous, wholesale emancipation, inclusive of millions of men, women,
and children."[22] One is hard-pressed to find any rationale for abol-
ishing such a positive institution! Especially intriguing is the role
that black Americans, including Crummell, had played in swaying
public opinion in favor of abolition. Perhaps this is yet another manifestation of the invincible "finger of God," to use Delany's phrase,
working to free and promote black Americans for a greater responsibility—to transfer the civilized values imbibed from slavery to Africa! Slavery and emancipation, therefore, were not accidents of history. They were God's mechanism for transforming black Americans
into colonists, merchants, missionaries, and teachers—agents for the
transformation of Africa from barbarity to civilization. The acceptance by leading black American nationalists of European definitions of progress and civilization—i.e., their appropriation of European values and institutions—blinded them to the imperialist
implications of their own schemes and those of the Europeans, and
even to the self-abnegating implications of those values.

Crummell spoke glowingly of Western values and institutions.
He also strongly urged the Europeans, as a matter of moral responsibility, to rescue Africa from the "barbarism" of indigenous languages
and cultures. This direct appeal, more than anything else he had
written, directly tied Crummell to the "civilizing mission." Even with
regard to industry, an attribute he acknowledged in indigenous Africans, Crummell still found shortcomings serious enough to warrant
the intervention of external powers. Their resourcefulness and industry notwithstanding, Africans manifested negative and essentially
primitive behavioral traits. As Crummell put it, the primitive indi-
gene possessed an "acquisitive principle"—he or she engaged in trade
to satisfy his or her wants, wants that were largely "undefined."
Crummell discerned a certain element of irrationality in the indus-
triousness of indigenous Africans, whom he viewed as a greedy and
selfish people, driven by an insatiable thirst for commodities. These
characteristics, according to him, were the cause of the tribal conflicts that engulfed the interior of the continent, slowing down, and
in many cases preventing, the progress of commerce and civilization. To remedy this situation and open up the interior for the flow
of legitimate commerce and civilization, he called for the introduction of a "grand police force" all over the continent.[23]

It is noteworthy that Crummell described Belgian atrocities in the Congo as "eminently practical" measures that would provide the discipline needed to advance the course of civilization. The policies and activities of King Leopold II of Belgium were, according to Crummell, acts of deliverance, in spite of the brutalities and violence perpetrated against the Congolese.[24] Crummell displayed this insensitivity to the plight of Africans at a time when even other European nations and Americans expressed outrage over the atrocities.[25] Crummell's embrace of Belgian colonialism contrasted sharply with his earlier opposition to colonization and denunciation of European influence. This public endorsement is significant, given Europe's depiction of colonialism as the vehicle for the regeneration and transformation of Africa. Like Delany, Crummell proposed a historical and providential rationalization for African colonization. The transplantation of blacks to America was not an accident but part of a comprehensive divine plan. He dismissed the theory of chance; all historical events were driven by "the moral economy of God." There was, consequently, a divine plan that inspired peoples and nations toward the realization of a divine end. As he put it, "We see every where God's hand in history. In all the movements of society, or the colonization of peoples, we see the clear, distinct 'finger of God' ordering, controlling, directing the footsteps of men, of families, of races." In Crummell's view, all human experiences, negative as well as positive, were thus infused with a divine purpose. This providential determinism perhaps explains why Crummell de-emphasized the cruelties and inhumanity of slavery, focusing instead on what he deemed its positive goal. Although God could not be the "author of evil," Crummell argued, he exercised a "masterful authority" over the "work and ways" of the wicked, redirecting them toward a positive and noble end.[26] Slavery represents God's capacity to effect Good out of Evil. God allowed slavery to exist, but intervened and reshaped it into a positive experience. According to Crummell, "Millions of the Negro race have been stolen from the land of their fathers. They have been the serfs, for centuries, on the plantations and in households, in the West Indies and the United States, of civilized and Christian people. By contact with Anglo-Saxon culture and religion, they have themselves been somewhat permeated and vitalized by the civilization and the Christian principles of their superiors."[27] Although an evil act, the enslavement of Africans consequently had a dynamic and positive sequel, reflective of God's intervention in reshaping slavery for a higher purpose. His "moral economy" required that the transformed former slaves function as bearers of light and civilization. Again, in Crummell's plan, as in that of Delany, the role assigned indigenous Africans was clearly a subordinate one. These plans treated indigenous Africans as objects, in very much the same way that Euro-Americans had related to black Americans. Africans were like a heap of clay at the disposal of Europeans and their black American partners, to be molded into whatever shape the colonizers deemed appropriate.

The Africa depicted by Crummell is a static environment, inhabited by peoples with backward, hideous, and demeaning cultural traditions. In his study of Crummell, Ottey Scruggs doubts that "Crummell contributed much to an accurate knowledge of the African people and African societies. His mind was simply too imbibed with Western missionary ideas to expand much beyond false, value-laden categories as paganism and barbarism. His views, ironically, may have contributed heavily to the negative image of Africa in the black middle-class mind at the turn of the century."[28] There is no doubt that Crummell's ideas did foster demeaning perceptions of Africans. Much more than this, his ideas corresponded with those of European imperialists and accorded legitimacy to their designs on Africa. There was thus an ideological convergence between European imperialists, in search of justification for moving into Africa, and black American nationalists and "Pan-Africanists," whose ideas and platforms provided the grist for the mill of imperial ideology. Left alone, Crummell argued, indigenous Africans "can never become spiritually enlightened. You cannot find one single instance where a rude, heathen people have raised themselves by their own spontaneous energy."[29]

Crummell identified two distinctive attributes that underlined the divine character of slavery. The process of enslavement illuminated both the retributive and restorative qualities of the "moral economy of God." Slavery constituted a retribution for the idolatries and barbarous practices of Africans. Crummell thus provided justification for the enslavement of Africans. The restorative process began in America, culminating in emancipation. Restoration, however, remained unconsummated until black Americans returned to pass the positive influences of the diaspora to indigenous Africans.[30] It is plausible to infer from Crummell's thought that the seeds that would germinate in the colonization of Africa were embedded in the very institution and experience that ravaged and destroyed the continent: slavery. There is thus a long divine chain linking slavery to colonialism. In fact, they were obverse sides of the same coin.

Crummell's declaration of support for imperialism was not intended solely for the black American public, but also for the American government whose isolationist and anti-imperialist policy he considered ill-advised, given the fact that other European nations were becoming increasingly involved in Africa and were actively backing their respective missionaries and traders.[31] Crummell sought similar support from the American government for American missionaries and traders. The acquisition and appropriation of Africa's resources, he said, constituted "one of the prime conditions of OUR existence," although it is not exactly clear to whom the "OUR" refers (177). In any case, Crummell urged the United States government to become more active in Africa, in accordance with the policies of "the new born states of modern times," an obvious reference to Germany and Italy (178). He perceived the preeminence of black Americans in Liberia as a solid foundation from which to launch a U.S. colonial policy in Africa, and he advocated the declaration of an American protectorate over Liberia (180-82). The call for a protectorate is indicative of his endorsement of the existing policies of the British, French, Germans, and Belgians, who were already proclaiming fraudulent protectorates over other African societies.[32]

By declaring a protectorate over Liberia, the American government would, Crummell opined, guarantee both the much-needed protection to American missionaries and traders and the stability that would facilitate their commercial and "civilizing" activities. He further called for the introduction of an "armed force" into Africa (like the British navy) to curb "petty native fights" that disrupted trade. Force was Crummell's answer to the internal conflicts among Africans. To be effective, force had to be applied decisively, unsparingly, and with little regard for the "democratic rights of the natives" (185). He denied the extension of democratic rights to Africans, "a rude people, incapable of perceiving their own place in the moral scale, nor of understanding the social and political obligations which belong to responsible humanity" (185). Although he commended the English for what he deemed their positive contributions to Africa, Crummell deplored the confinement of England's naval force to the coast and the hesitant and tentative use of that power. He regretted Britain's failure both to plant its flag in Ethiopia in 1868, when it had the opportunity after an encounter in which the Ethiopians were defeated, and to permanently cripple Asante and assert British hegemony throughout the empire after the defeat of the Asante army in 1874. If Crummell had had his way, the occupation of Africa would probably have occurred much earlier![33]

Crummell, however, seemed a little uncomfortable with his advocacy of using force against Africans. Although theoretically in favor of the indiscriminate application of force, he quickly qualified his stand with a moral conception of force. The force he proffered was one associated with the diffusion of civilized values—"the force that anticipates the insensate ferocity of the pagan, by demonstrating the blessedness of permanent habit and lasting peace, which forestalls a degrading ignorance and superstition, by the enlightenment of schools and training" (186). He envisioned a force whose impact transcended physical violence and pain. This would be a force with a moral and ethical conscience, the impact and effectiveness of which would be reflected in its transformative effect on the habits and condition of Africans. Crummell appeared a little uncomfortable with physical violence. It remains unclear, however, how this "moral force" would have effectively tamed Africans, given the depth and magnitude of the "rudeness" and "primitivism" he ascribed to them.

Crummell's advocacy of brute force is consistent with a perception of Africans as "rude peoples." Without the moral development of Africa backed by force, he predicted a "visitation of the sorest anguish" as Africans "combine together, along the line of our interior borders, in their several tribes, . . . who will come down to the sea-board, in sanguinary ferocity and terrible array, to destroy every vestige of religion, and sweep us, if possible, into the sea." Again, who is the "us"? The battle line imagined is certainly not between black Americans and Europeans but between these two and the "rude peoples." Like Delany, Crummell justified force as an appropriate response to the conflicts in the African interior. Crummell is thus implicated in the forcible European overthrow of African states. His pride in European values is remarkable. He proposed a "hierarchy of social development"—a progression from savagery and barbarism, through slavery, to civilization.[34] Britain, and Europeans in general, exemplified the latter at its best. Consequently, Europe's intrusion into Africa represented "the highest philanthropy and most zeal-ous religionism."[35] One is hard-pressed, finally, to find any substan-tive difference between Crummell's ideas and those of the Euro-pean racial classifiers of earlier epochs.

Once Crummell had accepted the intrinsic validity and superi-ority of European values, his sense of revulsion against African val-ues and culture assumed a virulent tone. The future of Africa de-pended on the extent to which those "superior" European values were transplanted. He thus embraced both dimensions of European imperialism—political and cultural. That is, he found strong vindi-cation for imperialism in both the political-economic and cultural conditions of Africa.

Much of the "barbarity" that Crummell abhorred and highlighted was found in indigenous African customs and traditions. He singled out indigenous languages for perhaps the most scathing condemna-tion. The languages perfectly mirrored the "backwardness" and "rude-ness" of the people.[36] If Europeans were to civilize the continent effectively, the languages would have to be changed; Crummell sug-gested the English language as a substitute. Perhaps no issue illumi-nates Crummell's disdain for indigenous African societies so much as his lionizing of the English language. The English language, in his estimation, possessed certain inherent qualities that elevated it to the standard of "those great charters of liberty" that were funda-mental elements of true governments and guarantees of personal liberty (22-29). He was particularly impressed by the "civilizing" impact of the English language. Liberians who spoke English seemed to exhibit a remarkable level of civilized behavior. Crummell was excited by the "Anglican aspects of our habits and manners and the distinctness . . . of our English names and utterances," and he urged the rapid Anglicization of Liberians (11, 12-22). The acquisition of Anglicized habits, accent, and names became for Crummell a mea-sure of civilization. He underlined the distinction, in civilized dispo-sition, between Liberians who had acquired elements of civilization through their ability to speak English and the vast majority who spoke the indigenous languages (30-34). He associated slavery with another "positive development": it had put black Americans in touch with the language of "Shakespeare, Milton, Wordsworth, Franklin, Bacon, Burke" (9-10). This modernizing experience had already diffused to some indigenous Africans through contacts with black Americans and with Europeans in Sierra Leone and Liberia. Crummell measured progress among Africans by how much of the English language they had mastered. Knowledge of English represented a transition "from low to higher and nobler civilization" (18). Crummell compared indigenous languages with English and found them worthless. They possessed the "definite mark of inferiority" and were remote from "civilized languages" (20). Echoing the views of Dr. Leighton Wilson, an American missionary, he concluded that African languages were distinguished by "lowness of ideas"— they were "the speech of rude barbarians, marked by brutal and vindictive sentiments, and those principles which show a *predominance of animal propensity*. . . . [T]hey lack those ideas of virtue, of moral truth, and those distinctions of right and wrong . . . of justice, law, human rights and governmental order which are so prominent and manifest in civilized countries. Those supernal truths of a personal, present Deity, of the moral government of God, of man's immortality, of the judgement, and of everlasting blessedness" (19-20, emphasis added). Dr. Wilson had confined his critique to the Grebo language; Crummell had no qualms about applying those negative qualities to every other language in Africa.

Crummell's invective against African languages underscores his failure to appreciate or understand the true meaning and essence of these languages. In this respect, he reflected the age in which he lived. European scholars, linguists, explorers, and missionaries had difficulty with the tonal complexity of indigenous West African languages. According to Philip Curtin, "Where the grammatical context or even the meaning of a word depended on tone, the Europeans were quick to assume that the language was 'primitive,' because it seemed then to lack grammatical regularity."[37]

Against the negative features of indigenous languages, Crummell juxtaposed the positive qualities of the English language. It was "the language of universal force and power—simple, intelligible, of freedom," and those who were exposed to it (such as black Americans) immediately developed the noble qualities of freedom, tolerance, and compassion (22-24). Consequently, acquiring knowledge of English was worth the high price black Americans had paid for it. The language had already unified many blacks in the diaspora (in the United States, Latin America, and the Caribbean), and placed them on a pedestal above Africans.

To ensure the spread of the language among Africans, and the enhancement of European values, Crummell recommended the systematic introduction of Africans to the orbit of Western and European culture (32-36). He was very specific about the right type of education for Africans—one that would inject in them "the staples of the Anglo-Saxon mind" (41). To accomplish this, Crummell recommended the following reading materials and subjects: Bacon's *Essays*, Locke on the Mind, *Life of Benjamin Franklin*, Watts on the Mind, Alison on Taste, Bunyan's *Pilgrim's Progress*, *Robinson Crusoe*, History of Rome, History of Greece, History of England, Butler's *Analogy*, Paley's *Natural Theology*, Wayland's *Moral Philosophy*, Channing's *Self-Culture*, Milton's *Poems*, Cowper's *Poems*, Burder's *Self-Discipline*, Todd's *Student's Manual*, Life of Mungo Park, and Life of James Watts (42). These subjects and reading materials are presented in exactly the way Crummell wrote them. They betray foresightedness. He anticipated, and possibly set the stage for, the content and character of colonial education.

Although Wilson J. Moses acknowledges that Crummell's nationalism was "marked by certain inconsistencies," he absolves him of responsibility. The inconsistencies, according to Moses, derive from the broader "inconsistencies and hypocrisies of American racism." Moses further contends that it is impossible to "create an ideology that responded rationally to an irrational system."[38] This assertion is not merely questionable; it is untenable. By absolving Crummell of responsibility for his inconsistencies and paradoxes, a familiar reductionist strategy in black biographical studies, Moses reduces Crummell, just as Delany and several of his contemporaries have been reduced by other writers, to a mere object: powerless in the face of overwhelming societal pressures, a helpless instrument of an irrational order, always reacting to external pressures rather than being the conscious architect of his designs. It is very difficult, but certainly not impossible, to respond rationally to an irrational situation. It is even more plausible to ascribe Crummell's inconsistencies to the inner conflict that he and other blacks experienced, associating them with the problematic of identity that W.E.B. Du Bois later appropriately called the "twoness" of the black American: both an African and an American, "two souls, two thoughts, two unreconciled strivings; two warring ideals in one dark body. . . . The history of the American Negro is the history of this strife—this longing to attain self-conscious manhood, to merge his double self into a better and truer self."[39]

Crummell, Delany, and Turner indeed responded rationally, as might be expected of members of an oppressed and marginalized minority, to the inconsistencies of American slavery and freedom. This is corroborated by their criticisms, objections, and propositions. The major irrationality or inconsistency occurred in their response to Africa, and this was itself a manifestation of the dynamics of their dual identities—including their internalization of Eurocentric cultural dichotomies. They had been socialized to accept the definitions of Euro-American identity as superior and African identity as inferior. Consequently, although compelled to acknowledge the African identity, black Americans remained uncomfortable with that connection and vigorously pursued the realization of the Euro-American identity. The elevation and imposition of the American and Anglo-European heritage over the African is a measure of the grip of Eurocentrism on black American consciousness.

The full implication of Crummell's ideas would become prominent after the imposition of colonial rule. The assertion by the colonial powers—Britain, France, Portugal, and Belgium—that Africa was primitive and inferior and that Europe was civilized and superior; their demeaning of African value-systems and languages; their use of education as a weapon of "civilizing" and alienating Africans from their original culture—all represented colonial implementation of Crummellian ideas. The colonial order that emerged, as several scholars have shown, proceeded along the lines of reshaping the culture and values of the colonized in the image of the colonizer.[40] This entailed a reductionist devaluation of Africans, their customs, and their worldview. Language was a major framework for this process of devaluation. Africans were induced to distance themselves from their own languages. As one critic put it, the process "systematically instilled a sense of inadequacy and inferiority into African people. This was done particularly through the conveying of racist images of Africa and the rejection of African languages, while promoting and glorifying the European philosophy of life and European languages. African languages constituted part of the 'blackness-that-needed-to-be-left-in-the-jungle.'"[41]

During the colonial period, education, through its propagation of European languages and curricula, became a vehicle for molding a personality conducive to colonial "enculturation" (to borrow Walter Williams's concept). While the suggestion of a relationship between the ideas and schemes of Crummell (and those of Delany and other black American nationalists of the epoch) and the shape and character of European colonialism in Africa may appear far-fetched, given the fact that the colonial enterprise was essentially controlled and managed by Europeans, it seems equally inaccurate to project the two as diametrically opposed and in conflict. Admittedly, the Europeans would have imposed their languages and belief systems on Africa, in order to facilitate and reinforce their rule and domination, regardless of what black American nationalists said or did. Nevertheless, it seems dishonest to ignore the links between the two varieties of nationalism and colonialism (i.e., black American and European), particularly the presence of the core values of European imperialism in black American nationalist thought.

Henry McNeal Turner:
The Cultural Imperative of
Imperialism

Henry McNeal Turner (1834-1915) was born in Newberry, South Carolina. His slave mother, who was said to have been the daughter of an "African king," was freed by the British during the Revolution. His father, of whom we know little, died when Turner was very young. Although born free, Henry, like most other free blacks, suffered the indignities and abuses that racism bred. Nevertheless, he remained optimistic and integration-minded, believing in the inevitability of change. After his mother moved to Abbeville, South Carolina, Henry began working as a servant in a law office there. It was in Abbeville that he learned to read and write.[1] Henry seems to have embraced religion early in his life; he joined the Methodist Church in 1848 and was licensed to preach five years later, becoming an itinerant preacher and spreading the gospel throughout the South. In 1857 Turner joined the Negro African Methodist Episcopal Church, and in 1862 he was appointed pastor of Israel Bethel Church in Washington, D.C., a position he held until the outbreak of the Civil War.[2]

Like other black leaders, Turner saw prospects for black freedom and elevation in the war, and he actively supported and campaigned for black enlistment. In 1863, he was commissioned by President Lincoln as a chaplain of Negro regiments, and he assisted in raising black troops. After the war, he retained his chaplainship and was assigned to the Freedmen's Bureau in Georgia. He became very active in radical Republican politics, serving as a delegate to the state constitutional convention of 1868 and subsequently being elected to the state legislature. But the year following his election, just as he seemed to have reach the pinnacle of his career, everything sud-

Henry McNeal Turner. Courtesy of Moorland-Spingarn Research Center,
Howard University

denly crashed when all black members of the Georgia legislature were ousted, effectively terminating radical Reconstruction in the state. This experience pushed Turner to the brink of complete alienation. He gave up on America and veered in the direction of emigration.[3]

Like Delany and Crummell, Turner believed in the "American Dream," a dream that he pursued most of his life. His nationalism and Pan-Africanism developed against the backdrop of the failure of this quest. His feeling of alienation following his ouster from the Georgia legislature gave rise to a new emigrationist consciousness and propelled him into national prominence as a nationalist. In an address to the Georgia legislature just before the vote to expel black legislators, Turner delivered a scathing rebuke and indictment of the racism that he felt was about to railroad his political career. He accused whites of deceit and betrayal: "The Anglo-Saxon race, sir, is a most surprising one. No man has ever been more deceived in that race than I have been for the last three weeks. I was not aware that there was in the character of that race so much cowardice, or so much pusillanimity." Turner proclaimed war against the country. He absolved himself and all blacks of any obligations of loyalty and patriotism to the United States. "You will make us your foes," he declared further. "You will make our constituency your foe. I'll do all I can to poison my race against democracy. . . . This thing means revolution." His speech had little impact. All the black legislators were expelled. Turner continued to participate in Georgia state politics and ran unsuccessfully for reelection to the legislature in 1871. He remained a steadfast supporter and advocate of radical republicanism until 1883, the year that the Supreme Court declared unconstitutional the Civil Rights Bill of 1875. This decision so appalled Turner that he publicly renounced the Republican Party. He described the decision as a "public outrage, and an invitation to murder all Colored persons who possess the element of true manhood." In his judgment, the decision represented a national betrayal of blacks. He denounced the Republican Party and declared that blacks had no future in the United States. He embraced colonization and implored fellow blacks to "rise up and organize or leave for a better land." The land he had in mind was Africa. Although Turner fully embraced emigration in 1883, his ouster from the Georgia legislature was the turning point. Once triggered, Turner's alienation was total and unequivocal, and few blacks, with the possible exception of Marcus

Garvey, have expressed the same degree of disdain and hatred for white values.[4]

Described as a radical egalitarian, Turner rejected the notion of black inferiority and championed the fight for equality. He felt intensely uncomfortable in a society that refused to recognize and respect his humanity. Believing that human beings were equal before God, he denounced all discriminatory acts as a violation of God's will. He declared a commitment to full equality for marginalized people and refused to compromise with those who advocated accommodation. Like Delany and Crummell, he espoused a strong nationalist position. He measured black acceptance in America by the degree to which blacks were "a self-controlling, automatic factor of the body politic or collective life of the nation," a principle very much akin to Delany's contention that "no people can be free who themselves do not constitute an essential part of the *ruling element* of the country in which they live."[5]

Turner equally believed that the threat to blacks transcended the boundaries of the United States. Like Delany, he discerned a deep, global chasm between blacks and whites—in the West Indies, Germany, France, Ireland, England, and South America.[6] In fact, Turner's concept of the essence of Negro nationality closely echoed the values enshrined in Delany's *Condition, Elevation, Emigration, and Destiny of the Colored People of the United States.* The realities of a global conspiracy and racial divide, plus the unlikelihood of an integrative order in the United States, compelled Turner to search for an independent black nationality abroad. "Nothing less than a nationality," he insisted, "will bring large prosperity and acknowledged manhood to us as a people."[7]

Turner visualized a distinct black nationality that would "cure the evils under which blacks labor." He scoffed at the belief that blacks could achieve progress and elevation on the same territory as their oppressors. Even if such a development were possible, Turner maintained, again echoing Delany, it would entail black Americans sacrificing their distinctive identity. According to him, "There is no instance mentioned in history where an enslaved people of an alien race rose to respectability upon the same territory of their enslavement and in the presence of their enslaver, without losing their identity or individuality by amalgamation."[8] He was especially critical of Booker T. Washington, whose accommodationist strategy he blamed for undermining the black struggle. He described Washington's 1895 Atlanta Cotton Exposition Address as a speech designed to comfort the "civil and political enemies" of the black race.[9]

Turner expressed a strong affection for and affinity with Africa. He offered emigration to Africa as the only viable solution left to blacks. His praise of Africa and defense of her culture and values system led him to an even stronger rejection and condemnation of American and European influence and imperialism.[10] Seeing black Americans denied the opportunity for advancement in the United States and threatened by racism on a global scale, Turner directed them to Africa. He evinced a strong Pan-African consciousness: Africa became for him "the thermometer that will determine the status of the Negro the world over." The destinies of Africans and black Americans were inextricably tied, and freedom for one was consequently inconceivable in the context of the enslavement or degradation of the other. As he put it, "We may boast of our American citizenship . . . but mark my word, the Negro will never be anything here while Africa is shrouded in heathen darkness. The elevation of the Negro in this and all other countries is indissolubly connected to the enlightenment of Africa."[11]

Even as he took up the mantle of black nationalism and Pan-Africanism, Turner refused to jettison the myth of Africa as the "dark continent." True to his "civilized" disposition, Turner described Africans as heathens and barbarians, and like other nationalists he placed the burden of responsibility for civilizing them squarely on the shoulders of black Americans. Like his contemporaries, Turner saw Africa as a land blessed with enormous economic resources but inhabited by people shrouded in "moral and spiritual blindness."[12] Although he had many positive things to say about Africa, his thought betrayed an extremely condescending and paternalistic attitude toward Africans. In his view, an African was "the most susceptible heathen upon the face of the globe. He is ready to lay down any habit, custom or sentiment for a better." Turner described Africa as "the grandest field on earth for the labor of civilization and the Christian church," and he opined optimistically, "There is no reason under the heaven why this continent should not, or cannot, be redeemed and brought to God in twenty-five years—say thirty at most."[13] His writings and utterances betrayed the depth of his subscription to Eurocentric values; his words, like those of Delany and Crummell, were suffused with Eurocentric platitudes, contrived to arouse the humanitarian and civilizing impulse of the age. Once Turner embraced colonization, there was no turning back. He perceived American society as inherently and irredeemably racist. Like Delany, he warned of a conspiracy by whites to subordinate and exploit blacks *ad infinitum*.[14] He predicted a bleak future for blacks in America. Underscoring his pessimism and cynicism, Turner declared, "I have had no faith in this country being the ultimate home of the Negro for fifteen years. . . . I believe that the prejudice of the white race would either drive us out of the country or reduce us to a state of vassal degradation that could be more intolerable than slavery itself."[15] After the official demise of Reconstruction in 1877, Turner saw conspiracy in every government policy. The choice was quite clear for blacks—emigrate or risk reenslavement. Whereas Delany referred to the Fugitive Slave Law as evidence of a national conspiracy against blacks, Turner focused on the collapse of Reconstruction and the 1883 Supreme Court decision that nullified the Civil Rights Act of 1875 (which had prohibited discrimination in public accommodations and facilities). The latter decision confirmed Turner's conviction that racism was deep and ubiquitous. Blacks urgently needed an African nation—a place of their own, free and distant from the restrictive and debilitating influences of Anglo-Americans.

Turner riveted his attention on Africa. Success in establishing an African nationality would give blacks in America and elsewhere in the diaspora a renewed sense of identity and an enhanced self-conception. In fact, Turner believed, Africa possessed all the prerequisites for the success of such a nationality. Underlining the urgency of emigration, Turner wrote,

> There is no [more] doubt in my mind that we have ultimately to return to Africa than there is of the existence of God; and the sooner we begin to recognize that fact and prepare for it, the better it will be for us as a people. We there have a country unsurpassed in productive and mineral resources, and we have some two hundred millions of our kindred there in moral and spiritual blindness. The four millions of us in this country are at school, learning the doctrines of Christianity and the elements of civil government. As soon as we are educated sufficiently to assume control of our vast ancestral domain, we will hear the voice of a mysterious Providence, saying, 'Return to the land of your fathers.'[16]

Notice Turner's positive rendition of the black American ordeal—it constituted a schooling in the elements of religion and good government, an experience allegedly alien to Africa! Equally noteworthy is the controlling and moderating influence of God. God was carefully watching over the experience of black Americans and would know the appropriate time to turn them in the direction of Africa. Further emphasizing the necessity, practicality, and divine character of colonization, Turner declared, "For myself, I am sure there is no region so full of promise and where the possibilities of success are so great as the land of our ancestors. That continent appears to be kept by Providence in reserve for the Negro. There everything seems to be ready to raise him to deserved distinction, comfort and wealth. Ample territory, rich in all the productions of the tropics and many of those of the temperate, with coal, iron, copper, gold, diamond, *awaits the trained hand of civilization.*"[17] In these two quotations, Turner amplifies two crucial Eurocentric ideas: the belief in the necessity and inevitability of colonizing Africa, and the image of Africa as a land blessed with rich natural resources but darkened by moral and spiritual blindness. Perhaps most intriguing is Turner's representation of enslavement as a schooling process, a civilizing experience that was preparing black Americans for duty in Africa. Throughout the centuries of enslavement of black Americans, Africa seemed to have remained in an arrested stage; it was awaiting the "graduation" of its kindred, who would return and cleanse the continent of moral decadence by introducing civil government, Christianity, and civilization.

Turner's depiction of Africa and rationalization of colonization appealed favorably to the American Colonization Society, whose agenda of repatriating free blacks to Liberia he had once opposed. During his early integration phase, like other black Americans, Turner opposed colonization and refused to embrace solutions that internationalized the black struggle. The majority of blacks perceived colonization as a sinister, proslavery ploy designed to rid the country of the troubling free blacks and render slavery secure. The American Colonization Society therefore found little support among blacks.[18] By the 1880s, however, Turner seemed to have been purged of his integrationist consciousness. He warmly embraced colonization and glorified the society, despite its odious reputation among blacks. The society's accomplishments, in Turner's opinion, far outweighed its failures. He presented the society as the most viable institution for the realization of black nationhood, referring to its members as "the best and greatest benefactors" of blacks, and as committed to helping them in doing what no civilized Negroes had creditably done: "founding and manning a government of their own creation." In 1876 the colonization society reciprocated by conferring upon Turner the title of honorary vice president. With this, Turner felt freer to solicit financial support from the society and to use its name to promote colonization and emigration.[19]

Turner's nationalism embodied the three cardinal C's. His depiction of Africa as a treasure house of economic resources, and his contention that indigenous Africans lacked the intelligence and morality to effectively develop those resources, established the need for commerce, Christianity, and colonization. He seemed particularly disturbed by the depth of what he viewed as Africa's primitivism and moral decadence and, like Crummell, he implored black Americans to assume a greater responsibility in the task of rescuing their brethren from the depths of cultural and moral decay. When he was ordained a bishop of the African Methodist Episcopal Church (AMEC) in 1880, Turner immediately took up the cause of the "African mission." He implored the church to make Africa the centerpiece of its missionary activities, and he argued forcefully against a view of Christianity that precluded concerns for the miseries of that continent. He was particularly worried that the AMEC leadership seemed fixated on compromise, accommodation, and integration.[20]

Turner offered black Americans only one alternative to emigration: extinction. He identified the disastrous consequences of integration: it would imprint on blacks an indelible badge of subordination and deny them any semblance of respect and dignity. Furthermore, integration implied a voluntary relinquishing of the black American claim to Africa. Africa had the resources for a black nationality, and until that nationality materialized blacks would have no legitimate grounds for claims of equality with whites.[21] The capacity for self-governance, in Turner's judgment, was the hallmark of civilization, and no people deserve respect and consideration "who do not show themselves capable of finding and manning a government of their own."[22] History, he affirmed, had yet to reveal evidence that the Negro possessed this ability. It is obvious here that Turner either did not include Africans among "civilized Negroes" or did not regard the states, kingdoms, and empires of Africa (that is, if he was aware of them) as authentic and credible. With a stroke of the pen, he nullified the civilizations of ancient and classical Africa.

The bleak portrait of African societies and culture, particularly the alleged absence of civilized or organized states, justified external intervention. Turner initially placed greater responsibility on black Americans. He had lost faith in whites, having, like Delany, developed a deep suspicion of a white conspiracy against blacks. He wished that black Americans would realize the reality and enormity of this conspiracy, a realization that would have compelled them to close ranks and commit their energies and resources to the creation of an African nationality. In consequence, Turner appealed strongly to the black American middle class, emphasizing their kinship ties to Africa. Stressing the futility of integration, he called on them to pull together their resources and focus attention on the continent.[23] Like Delany and Crummell, Turner presented Africa's economic base as the solution to the predicaments of black Americans. His ideology also reflected his religious persuasion. He had faith in divine intervention and believed that God approved of colonization. Africa appeared to have been kept in reserve for black America by God. Everything in the continent—the land, the untapped mineral and natural resources, the immense manpower—had been reserved specifically for exploitation and utilization by, and for the development of, black Americans.[24] This unquestionably establishes Turner's subscription to the normative paternalistic and racist perceptions of Africa. The notion of a static, ahistorical Africa, held in reserve for "black graduates" of the School of Western Civilization, prevailed among black Americans. However, the black American middle class was predominantly integration-minded. Many hoped that, despite the depressing and discouraging realities, the "American Dream" remained within the realm of possibility. Turner's doomsday philosophy therefore convinced few. Like Delany before him, Turner failed to garner enough support and strength within the black community. He turned to the U.S. government.

Turner initially couched his appeal to the government in the language of reparation. He demanded the sum of $40 billion, which he estimated the American government owed blacks for centuries of enslavement and exploitation. Possession of this sum would enable blacks to finance relocation to Africa. The U.S. government simply ignored him. When he realized that reparation was not forthcoming, he appealed to American economic and national interest, stressing the necessity for an American foreign policy that harmonized with that of "the civilized world." He implored the U.S. government to jettison isolationism and assume its "share of duty in this great movement." Like Delany and Crummell, Turner represented the colonization of Africa as a historical phenomenon—indeed, the realization of a divine plan. He promised whites enormous profit from investing in Africa. Aside from the economic and material benefits, the colonization of Africa held another promise that was dear to all Americans, black and white—that of finally resolving the intractable "dark problem."[25]

To justify colonization, Turner applied the same rationalization of slavery as Delany and Crummell. He described slavery as a divine "civilizing" instrument, God's "primal factor" in the colonization and Christianization of the "dark continent."[26] Although the "greed and avarice of the white man" led to the enslavement of blacks, whites were actually unconsciously acting out the will of an "over-ruling Providence" to actualize a "great and grand purpose." God consequently intended good to come of "a temporary evil." Humanity had yet to realize and appreciate the inherent benefits of slavery. In the future, Turner argued, humanity would develop a greater appreciation of the institution, that is, when the ultimate benefit of slavery was manifested in the uplifting of primitive Africa through colonization and Christianity. At that time, Turner declared, "millions will thank heaven for the limited toleration of American slavery."[27] Those who opposed colonization, therefore, were battling against the force of God, for only through colonization would the positive dimension of slavery be realized.

To galvanize support for colonization, Turner, like Delany and Crummell, thus "purified" and rendered positively a negative and painful historical experience. Slavery became a divine strategy meant to bring heathen and backward Africa in contact with civilization, slavery's attendant pain and anguish notwithstanding. According to Turner, God sanctioned the violent and dehumanizing character of slavery. As he maintained, "When the Negro was being captured and brought to this country and subjected to a state of unrequited servitude, [God] knew of the horrors of their past and present condition and foresaw . . . the termination of their slave ordeal." Not only did God sanction slavery, but emancipation itself seemed predetermined.

Turner referred to slavery as "the most rapid transit from barbarism to Christian civilization for the Negro." God's ultimate goal in allowing slavery was to effect its redemptive *raison d'être*—the elevation of Africa. Slavery, Turner argued, was *"evolution* in its fullest grandeur." Those enslaved and brought into proximity with a superior culture and civilization *evolved* into superior beings. The evolutionary process entailed the diffusion of the values of the superior culture. It remained unconsummated, however, until the superior values were implanted in Africa.[28]

Just as slavery possessed a positive and divine side, Turner held, so too did racism. The purpose of racism was to instill in black Americans a consciousness of their nationality and inspire them to take appropriate actions to relieve their sufferings. Embedded in the harsh and ugly realities of slavery and racism, then, were what he viewed as ennobling and positive experiences. The same Supreme Court decision that Turner had earlier condemned, and presented as evidence of a national conspiracy against blacks, suddenly acquired a positive complexion. He recast the decision as a design by God to "arouse the Negro to a sense of his responsibility." Such accommodation and legitimation of racism later resurfaced in Garveyism: an intriguing aspect of Marcus Garvey's nationalism remains his commendation of the Ku Klux Klan.[29]

In his most recent publication, Wilson J. Moses acknowledges the religious historicist character of classical black nationalism. Divine providence functioned as a guide toward the fulfillment of the goal of nationalism. This "religious optimism," Moses suggests, strengthened black nationalist "psychological resistance to the slavery, colonialism and racism imposed by Europeans and white Americans."[30] Moses errs, however, in equating religious historicism with resistance. In fact, providential determinism seemed geared more toward bridging the gap between black Americans and Euro-Americans, which had been accentuated by slavery and racism. By absolving Europeans of guilt and responsibility for slavery, religious historicism provided the basis for cooperation and for the construction of mutuality. It established a kind of consanguinity defined by the word *civilization*. In this view, slavery, a divinely sanctioned institution, had brought blacks and Euro-Americans together for a purpose: the redemption of Africa. The problem, however, arose when Europeans claimed a monopoly on civilization. Black Americans responded with a strong affirmation of the "civilized" state they had achieved through enslavement.

If slavery constituted the "most rapid transit to civilization for the Negro," as Turner and Crummell seemed to agree, would it not have been logical and more effective to simply enslave the rest of Africa? This would have been the ideal solution to Africa's primitivism, had the situation in Africa not changed fundamentally from what it was in the fifteenth century. In fact, had the Europeans tried enslaving the rest of Africa, they would have received a different reception and response. But this was not an option they considered. Instead of slaves, Europe now needed tropical products, and by the beginning of the nineteenth century Britain had begun to spearhead abolitionism and advocate the replacement of the slave trade with "legitimate trade." Because African labor was no longer in demand abroad, slavery suddenly became abhorrent! The first phase of African enslavement had served its purpose. It had produced the raw materials that launched and serviced the industrial revolution. The revolution in turn shifted European demands from slave labor to tropical products, the raw materials that Africa possessed in abundance. Africans would remain at home and perform precisely the same function that slaves performed in the New World—to produce the tropical raw materials that were to service the expanding industrial base of Europe. Africa was thus entering the second phase of enslavement, distinguished by its domestic application (i.e., colonialism). The setting for enslavement shifted from Europe and America to Africa. Africa's previously enslaved brethren (now free and presumably civilized) enthusiastically endorsed the second enslavement and sought to participate in it as partners of the Europeans. There was, consequently, one continuous chain between slavery and colonialism.

A hidden dimension to the second enslavement is the ingenious manner in which black American nationalists tried to maneuver Europeans into accepting them as partners. Still bedeviled by an endemic crisis of identity, black American nationalists sought a validation of their Anglo-American identity as a qualification for assuming the same role as the Europeans in Africa. Slavery became the evidence for this validation. The purifying and cleansing quality of slavery was supposed to have bridged the cultural and civilizational gap between whites/Europeans and black Americans. It was the experience of slavery that set black Americans apart from "primitive Africa." Slavery drew black Americans closer to Europeans and inculcated in them the rudiments of civilization. Slavery, therefore, was the essence of the new identity cherished by leading black American thinkers. Such slavocentric consciousness situates black American identity in its truly Anglo-American context. This is a classic moment in the identity-complex problem. A curious side to all of this is that the slavocentric identity was proposed and upheld as the antithesis of, and an advancement over, the African identity. Slavery became both the means of affirming the Anglo-American identity of black Americans and their passport to hegemony over Africa. While not denying their African roots, Delany, Crummell, and Turner distanced themselves from Africa by projecting slavery as the basis of a new identity.

It is worth noting that this slavocentric consciousness is a crucial component of modern discourse on black American identity. An increasing number of black Americans are beginning to accord slavery, sometimes disguised in the phrase "American experience," a central position, as the substantive basis of their history and identity construction. Slavocentrism, therefore, identifies slavery and the American experience, rather than Africa, as the foundation for constructing a black American identity. Among the most vocal proponents of this view are playwright Douglass Turner Ward, journalist Stanley Crouch, actress Whoopie Goldberg, and former *Washington Post* African bureau chief Keith B. Richburg.[31] Richburg's *Out of America: A Black Man Confronts Africa* presents slavocentrism in perhaps its most articulate and scholarly form. After a three-year sojourn in Africa, during which he was horrified by the depth of corruption and carnage, Richburg expresses gratitude to God and to slavery for rescuing his ancestors from the continent. He is most appreciative of his American identity and depicts slavery as an institution with positive consequences, in spite of its evil character. According to Richburg, "Condemning slavery should not inhibit us from recognizing mankind's ability to make something good arise often in the aftermath of the most horrible evil."[32] Richburg and other slavocentrists before him have fulfilled Turner's nineteenth-century prophesy that the world would someday develop a greater appreciation for the benefits of slavery.

Turner's attempt to generate national support for colonization failed. Neither the black American middle class nor whites responded with the degree of enthusiasm he expected. He began to publish *The Voice of Mission*, which became the organ of colonization. In 1891 he made his first trip to Africa, under the auspices of the AMEC. Between 1891 and 1898, he visited Africa four times.[33] His contact with Africa was indeed an enlightening experience. Like other black Americans who visited Africa for the first time, Turner came with the prejudices he had imbibed in America, some of which he had already revealed in his writings. The reality that confronted him, however, shattered these preconceived notions. His baptism began on the ship en route to Africa. He shared a cabin with an African named Matthew Thomas, of what Turner referred to as Lagas, whom he described as "black as ink." Thomas was fluent in English, French, German, Italian, and Spanish. This was a stunning revelation, for such linguistic ability, in Turner's judgment, qualified Thomas to head the language department in any American University.[34]

His arrivals in Sierra Leone and Liberia further unsettled Turner's preconceived notions. He saw enormous natural resources and an industrious and intelligent population. He was surprised by the degree of urbanism and development. Instead of a dark jungle, he saw cities, buildings, and infrastructures similar to those of major American cities.[35] He saw clean and well-dressed people engaged in professions, private enterprises, education, religious institutions, publishing, and so on. He observed social distinctions among Africans, particularly the gulf between the ruling class and the commoners. He found the people generally to be amiable, industrious, and morally upright, and he concluded that they were "the most honest people on earth."[36] These findings significantly reduced, in Turner's consciousness, the civilizational gap between Africa and America. Africa presented a different spectacle from what he had been socialized to expect.

Turner wrote some fourteen letters detailing his findings. What he found in Africa compelled him to question the characterization of the United States as a civilized society. For him, "civilization" meant much more than economic development. As he observed, possessing "the highest form of civilized institutions that any nation has had" did not make the United States a civilized nation, given "the barbarous condition" of a country that dehumanizes part of its populace.[37] Collectively, the letters highlight positive aspects of Liberian society—lifestyles, occupations, economic activities, urbanization, moral and social conditions of the inhabitants. Nevertheless, the letters confirm certain shortcomings in the condition of Liberians that justify the "civilizing mission." Although they appeared neat, organized, industrious, peaceful, and intelligent, Africans were essentially heathens who were chronically divided along tribal lines. Consequently, Africa remained "the grandest field on earth for the labor of civilization and the Christian Church."[38] In essence, the challenging discoveries did not significantly affect Turner's Eurocentric consciousness. Although indigenous Africans were not completely backward, they nevertheless retained certain anachronistic habits and customs and remained in need of spiritual salvation. The need for the infusion of the "superior" skills and intelligence of Americans, black and white, remained prominent.

This shift between praise and denigration of Africa suggests that Turner, like Delany and Crummell, was torn between his conflicting cultural experiences. Despite his alienation from American society, Turner could not transcend his Western acculturation, an experience that had instilled an appreciation and respect for Western values. Like Delany and Crummell, Turner rationalized this by proposing the existence of a divine plan, boldly proclaiming his belief "that the Negro was brought to this country in the providence of God to a heaven-permitted, if not a divine-sanctioned manual laboring school, that he might have direct contact with 'the mightiest race that ever trod the face of the globe.'"[39]

The discovery of ennobling qualities among Africans and the shattering of some of his preconceived values did not shake Turner's faith in colonization. Generally, he had no reservations about European intrusion into Africa. Although he voiced concern over the intensity of European activities, Turner was more troubled by the isolationist stance of the U.S. government.[40] He was particularly apprehensive of British, French, and German naval activities. In combination, these nations assembled about eighty steamships on the African coast, all of them engaged in the lucrative African trade. He decried the absence of the U.S. government, an unfortunate situation given, according to him, the preference of indigenous Africans for Americans. Remarkably, he ascribed the reluctance of black Americans to challenge European economic hegemony in Africa to a characteristic American disdain for commerce: they had imbibed the prevailing white American lack of appreciation of commerce and its utility. Turner's apprehensions increased as Europeans intensified the race to plant their respective flags and accumulate wealth in as many African territories as possible. He could not understand why fellow black Americans, and the U.S. government, would fail to appreciate the immensity of the economic opportunities available in Africa. What Turner desperately sought was precisely the kind of support and national backing that British, German, and French traders and missionaries demanded and received from their respective governments, as the competition intensified for the appropriation of African resources. He sought for black American entrepreneurs a function similar to that of European traders in Africa—an active role in the economic exploitation of the continent.

Turner condemned the seizure by France of a large tract of Liberian territory and objected to the Anglo-French compact to partition and appropriate a portion of Liberia. His concern, however, had more to do with the marginal role of black Americans in such proceedings, and the conspicuous absence of the U.S. government from them, than with the independence of Liberia. He especially regretted the inability of black Americans, "who have been brought in contact with civilization and Christianity, . . . to take intelligent *possession* of . . . [their] fatherland."[41] The word *possession*, which Delany had also used to proclaim black American rights to Africa, betrays the imperialist or, as some have called it, Zionist character of black American nationalists. Turner's consternation over European activities in Africa was largely because Europeans appeared to be usurping what he and other black American nationalists claimed for black America.

What is most striking about Turner's nationalism, Darryl Trimiew contends, is the notion that Africans were culturally inferior to Westerners. Turner failed to distinguish between "qualitatively different concerns—that is, between economics, technological competence, and efficiency and cultural competence. Thus he confused the technological deficiencies in Africa—for instance, the lack of modern infrastructure and industries—with the state of Africa's culture, which was, of course, in no way primitive or inferior to that of any other culture. As a result he was not really prepared to go to Africa and work with and under Africans, and he was equally unready to develop the tribal nations that were already in place."[42] True to his socialization, Trimiew suggests, Turner identified civilization with material and technological advancement, and in consequence depicted

Africa's technological backwardness as the quintessence of African culture. Contrary to Trimiew's claim, however, Turner (and Delany and Crummell as well) in fact distinguished between these "qualitatively different concerns." This is exemplified in the dual conception of civilization implicit in their thoughts. First, they endorsed a Western technological and materialist definition of civilization. Second, they proposed the inclusion of ethical and moral values. In other words, they theorized a dual construction of civilization that combined Western elements, based on criteria that are empirical and rational, with a fundamentally African conception, based on intangible, immaterial, nonrational values that are measurable and appreciable solely in ethical, moral, and behavioral terms. These nationalists utilized the doctrine of dual cultural space, in other words, to initially assert and proclaim Africa's "efficiency and cultural competence." The plain fact, however, is that they all equated civilization with material progress. Consequently, though believing on one level in the "efficiency and cultural competence" of Africa, they seemed reluctant and unwilling to declare it as evidence of civilization according to the Western conception of the term, which they acknowledged as universal and normative.

Trimiew is right in another respect, however. Turner, the black nationalist and advocate of the rights of marginalized people (black Americans), could not have seriously considered Africans to be among those deserving of the equality for which he fought so ferociously, despite his radical nationalist and "Pan-Africanist" postulations. His primary constituency, and rightly so, was black America. His Pan-African rhetoric was fraught with hegemonic ambitions. Africans and black Americans were to unite not as equals in a struggle for mutual development but as partners in a relationship in which black Americans held dominance and preeminence. Turner did not see Africans as kindreds, people to work with and under, but as ignorant and backward, and he presented himself as someone with the superior and civilized values to transform Africans culturally. In this respect, Turner, like Delany and Crummell, adopted a "banking" conception of enlightenment and civilization, to borrow Paulo Freire's construct.[43] They all conceived of the enlightenment of Africans as a one-way process—with the superior, enlightened, educated, and civilized Westerners (Europeans and black Americans) coming to "deposit" knowledge and civilization in the abject and inept receptacles—Africans.

Turner's activities in Africa were not confined to the west coast. In 1898, as a senior bishop of the AMEC, he led a delegation to South Africa to discuss modalities for union with the dissident "Ethiopian Church" of South Africa. His observations, at a critical period when blacks in South Africa were being denied their lands, rights, and liberties and subjected to dehumanizing experiences similar to the conditions he criticized in the United States, illuminates the curious ambivalence in his nationalism. He went out of his way to minimize racial prejudice in South Africa. Turner praised the Boers, especially the president of Transvaal, Paul Kruger, whom he called a "statesman of large caliber and shrewdness." While acknowledging the existence of prejudice in South Africa, he characterized it as prejudice of condition rather than of race, and therefore fundamentally different from practices in the United States and ultimately justifiable. Blacks in South Africa deserved their treatment, according to Turner, because the "Europeans came with their civilized ideas among a heathen people, inferior in knowledge and religion. They came with civilized forms of government, and as a natural consequence the natives were rated as any people in a similar condition would be."[44] Here, Turner echoes the classic Eurocentric reasoning. He seems to advance the old "might is right" or "just war" argument, justifying subordination on the basis of conquest. In this case, the subordination of South African blacks is justified by their defeat at the hands of the "civilized" Dutch. Turner's philosophy of subordination de-emphasized race. He found nothing wrong or extraordinary about Boer subordination of blacks. The Romans, he argued, treated the Britons in much the same way when they conquered Britain. It is a universal precept, Turner implied, that the conqueror should by right dominate the conquered. Turner's rationalization of racism and domination in South Africa on the grounds that the Boers were civilized, finally, provides further insight into his conception of the relationship between black Americans and Africans: exposure to Westernization had civilized black Americans and rendered them superior, and logically they deserved to exercise dominance and authority over indigenous Africans.

It is interesting that Turner denied the reality of race in South Africa while acknowledging its existence and pertinence in the United States. He portrayed the situation in the United States as essentially structured by *race*, whereas he ascribed that of South Africa to *condition.* Black Americans suffered due to systemic and ideological problems over which they had little control. The experience of black South Africans, on the other hand, was the consequence of a situation over which they had greater control and for which they should therefore bear responsibility—their condition. Turner apparently mistook the hospitality showered on him by the Boers as indicative of their liberal disposition on race, and he concluded that black South Africans would someday overcome racism as their condition improved. The conditional or situational deficiency argument had historically been applied to blame racism and segregation on alleged deficiencies in the material and moral condition of American blacks. By adopting this rationalization, Turner thus situated the cause of black oppression in South Africa not in the racism of the oppressors but in the condition of the oppressed, just as the apologists of slavery had done in the United States. Paradoxically, Turner had objected strongly to, and contributed to debunking, this same thesis when it was applied to the black experience in the United States. Yet in South Africa, and indeed in the whole of Africa, Europe's civilized traditions and values legitimized the subordination and dispossession of indigenous peoples. Delany and Crummell shared Turner's convictions. The appropriation of and adaptation to Eurocentric values induced all three to assume a paternalistic and disdainful posture toward Africans. This also explains why none of them recognized the glaring ambivalence in propagating nationalist and Pan-Africanist ideas while simultaneously endorsing policies and measures calculated to reduce Africans to second-class citizens in their own land.

Black American Nationalism and Africa: Ambivalence and Paradoxes

The golden age of black American nationalism was also the apogee of European nationalism. Although products of fundamentally different sets of circumstances, both varieties of nationalism paradoxically converged on the same spot—Africa. European nationalism unleashed expansionist ambitions that directed Europeans toward Africa. Black American nationalism also nudged black Americans toward Africa in search of a black nationality that, many hoped, would combat the growing and threatening tide of European nationalism and imperialism. In the end, however, the force that unleashed the quest for a black nationality succumbed to, and was absorbed into, the more powerful force of European nationalism. Combined, the two laid the foundation for the colonization of Africa. It seems reasonable, therefore, to suggest that the traditional context for the study and analysis of the advent of colonialism in Africa be broadened to include black American nationalism, which was also a dynamic force in African colonization. As this study demonstrates, Europeans and black American nationalists constituted two rival groups of imperialists, of unequal force, who converged on Africa in the second half of the nineteenth century. The Europeans were successful because of their technological and economic power as well as their ability to mobilize national support. As an independent force, black American imperialism failed to mature beyond the stage of theoretical posturing, due to a combination of factors—the lack of national backing, the failure to attract and mobilize a significant portion of the black middle class, and the conflicting nationalist agendas of its proponents. The majority of black Americans identified themselves primarily as Americans, and they remained indomitably committed to the struggle for the realization of their potentialities within the United States. But Richard Blackett provides another explanation for the collapse of the imperial ambitions of black American nationalists: the failure of their attempts to secure the partnership of the Europeans.[1] Attempts to forge cooperation with Europe failed because Europeans proved reluctant to relate to black Americans as equals, however attractive the proposals they presented.

European imperialism in Africa went through three distinct stages. First was the stage of imperial disposition—that is, the propensity to intervene. As already demonstrated, this stage evolved logically from the notion of European superiority. The second stage entailed the development of ideological justification for foreign intervention. While the justification developed initially from the lack of an understanding and appreciation of Africa's cultural nuances and complexities, later it relied on deliberate and calculated misrepresentation and denigration of the lifestyles and values of Africans. The third and final stage was that of occupation, set in motion by the Berlin Conference of 1884-85. Black American imperialism, or what some call the black American emigration scheme, evolved along a similar trajectory. Leading black American nationalists had a strong disposition to intervene in Africa due to a presumed superiority over indigenous Africans. This easily evolved into a full ideological justification for intervention in Africa because of their exposure to, and acceptance of, a Eurocentric worldview. Unlike the Europeans, however, they did not reach the final stage of occupation.

The underlying impulse of late-nineteenth-century black American nationalism was the pursuit and realization of American nationality. Frustrated at home, black Americans picked Africa as the base for a nationality whose power and influence, they hoped, would have a positive impact on the cause of freedom and citizenship in the United States. Their response to Africa, therefore, seemed tied to the changing dynamics of the American sociopolitical milieu. The slightest indication of a move toward liberalism in the United States almost assuredly compelled black leaders to abandon thoughts of Africa. Martin Delany jettisoned emigration and turned to America at the outbreak of the Civil War. Henry McNeal Turner's plan collapsed in the late 1890s, partly because of the lukewarm response and even opposition of the black American middle class, but largely because of the emergence of a new leader, Booker T. Washington, whose values inspired hope and optimism for the "American Dream."

Although legally a Liberian, Alexander Crummell returned to the United States in 1872, where he continued his struggle for black elevation. He abandoned Africa and, in fact, as Wilson J. Moses demonstrates, became very critical of emigrationist projects. The realization of the "American Dream" and American nationality became Crummell's primary consideration in the 1880s. He devoted most of his energy in the latter phase of his life to strengthening his American nationality.[2] The values that he propagated in advocacy of American nationality were adapted from the sermons that had once served to advance his quest for an African and Pan-African nationality. According to Moses, the crux of Crummell's thought in later years was "distinctly American," and his values were designed to "suit the goal of full participation in American life."[3] The ease with which all three nationalists disposed of their African schemes itself speaks to the frailty and superficiality of their African and Pan-African consciousness. Perhaps this fragility, more than anything else, demonstrates the degree to which black American nationalism was centered in America.

As hard as Delany, Crummell, and Turner fought to advance the cause of black nationalism and Pan-Africanism, their ultimate objective was the enhancement of their American nationality. Hence their willingness to consider and exploit every conceivable opportunity to actualize this American identity. Had they been inspired and driven by a deep commitment to an African nationality, and an equally deep consciousness of cultural and historical affinity with Africa, their attitudes toward Africans and response to Eurocentric values would have been demonstrably different. What pushed them in the direction of Africa was not the paramount importance of African identity but the rejection, subordination, and exploitation of blacks in the United States. It was this negative experience that impelled many black Americans to situate the idea of Africa *temporarily* in the place of the much-cherished but elusive American identity, an interpretation that remains valid regardless of the depth and strength of the nationalist and Pan-Africanist professions in question.

Concomitant with championing emigration and African nationality, Delany lamented his rejection by and alienation from the United States. Although angered, alienated, and compelled to turn outward for succor, he refused to sever ties completely with the United States. Instead, he characterized the relationship of black Americans to emigration as an adoption, undoubtedly to underline its temporality. As he bemoaned, "We love our country, dearly love her, but she don't love us. . . . She despises us, and bids us begone, driving us from her embraces, . . . but when we do go, whatever love we have for her, we shall love the country none the less that receives us as her *adopted children.*"[4] Delany's love for America, his predisposition to sacrifice almost anything for his American nationality, and the superficiality and fragility of his emigrationist and Pan-Africanist thought are graphically illuminated in his response to the Civil War. He needed no persuasion or prodding to drop the idea of emigration in favor of the American nationality whose prospect seemed brightened by the war. He later confessed to William Coppinger of the American Colonization Society that, though he had set his mind on emigrating permanently, "the War coming on for the time being changed everything."[5]

Deconstructing European imperialist theory did not seem to be a major concern of Delany, Crummell, and Turner. Their counterattacks on European imperial ideology were conceived essentially to effect a blending of their own agenda with that of the Europeans— primarily to justify, at the very least, a joint enterprise in Africa. The process of "civilizing" Africa entailed the economic enhancement of black Americans and their European partners or competitors. All three nationalists persistently stressed this "mutual benefit" factor. The spreading of literacy among indigenous Africans, the mobilization of cheap African labor to produce commodities that were in demand in Europe (rather than those of immediate benefit to Africans), the attempts to erode the essence of indigenous African customs and languages, the imposition on Africa of European languages and values—these strategies endorsed by black nationalists were all aimed at creating an atmosphere conducive to maximizing the "mutual benefits" anticipated from the "civilizing" of Africa.

When black Americans and the Europeans talked of extending civilization to Africa, they meant the creation and imposition of a "rational" order, defined and conceived by outsiders, which would expedite the exploitation of the resources of the continent while transforming the lifestyles and mannerisms of indigenous Africans. In fact, the calls by Turner and Crummell for American intervention in Africa occurred in the context of the debate between the pro- and antiimperialist forces in the United States. For different reasons, both sides forwarded racist rationalizations to justify their positions on American participation in global imperialism. The anti-imperialist forces balked at the prospect of bringing into the United States peoples of inferior race who could never be assimilated and who would consequently contaminate the racial purity of the nation. Those in favor of imperialism, on the other hand, advanced a similarly racialist argument in favor of the conquest of aliens: that it was imperative to improve their alleged primitive condition.[6] Delany, Crummell, and Turner applied the principle of the pro-imperialist school. They used the African condition—political, cultural, economic, and social—to justify the imposition of foreign rule. Their economic justification of foreign intervention in Africa echoed many of the ideas of the European merchants and traders, who also urged their respective governments to intervene in Africa on the promise of immense economic benefits.[7]

A distinguishing feature of nineteenth-century black American nationalism, therefore, is not so much its adaptations of Anglo-Saxon values as its relation to imperialist culture and ideology and the way that this connection helped to shape, legitimize, and strengthen the imperial onslaught on Africa. The nationalists in this study eventually concurred with much of the rationale for European imperialism, some of which they had previously rejected and condemned. In their attempts to harmonize with Europeans and distance themselves from the historical and cultural Africa that the Europeans had invented, they not only jettisoned many of their earlier nationalist and Pan-Africanist postulations and contentions, but they also accepted many of the negative and racist values characteristic of Eurocentric ideology.

The reflection of European imperial ideology in black American thought corroborates Bernard Magubane's poignant depiction of history as "man's autobiography and his biography."[8] Black American nationalists interpreted their history through the perspective of their historical interactions and experience with whites. Their story about themselves and, by extension, about Africans was told "biographically," from the experiential locus of Western socialization. The values they cherished and the basis of their self-definition and identity, especially in relation to their African historical and cultural heritage, echoed essentially the same values as those embedded in Eurocentric thought. Put differently, the empirical and ideological realities of black American historical experience in America, in a tragic but significant sense, shaped both black American self-perceptions and the understanding of African reality. Eurocentric ideology thus acquired universal and intrinsic validity. Consequently, as Peter Worsley rightly contends, the internalization and acceptance of the total superiority of European culture, and not force alone, became responsible for the "lengthy psychological subordination" of non-Europeans. European superiority "seemed self-evident to both conquered and conquerors. It induced in the conquered a sense of inferiority and dependence, and its rational correlate, a belief in the inevitability, even the rightness, of White rule."[9] Black American socialization was thus infused with values that affirmed white supremacy. The ideology that underpinned slavery and segregation induced internalization of the racial hierarchy, leading to self-denial and self-hatred. Little wonder then that it was easy for black Americans to accept the concepts of African inferiority and of Africa as the "dark continent" as sufficient grounds for subjugating the continent. In essence, the *mission civilisatrice* acquired some measure of legitimacy from its ideological control of the consciousness of black diasporans. As Magubane contends, "The black, sharing the same soil with the white people in the United States, was taught to admire the Hebrews, the Greeks, the Romans, and the Gentiles, but to despise the African."[10] This education induced a diminutive and denigrating self-conception and a disdain for one's cultural heritage, a condition that is exemplified by Delany's critique of African living habits and Crummell's vilification of indigenous African languages. Whatever significance the Europeans attached to the writings and reports of their explorers and missionaries who "discovered" and began the process of opening up Africa, they certainly attached equal, if not greater, importance to the views and utterances of black American nationalists.

The ambivalence these nationalists displayed was a symptom of their complex cultural and historical experiences. Although exposed to and affected by the prevailing European denigration of Africa, all three responded not only with acknowledgment of the validity of the Eurocentric devaluation of Africa but also with a counterimage of Africa that seemed to directly contradict the one in European thought. They envisioned a different Africa, with ennobling qualities in ethics and morality, that counterpoised the European image.

They then conferred upon this Africa some degree of legitimacy and perhaps even superiority over the technological and materialist worldview of the Europeans. Both Turner and Delany advanced Africa's moral authority and superiority over Europe. This is evident in the praises and expressions of admiration for Africa's traditions and customs contained in their writings and in their complex conceptions of civilization. In essence, all three seemed to have constructed a dual cultural space by positing a complex conception of civilization that combined both the technological, materialist, and positivist criteria of the West and the moral, qualitative, and ontological realities of Africa.

In Crummell's thought, for instance, civilization encompasses not only the elements of technology and materialism but also abstract qualities and conditions such as "the clarity of the mind from the dominion of false heathen ideas . . . the conscious impress of individualism and personal responsibility . . . the recognition of the body, with its desires and appetites and passion as a sacred gift . . . the honor and freedom of womanhood, allied with the duty of family development . . . the sense of social progress in society . . . the sense of new impulses in the actions and policy of the tribe or nation . . . an elevated use of material things, and a higher range of common industrial activities . . . the earliest possible introduction of letters, and books and reading."[11] This definition of civilization incorporates complex values. Turner, on the other hand, views civilization as a contemplation of "that fraternity, civil and political equality between man and man, that makes his rights, privileges and immunities inviolable and sacred in the eyes and hearts of his fellows, whatever may be his nationality, language, color, hair texture. . . . Civility comprehends harmony, system, method, complacency, urbanity, refinement, politeness, courtesy, justice, culture, general enlightenment and protection of life and person to any man, regardless of his color or nationality. It is enough for a civilized society to know that you are a human being, to pledge surety of physical and political safety to you, and this has been the sequence in all ages among civilized people."[12] Like Crummell's, Turner's definition combines complex values. Implicit in both definitions is an attempt to highlight what is wrong with, and missing in, Western civilization—an acknowledgment of its imperfections. Despite the advanced state of Western societies, therefore, measured by technological and materialist accomplishments (one cultural space), the paradigms of civilization that Turner and Crummell proposed underlined other values that are conspicuously missing in, and perhaps even alien to, Western civilization—political equality, social equality, respect for the rights and privileges of fellow beings, civility, justice, courtesy, and so forth (a second cultural space).

All three nationalists at some point attempted to illuminate positive aspects of Africa, primarily to debunk the myth of the "dark continent." Delany, both before and after his trip to Africa, praised Africa's worth in the arena of morality and ethics. Turner's letters from Liberia are full of admiration for the moral character of Liberians and praises for their accomplishments. In proposing a second cultural space that affirms Africa's preeminence, these nationalists attempted to qualify, not necessarily invalidate, the universalist and absolutist claims of Western civilization.

Crummell invoked his "nigh twenty years" of sojourn in West Africa to proclaim the ethical and moral superiority of indigenous Africans. He identified London and New York as exhibiting more indecency than found anywhere in Africa. Despite ethnic and cultural heterogeneity, Crummell found certain universal values and qualities among the Africans he encountered: orderliness, inventiveness, honesty, and hospitality. Furthermore, Africans held their women in high esteem, spurned prostitution, and respected "maiden virtues, and the instinct of chastity." In fact, Crummell characterized indigenous Africa as a "very honest" and "most orderly" society, the extent of paganism notwithstanding.[13] These validations of Africa suggest a relativist conclusion: despite its technological and material backwardness, Africa possessed ennobling values and qualities that were conspicuously missing in Western civilization.

However, regardless of this dual cultural construct that challenged Europe's claim to a monopoly on civilization, black American nationalists confronted a troubling dilemma. The theoretical framework they developed combined two contradictory elements—an acknowledgment of Europe's superiority and a defense of Africa's claim to civilization. The troubling factor was the self-incriminatory implications of their subscription to Europe's depiction of Africa as primitive and, by extension, of all blacks as inherently inferior. Black Americans refused to conceive of themselves as belonging to this "dark and primitive" Africa. Unfortunately, the dual cultural space failed to satisfactorily resolve this curious predicament. Acknowledging Africa's primitivism lent credence to Europe's blanket vilification of blackness. It meant a validation and strengthening of a fundamental pillar of Eurocentric diffusionism. Essentially, the self-abnegating factor in black Americans' close tie to Africa's primitivism remained untouched.

Desperately in need of an experience that could effectively isolate black Americans from the implications of Africa's primitive state, these nationalists turned to the one unique and peculiar institution that had both separated them from Africa and drawn them closer to Europe: slavery. They all contended that slavery, and centuries of association with European civilization and Christianity, had liberated and set them apart from indigenous Africans. If there were still black savages, therefore, they all seemed to suggest, they were to be found not in black America but in continental Africa. The institution of slavery and the contact with European culture that accompanied it established black American cultural identity with Europe. This relationship with Europe was solidified by its antithesis—cultural distance from Africa, a distance that, in turn, conferred legitimacy and recognition upon black Americans as they sought to become partners of the Europeans in the task of civilizing "primitive" Africa.

Delany, Crummell, and Turner thus proposed two contradictory images of Africa. The first, a negative Africa, enabled them to subscribe to and justify the "civilizing mission." Put bluntly, this image legitimized their imperialist schemes. The second represented a positive Africa, blessed with admirable moral qualities. The latter was conceived to counter some of the negative Eurocentric values that had sustained the ill-treatment and subordination of black Americans in America and to affirm their right to better treatment. Both images mirror the dual cultural space that the nationalists created, which allowed them to condemn European civilization and to assert the inherent goodness and validity of African culture. By conceding that Africa was "backward and barbaric," Delany, Crummell, and Turner acknowledged the need for a "civilizing mission." However, by counterpoising this "barbarity" with Africa's moral and ethical qualities, they sought to invalidate many of the proslavery rationalizations that had justified their own enslavement and subordination.

The problem of the dual cultural space, however, lies in its inherently contradictory nature. Rather than being complementary, the two cultural spaces seem at odds. The Europeans, by virtue of technological and economic power, claimed the right to dominate the "other," Africans. In essence, the respect and recognition that the nationalists hoped to gain by positing a dual cultural space, with the African space serving as a stepping-stone for cooperation with Europe, failed to materialize. It is difficult to see how their proclamation of the essential morality of Africa would have effectively counterbalanced the technological, materialist, and civilizational authority of Europe that they had equally conceded and even boldly proclaimed. What precisely they hoped to accomplish by asserting Africa's moral authority *after* they had conceded the preeminence of European civilization is not clear. This is yet another manifestation of the subconscious, inner conflict caused by their dual or complex identity.

All three nationalists accorded slavery a positive significance beyond that imagined and projected for it by even the most ardent white proslavery advocate. Crummell and Turner depicted slavery as a divinely sanctioned institution for "civilizing" diasporan blacks in preparation for a greater mission—the civilizing of Africa. Although slavery represented a "civilizing experience" for black diasporans, for Africa the "civilizing" experience was encapsulated in Christianity and commerce (legitimate trade). However, despite the emphasis on Christianity, a greater portion of the schemes of these nationalists was devoted to trade in "legitimate" products—that is, economic consideration. The concept "legitimate trade" was coined by the Europeans to distinguish trade in tropical products from the slave trade, which had become illegal. The pursuit of "legitimate trade" became Europe's strategy for permanently obliterating the slave trade. "Legitimate trade" acquired the veneer of a humanitarian venture— an alternative to the obnoxious and inhuman slave trade. The Europeans, particularly the British, projected the crusade for "legitimate trade" as a humanitarian venture, effectively masking the underlying economic motives—that the European economy no longer needed the slave trade, and that European and British industries now demanded tropical products. Instead of shipping Africans to America to be enslaved, they were now needed to produce those tropical commodities locally in Africa.

This shift in European demand is central to the changing dynamics of Euro-African relations in the second half of the nineteenth century. The conception of Africa as primitive, economically under-developed, and heathen rendered it a prime candidate for the application of the gospel of Eurocentrism, with its belief in the potency of capitalism and Christianity as civilizing forces. Raised and socialized in this cultural context, black American nationalists acknowledged the legitimacy of European ideas and acceded to justifying and accommodating the subversion of African sovereignty and the exploitation of her resources. From the standpoint of this Machiavellian disposition, these were necessary if Africa's untapped material and natural resources were to be developed and if her human resources were to emerge from centuries of isolation, decadence, and primitivism. The commitment to legitimate commerce became itself a justification for interfering in the internal affairs of African states. Underneath the cloak of commerce and Christianity, however, lay the skeleton of European imperialism, an enterprise whose legitimacy depended on the denial of the authenticity and the essence of African culture and civilization.

Delany, Crummell, and Turner appropriated the language and values of Eurocentrism in their attempts to generate support among black Americans for the *repossession* of what they deemed their rightful inheritance—Africa. To excuse and rationalize a contradiction of mind-boggling proportions (i.e., the profession of commitment to African/black interests *and* the advocacy of cooperation with Europeans), all three nationalists whitewashed slavery and racism, cleansing both of their iniquitous and negative features, and then rewrapped them in providential robes. Slavery and racism were depicted as essential mechanisms of a divine plan: God intended both evils in order to bring to fruition a divine order. If slavery and racism possessed such historical and divine validation, it logically followed that those who perpetrated the twin evils, or wrote the obnoxious laws that sustained them, could not and should not be held responsible, since they were merely executing a function over which they had little control. As Crummell emphasized, "All human events . . . [are] elements and instruments in [God's] hand, for the accomplishment of the august objects of His will. . . . The Will of God overrules all the deeds, the counsels, and the designs of men. . . . While men act on their own personal responsibility, they nevertheless act either consciously or unconsciously as the agents of God."[14] The projection of providentialism as the dynamic of human development explains why, in spite of their sense of outrage and alienation, these nationalists were willing to cooperate with and defend, rather than forcefully challenge, European imperialism in Africa. They portrayed the European presence in Africa as the final phase in the actualization of a divine plan set in motion by slavery. White Americans and Europeans who enslaved and degraded Africans were, therefore, absolved of direct responsibility, since they were unconsciously executing a divine plan—a divinely sanctioned *evolutionary* experience that brought "African savages" in touch with a "superior culture."

All three nationalists proclaimed the transformative and positive impact of slavery on black America (that is, its civilizing effect), while forgetting the equally transformative but negative impact it had on Africa: the demographic shockwaves, the violence, and the rape and plunder of invaluable human resources—precisely those resources which, as Walter Rodney and other scholars have argued, were needed to develop Africa.[15] Delany, Crummell, and Turner failed to perceive the enduring impact of slavery on Africa, how the same slavery that had "positively" transformed black Americans had created the very conditions of decadence and backwardness that they and the Europeans later used to justify the colonization and despoliation of the continent.

The idea of slavery as a positive institution is perhaps a precursor of modern-day modernization theory. Modernization theorists tie progress and development in Africa and other third world societies to contact with, and the infusion of, European values and institutions.[16] Leading European racial classifiers and proponents of Negro inferiority espoused and vigorously defended the view that contact with Europeans civilized black Americans and therefore distinguished them from Africans, thus propagating an erroneous linkage between whiteness and culture. In fact, by the beginning of the nineteenth century, leading defenders of the concept of Negro inferiority had shifted from the virulent racism that characterized earlier writings to a paternalism that barely disguised the essential racism of their thoughts. Blumenbach exemplified this shift. He jettisoned his classificatory paradigm and developed a new paternalistic theory based on biographical sketches of "Noble Negroes," who had become civilized and accomplished in consequence of contacts with and immersion in Western societies.[17] His objective, ostensibly, was to argue for some concession to the "Noble Negroes." Contact with Europe became proof of Negro adaptability and susceptibility to civilization. According to Blumenbach, "There is no so-called savage nation known under the sun which has so distinguished itself by such examples of perfectibility and original capacity for scientific culture, and thereby attached itself so closely to the most civilized nations on the earth, *as the Negro.*"[18]

This new theory greatly influenced other European writers. Abbé Grégoire saw Christianity and civilization as cures for Africa's primitive and savage traits. Extending Blumenbach's work, Wilson Armistead wrote *Tribute to the Negro* (1848), a massive text devoted to establishing "proofs of Negro equality." By the second half of the nineteenth century, black diasporans had themselves become seduced by the compelling force of these biographical sketches. Edward Blyden, in fact, invoked the list of "Noble Negroes" to counter racist claims of the innate inferiority of the Negro.[19] As this study demonstrates, the perception that Negroes became civilized by contact with Europeans, and therefore could not be lumped together with the rest of Africa, was popular among leading black Americans. It became the basis of their claims for better treatment and for consideration as partners of the Europeans in the expanding field of the *mission civilisatrice.* Delany, Crummell, and Turner all embraced this notion, subscribing in the process to the prevailing European tendency to define blacks as culturally deficient.

By the late 1870s and early 1880s European imperialism had entered its third and final stage: the application of force against African polities and the conquest of the entire continent.[20] During this final phase, Europe massed its military and technological resources against African states, unleashing a systematic destabilization of the continent. This period was by no means a politically, economically, and culturally sterile epoch in Africa, the propaganda of European imperialists and black American nationalists notwithstanding. The rise of European imperialism coincided with a progressive but painful process of political integration and nation building in Africa. This process, which also entailed programs of economic, social, and cultural development, occurred in many parts of the continent, spearheaded by leaders who envisioned the unification, stabilization, and modernization of their respective nations. The result was the unification of the entire northern Nigeria region under the Sokoto Caliphate, the consolidation of the Asante in the Gold Coast, the rise of the Mandinka empire and the Caliphate of Macina in the West and Central Sudan, revolutionary crises and political consolidation in Yorubaland, and the *Mfecane* movement in southern Africa.[21]

Whatever European scholars thought of these crises, for Africans they represented a process of political alignment and realignment, not unusual in a fluid political environment. Left alone, many scholars believe, these political movements would eventually have stabilized into even stronger polities and nation-states. Unfortunately, this embryonic nation-building process threatened the imperial interests of the Europeans and had to be arrested and destroyed to give way to colonialism. European scholars and black American nationalists represented these crises as manifestations of Africa's barbarism and therefore as obstacles to the progress of the three C's: colonization, commerce, and Christianity. The British engaged the Asante in a series of battles in the 1870s and 1880s; the French fought both Al-hajj Umar of the Caliphate of Hamdallahi and Samouri Toure of the Mandinka Empire at about the same period. Both powers justified the use of violence against African states on the premise of controlling the proliferation of interethnic and interstate conflicts. For the Europeans, as for Delany and Crummell (who equally sanctioned its use against Africans), violence became a viable solution to the problem of "political instability" in Africa.

The conflicts that Europeans represented as political anarchy, and as an obstacle to the peaceful progression of commerce, Christianity, and civilization (for which they had the blessing of leading black American nationalists), actually reflected the fluidity of the African political landscape. African states were undergoing a process of political consolidation and nation building that often entailed violent confrontations, not unlike the developments that occasioned the emergence to nationhood of European states in the 1860s, 1870s, and 1880s, most notably Italy and Germany. What was considered a positive development in Europe was denigrated in Africa. However, the Europeans opposed this development in Africa not because it undermined the progress of civilization, as they claimed, but primarily because it posed an obstacle to the imposition of imperial rule. The success of nation building in Africa might have been the nemesis of European imperialism, and it had to be resisted and nipped in the bud. To destroy this process of political integration, the European powers adopted the technique of "divide and conquer." They exploited existing differences among African statesmen and polities by playing one against the other. The British adopted this strategy against the Asante and the Fante; the French used it against Al-hajj Umar and Samouri Toure; and the Portuguese applied it in Mozambique and Angola.[22] It seems inconceivable, finally, that black American nationalists who endorsed the use of force against Africa were unaware of these underlying imperialist designs on African sovereignty.

In a recent publication, the renowned Africanist Basil Davidson illuminates the state of Africa on the eve of colonialism. African societies were at varying stages of development, with many in the process of being transformed into stronger political entities. A "community consciousness," a strong sense of belonging and identity, permeated African communities. The values that sustained the survival, growth, and development of these communities were authentically African, derived from African cosmology. The seeds of community consciousness or ethos germinated into the nationalism that in turn unleashed movements for political consolidation. Left undisturbed, this nationalism and the attendant political consolidation would have proliferated. According to Davidson, "There is much to suggest that the modes of self-organization of a significant number of African peoples in the nineteenth century had reached a point of growth where *forms of large organizational change were in course, or at least in prospect.* Kings in some polities acquired more power than before. Peoples without kings developed new forms of central authority. Groups of neighboring communities were perhaps on the verge of forming new constellations of multiethnic composition. As it was, there came instead the colonial intrusion."[23] In this respect, colonialism arrested the progressive consolidation of African states. Consequently, the anti-African invectives of black American nationalists—the justifications of the use of force against Africans by Delany in the 1850s and 1860s and by Crummell and Turner in the 1880s and 1890s—rendered them equally responsible for the interruption of Africa's development and the loss of its independence. Even if they did not physically participate, the ideological cushioning they gave colonialism implicated them in the process of dismantling and subverting Africa's sovereignties.

In his seminal publication, *Pedagogy of the Oppressed*, the Brazilian scholar Paulo Freire provides an appropriate theoretical framework for comprehending the ideological dynamics and values embedded in the nationalist programs of leading black American nationalists. Freire bases his theoretical construct on the contradictory and antithetical relationship of the oppressor to the oppressed and on the pedagogical component of that relationship, especially with regard to the strengthening of the cultural hegemony of the oppressor and the potentiality for a revolutionary overthrow of oppression. Nevertheless, he does highlight issues that are relevant to comprehending the relationship between black American nationalists, in their capacity as leaders of thought, and indigenous Africans, whose interests and liberation they professed to be advancing. Black American nationalism reflected the same pedagogical dynamics that Freire identifies as central to a relationship of oppression and exploitation. That nationalism, and the schemes that sustained it, evolved in reaction to oppression, dehumanization, and deprivation, and consequently it assumed in its early stages a critical anti-European character. However, this anti-establishment character does not, in absolute terms, suggest the concretization of a revolutionary consciousness. A revolutionary ideology has to advance beyond the verbalization of alienation. There has to be a linkage between a revolutionary ideology and the objective condition of oppression. In other words, a truly revolutionary ideology has to embrace, in principle and practice, the very oppressed in whose struggle *alone* it is validated. Freire emphasizes the need for integration and communion between ideological leaders and those whom they profess to lead and whose interest they claim to uphold.[24] Put differently, there has to be a correspondence between the theoretical formulations of revolutionary leaders (in this case the nationalist leaders Delany, Crummell, and Turner), and the objective factor, defined as the constituency of the oppressed and objectified (in this case Africans).

The nationalist ideas of Delany, Crummell, and Turner reveal a curious disjuncture in this regard. There is a wide gulf between their militant rhetoric and the objective reality. Although they included African concerns and interests in their theoretical formulations of the problematic of marginalization and subordination, in proposing practical measures designed to obliterate the problems, they sought and declared affinity not with Africans but with the Europeans, the very source of the problems they professed to be attacking. Subordination of Africa became the foundation for the mutual progress of Europeans and black Americans. The hope, of course, was that this confluence and stabilization of imperialism would lead to the redemption of Africa. Freire further emphasizes the importance of dialogue to any scheme designed for the obliteration of oppression. This dialogue, of course, is not just between the oppressor and an elite segment of the oppressed, acting in the role of leadership, but also between this elite and the mass of oppressed people. It is this latter dimension of the dialogue which breeds and sustains the "unshakable solidarity" fundamental to mutual liberation.[25]

Unfortunately, even in the crucial late nineteenth century, leading black American nationalists foreclosed the possibility of any meaningful dialogue with Africans. Delany, Crummell, and Turner came to Africa infused with cultural arrogance and a sense of superiority, just like the Europeans, and they objectified Africans as primitives who lacked the capacity for self-enhancement. Rather than initiate a dialogue with Africans and develop the solidarity implied in their theoretical formulations, they came determined to impose "modernizing" values and foreign solutions on the traditionalism and perceived primitivism of Africa. They engaged the Europeans in a dialogue on how best to harmonize their respective schemes, with an eye toward maximizing mutual rewards. Although they presented themselves as leaders of thought who articulated libertarian ideas on behalf of all blacks and Africans, the latter were deemed incapable of benefiting from those principles until they had attained civilization. Vis-à-vis Africans, then, these nationalists maintained essentially antidialogical postures and a disposition of cultural alienation, as they justified the conquest of, and imposition of foreign values on, Africa. The renunciation of African cultural values evident in late-nineteenth-century black American nationalism underscores the depth and pervasiveness of what Walter Williams describes as "Western enculturation."[26]

In *Black Marxism: The Making of the Black Radical Tradition*, Cedric Robinson observes that the identity of the twentieth-century black middle class develops from "abilities to absorb the cultures of their ruling classes and the reading and speaking of European languages. Deracination, social and cultural alienation, had become the measure of their 'civility,' loyalty and usefulness."[27] This contention applies with equal force to the nineteenth-century black American middle class, particularly those who assumed the ideological leadership of the freedom struggle. They constructed their identity on the foundation of the "cultures of their ruling class."

Cultural hegemony, Clovis Semmes contends, effects a "rotation" in the perspective of an oppressed class or group, inducing it to perceive reality as given by the oppressor—the reality or world of the oppressor acquires legitimacy and is deemed fundamental.[28] Within this context, subordination becomes normative as the oppressed are socialized to acknowledge subordination as both an effective panacea for, and the consequence of, backwardness. This explains the inability of black American nationalists to see anything wrong in recommending the subordination of Africa. The ideas of Delany, Crummell, and Turner demonstrate clearly that, though they were aware of the possibility and consequence of deracination, of the negation and distortion of their history (especially Delany and Turner), they were most unwilling to maintain a consistently counterimperialist and countercultural posture. Instead, they chose to embrace and seek validation in their Anglo-Saxon and Euro-American heritage. In consequence, they found African indigenous customs aberrant, repulsive, and primitive. This is a measure of the depth of their self-hatred and cultural alienation—a curious paradox, given their declared opposition to hegemonic culture and values.

In "The Eighteenth Brumaire of Louis Bonaparte," Karl Marx observes, "Men make their own history, but they do not make it just as they pleased; they do not make it under circumstances chosen by themselves, but under circumstances directly encountered, given and transmitted from the past."[29] Although Marx's contention is valid, the experiential locus of history is equally the product of circumstances that are deeply personal to, and directly encountered by, the subjects. In other words, history is not solely a remote and inherited experience from the past. History is also the consequence of experiences that unfold in full view of the actors and subjects. Delany, Crummell, and Turner participated in the making of a people's history—the development of a movement aimed at the liberation of Africans, and blacks in general, from centuries of domination and exploitation. In participating in this exercise in liberation ethics—in attempting to develop a theoretical basis for a transatlantic nexus of resistance to centuries of oppression—they were influenced not just by the dictates of their past experiences as descendants of Africa in the New World but also by the more recent and profound experience of being black in a global environment that was rapidly abandoning one form of exploitation (slavery) for another (imperialism).

In the United States, slavery gave way to Jim Crow, while in the global context, "legitimate trade" displaced the slave trade. Both transitions were backed by strong ideological rationalizations, with profound consequences for the fate of black Americans and Africans, respectively. In the United States, Jim Crow culture sustained and strengthened white supremacy. Globally, European hegemony prevailed.[30] Both developments reinforced the black nationalist and the Pan-Africanist ethos. The Pan-African slant of late-nineteenth-century black American nationalism was both a reflection of and reaction against the global projection of European hegemony. Black Americans responded to the threat of European hegemony by invoking nationalist and Pan-Africanist values. Paradoxically, the ideologies of black nationalists also revealed the hegemonic and racialist values they had imbibed from Eurocentric culture. The history that Delany, Crummell, and Turner helped to create, therefore, bore the imprints of the complex black American experience. In other words, despite its radical theoretical foundation, late-nineteenth-century black American nationalism failed to transcend the boundaries of the Euro-American cultural world. Black American nationalists conceded to the projection of Europe as the quintessence of civilization, and they accepted that civilization as the standard against which to measure other societies. This concession notwithstanding, they seemed uncomfortable with Europe's cultural narcissism and countered with a relativist conception of civilization designed to enhance their own claim for recognition and equality, a claim they also fortified through a curious reconceptualization of slavery.

The adoption of an antidialogical posture toward Africa captures the true character of the black American experience. Slavery, segregation, and racism were not based on dialogue. They were imposed experiences, based on and justified by European perceptions and convictions. The choice of whom to enslave and the ideological justification for enslavement were exclusively European. The domination and exploitation of black Americans were perpetrated with utter disregard for their feelings. Socialized in such a blatantly racist and hegemonic culture, black Americans in turn attempted to subject Africans to a similar experience. The schemes and programs they proposed for the "civilization" and "development" of Africa were not discussed with Africans. Given the very low opinion held of Africa, indeed, it seems illogical to expect that there would have been such a dialogue. The art of dialogue is conventionally practiced between parties with mutual interests and respect, but the attempt to alienate Africans from their traditions, languages, and cultures and to impose Eurocentric values on their societies strongly suggests a wider and deeper cultural chasm between black America and Africa than is often acknowledged—a chasm that is often ignored, or at least de-emphasized, in postmodernist discourse on black nationalism and Pan-Africanism.

The black American response to Africa, therefore, reflected desires and aspirations shaped by their American and European exposures and consciousness. One can bluntly and safely suggest that had American society been open and liberal, and had blacks been accorded their rights and privileges as citizens, the need to "civilize" and uplift "heathen and primitive" Africa would probably not have arisen. As Walter Williams suggests, "The attitudes of blacks toward their hopes of assimilation in the United States was the frame of reference upon which they based their attitude toward Africa. If they were disillusioned with America, their interest would be more likely to identify with Africa. Conversely, if they considered themselves as primarily American, their antipathy to Africa reflected their enculturation."[31] Contrary to popular assumptions, therefore, the emigrationist or back-to-Africa slant of black American nationalism did not necessarily suggest a strong desire to identify with Africa. It underscores more the depth of alienation from the United States. Theodore Draper was therefore perfectly right in relating black American nationalism more closely to frustration over the failure to secure American nationality than to interest in Africa.[32]

All three nationalists in this study began with a strong commitment to black and African identity and interests. They also condemned the persistence of racism (particularly Delany and Turner), and strongly rejected the hegemony of European values and civilization. They pledged, theoretically at least, to develop and sustain a countercultural nationalism. In essence, they attempted to galvanize a black consciousness and Pan-African ethos, and they strongly affirmed the essence and utility of the African and black cultural heritage. Paradoxically, this Afrocentric posture soon dissipated, as their needs and interests as Americans and "Anglos" assumed preeminence. They executed a *volte-face*, embracing not only the ideas and ideology of the previously rejected and dreaded Euro-American civilization but also its program of gradually displacing African civilization and destroying African sovereignty.

The Afrocentric character of late-nineteenth-century black American nationalism was soon submerged under the weight and force of Eurocentrism. Perhaps without realizing it, black American nationalists facilitated the triumph of Eurocentric nationalism in Africa. One can plausibly argue, therefore, that the partition and colonization of Africa was a triumph not only for European missionaries, explorers, and politicians, as is traditionally believed, but also for black American nationalism. The link between late-nineteenth-century black American nationalism and European imperialism in Africa was very strong. Given the strength of this connection, the prevailing practice of discussing the European colonization of Africa, in both its theoretical and practical ramifications, without acknowledging the contributions of black American nationalists, remains inexplicable.

Perhaps more than any other critic, Bill McAdoo captures the imperialist character of pre–Civil War black nationalism. He identifies two fundamental strands of nineteenth-century black nationalism—revolutionary and reactionary. Revolutionary nationalism sought to effect change within the United States. It was driven by a strong faith in the potency of revolutionary violence and in the revolutionary potentiality and essence of the black masses. He describes David Walker and Henry Highland Garnet as the leading revolutionary black nationalists. Reactionary nationalism, on the other hand, was directed outward, toward the creation of an independent black nationality. McAdoo depicts reactionary nationalism as essentially Zionist in orientation, and he identifies Martin Delany as its leading advocate. Black Zionism proffered elitist solutions meant to advance the exploitative and imperialist agenda of the elite black middle class, the wealthy and resourceful few who supposedly had the capacity to initiate change from abroad. Reactionary nationalists, or Zionists, directed their attention abroad, due to a lack of confidence in the revolutionary potentiality of the black masses. They gave up completely on the possibility of change within the United States. The grand design of black Zionism, McAdoo contends, was to possess and exploit Africa for the fulfillment of the capitalist aspirations of the black American bourgeoisie. McAdoo thus underlines the eclectic (or was it Janus-faced?) character of late-nineteenth-century emigrationism. Emigrationists espoused very strong pro-African values in defense of their quest for a black/African nationality. In fact, few nineteenth-century nationalists stressed the national question as forcefully as the "Zionists," most notably Delany and Turner. McAdoo describes the quest for a black nationality as the element that distinguished black Zionism from the establishment-oriented and sponsored colonization scheme.[33]

However, this "radical" nationality factor was soon coupled with a program of economic cooperation with Europeans that bore ominous implications for the future of Africa. Black Zionism, or what this writer prefers to call black imperialism, consequently possessed dual and inherently contradictory features: a revolutionary side that forcefully foregrounded the nationality question and affirmed the right of blacks to self-determination, and a reactionary and self-abnegating counterrevolutionary strategy. Essentially, black imperialism combined a superficially radical objective with an essentially reactionary and defeatist strategy.

The goal Delany espoused, amplified later by both Turner and Crummell, of developing a strong black nation in Africa was in essence compromised by the imperialist character of both the strategies devised for its realization and the context within which it was conceived and projected. Each of these activists took an approach to Africa that combined elitism and condescension with disdain for, and lack of faith in, the revolutionary potentiality of the African masses. They based a black nationality too narrowly on the elite, the few who comprised the wealthy, resourceful, and enterprising black American middle class. Although wealth and a viable economy are indispensable to the success of any nation, the marginalization of the masses denied the elite the kind of broad support that was equally fundamental to a successful nationality. Since Delany, Crummell, and Turner could not garner enough support among middle-class black Americans, they had no choice but to turn to the very class against whose threat the black nationality quest was conceived— Europeans and Anglo-Americans. The disdain of these men for the black American masses was also echoed in their complete relegation of the African masses to the role of laborers. The cultural bias derived from Western socialization inspired disdain for Africans and made it all the more difficult for Delany, Crummell, and Turner to consider Africans fit for any but subordinate roles.

The success of European occupation of Africa constituted the maturation of that external authority, force, and social structure that Crummell and Delany, in particular, had insisted "primitive" and "backward" Africans needed in order to become elevated and civilized. Denied power, subordinated, and exploited in America, these black nationalists had turned to Africa for succor and an effective power base upon which to fight back. Unfortunately, the power base they envisioned bore destructive implications for the future of indigenous Africans. Africans were placed in precisely those roles that black Americans had confronted and were attempting to avoid. This, at least, is the implication suggested by the joint ventures that Delany, Crummell, and Turner proposed with the Europeans. The three nationalists seemed driven more by a compulsive desire to appeal to and appease the Europeans, whose sympathies and respect they valued, than by the Pan-African imperative of initiating a strong black American and African cultural and nationalistic nexus.

The ambivalent and self-abnegating aspect of late-nineteenth-century black American nationalism has not been fully explored. Milfred Fierce's recent publication, however, though focusing on the twentieth-century development of Pan-Africanism, with only a cursory glance into the past, provides an excellent summation that captures the inherent contradictions of nineteenth-century black nationalism. Of Henry Turner, he writes, "Sometimes Turner was contradictory, at other times he was condescending and paternalistic toward Africa. Often he was presumptuous and ill-informed. On occasion he was guilty of perpetuating pseudo-scientific notions about race, and his remarks were frequently couched in the platitudes of the day."[34] Fierce's conclusions apply equally to Delany and Crummell. The three nationalists approached Africa, just as the Europeans did, intending not to understand the nature of African societies and traditions, and to appreciate their peculiarities, but to measure how Africans fit into the framework created by Europeans. They seemed more preoccupied with transforming African societies according to the dictates of Europe than with understanding and mobilizing those societies to constitute a common front against what they had each, at some point, identified as a threat to the existence and freedom of all blacks—European imperialism. The more indigenous an African society was, the more it was presumed primitive and in need of the infusion of European values. Black Americans who had come in contact with European civilization through the fortuitous experience of slavery could not be deemed primitive or lumped together with indigenous Africans. Slavery had thus "civilized" black Americans, distinguishing them qualitatively from "primitive Africans." The depiction of slavery as a positive good had always been a popular proslavery viewpoint, one that black Americans, including Delany and Turner, paradoxically, had at points vociferously opposed.

Overwhelmed by the depth and virulence of racism in America, black American nationalists ignored the global character of racism, an issue of which they were certainly aware. Once in Africa, Delany and Turner seemed afflicted by a state of amnesia. How else could one explain Delany's flirtation with the British, the same Anglo-Saxons whom he had once identified as collaborators with their Anglo-American cousins in a plot to keep blacks permanently subordinate? How could one explain Crummell's fascination with the English language and culture and Turner's call on the American government to enter into the race for the occupation of Africa?

Unfortunately, from their standpoint, the flirtation of these nationalists with European imperialism and their attempts to gain the respect and confidence of the Europeans failed. Being cleansed and civilized by enslavement was not sufficient grounds, in the judgment of the Europeans, to be accorded recognition as partners in the spread of civilization. As Richard Blackett argues, the cooperation and partnership envisaged by black American nationalists proved difficult in the context of the expanding field of European imperialism.[35] The basic premise of European imperialism was a belief in European superiority. This conviction justified the subordination of all non-Europeans, regardless of their state of civilization, their proximity to Europe, or the compatibility of their agendas. Consequently, though the premise undergirding the social and economic ideas of Delany, Turner, and Crummell was compatible with the ideas of the Europeans, the equality implied in the notion of cooperation and joint venture was unacceptable. The European agenda had no place for joint cooperation with representatives of a race considered primitive. Once it was decided that Africa held the answer to the economic problems of Europe, that force was necessary, and that formal empires were the answers to Europe's problem, all ideological weapons were marshaled to justify the impending rape of Africa.

The Europeans then concentrated their energies and efforts on effectively dismantling African sovereignty, and they would not countenance or accommodate any scheme of joint cooperation, especially one that directly contradicted the basic premise of white supremacy. By 1900, however, for a variety of reasons, black American nationalists had all but disappeared as viable participants in the colonization enterprise they had endorsed, leaving the Europeans to carry through the programs both had worked out and propagandized. One can plausibly contend that, though effectively out of the African scene by the first decade of the twentieth century, Delany, Crummell, and Turner had accomplished quite a feat—they had contributed to laying the foundation for the colonization of Africa. It would be left to a new brand of nationalists, with a deeper appreciation of the essence and value of Africa, and who were horrified and appalled by the excesses of colonialism and the global thrust of imperialism, to develop a new nationalist framework, albeit one based on the same transatlantic and Pan-African considerations that had inspired Delany, Turner, Crummell, and earlier nationalists. This new generation evolved a truly counter-European nationalist ideology. W.E.B. Du Bois of the United States, George Padmore, C.L.R. James, and Henry Sylvester Williams of the West Indies, Jomo Kenyatta of Kenya, J.L. Dube and D.D.T. Jabavu of South Africa, Wallace Johnson of Sierra Leone, Hastings Kamuzu Banda of Nyasaland (Malawi), Nnamdi Azikiwe of Nigeria, and J. Casely-Hayford and Kwame Nkrumah of the Gold Coast (Ghana) all turned "to the historical tradition of black liberation and became black radicals."[36] These black diasporans embraced Africa and Africans in a relationship that was truly designed for the defense and advancement of mutual interests. Black nationalism and Pan-Africanism assumed an ideologically combative posture, with a truly anti-imperial program that distinctly avoided the contradictory and self-abnegating character of earlier traditions.

Sylvia Jacobs's seminal study explores the attitudes and responses of black Americans to the European partitioning of Africa.[37] Jacobs touches only marginally on the three nationalists in this study, concentrating instead on the first two decades of the twentieth century. By 1920, black Americans had the benefit of an informed practical knowledge and understanding of European imperialism. Their perspective, not surprisingly, became very critical of imperialism in east, central, and southern Africa. They developed a very cynical and negative perception of the "civilizing mission." In essence, they were able to see through the cloak that had blinded the visions of Delany, Crummell, and Turner. Jacobs does an excellent job of illuminating this new, critical, anti-imperial character of black American nationalism. Anthony Appiah traces the origination of this character to the emergence of a new breed of nationalists in the post–World War II period, those he calls the "African Pan-Africanists," who manifested a much more positive attitude toward Africa. Appiah emphasizes the depth of their African consciousness. Socialized in Africa, cognizant of her wealth and value, and appreciative of her traditions, this new breed of nationalists refused to dismiss Africa as primitive. Their conceptual approach to Africa was directed at building on and celebrating the African essence and its values.[38] Unlike the "exiles of the New World," who "could show their love of Africa by seeking to eliminate its indigenous culture," the "African Pan-Africanists," as "heirs to Africa's civilization could not so easily dispose of their ancestors." Appiah thus discerns a perceptual and conceptual chasm between indigenous Africans of the post–World War II generation and black diasporans.

Although Appiah's contention is valid, World War II is not the ideal point at which to locate the signs of an emerging transformation in the way black diasporans and indigenous Africans saw Africa. The rise of colonialism was perhaps the much more potent factor instigating this change. By the second decade of the twentieth century—by the time Africa's resistance to colonialism had been effectively suppressed and the essence of colonialism illuminated—there evolved a convergence in how black American nationalists, black diasporans in general, and Africans perceived and defined the challenges they confronted. In other words, a greater awareness and understanding of the true character of the "civilizing mission" bridged the perceptual gap between Africans and diasporans. It was this strengthened sense of mutuality which shaped the cooperation exemplified by the Pan-African Congress movement. In fact, by the fourth Pan-African Congress in 1927, the framework for a genuine solidarity between Africans—from Nigeria, Sierra Leone, Liberia, and the Gold Coast—and black Americans was already in place. Continental Africans and blacks in the diaspora identified colonialism as the problem and consequently focused attention on it. Black Americans acquired a better insight into the real purpose of the *mission civilisatrice* and grew increasingly critical of it.[39] As Horace Campbell argues, "The struggle against the political, economic and cultural imperatives of imperialism sharpened the philosophical basis of Pan-Africanism in the twentieth century. And for much of the century the focus has been to unite the subjective reservoir of African identity into a social form capable of *confronting imperialism* in all its forms."[40] Campbell here underlines a transformation in the orientation of the black struggle, characterized by the jettisoning of the collaboratory ethos that had tied earlier nationalists to the apron strings of European imperialism.

W.E.B. Du Bois influenced the agenda and set the tone of this aggressively anticolonial and anti-imperial black nationalist and Pan-Africanist movement. In both utterances and policy formulation, black diasporans demonstrated an awareness of the centrality and pertinence of race in the shaping of the relationship between Europeans and the rest of humankind. They concurred with Du Bois's identification of the "color line" as the critical problem of the twentieth century. As one scholar puts it, they realized "how far differences of race, as manifested in skin color and their texture, were going to be used as criteria for denying more than half the population of the globe the right to share, to their utmost ability, the blessings of modern civilization. It was conceded that the darker races of the time lagged behind their European counterparts."[41] Paradoxically, this "primitive" and "backward" darker race seemed earmarked as the foundation for the nourishment and sustenance of the "superior" and "civilized" European! Put differently, Europeans seemed to harbor a *Herrenvolk* conception of civilization—that is, they assumed Europe's "civilized" condition would be sustained by the dislocation, subjugation, and exploitation of "primitive" Africa.

The new breed of black nationalist and Pan-Africanist, imbued with a clearer vision of imperialism and a more positive outlook toward Africa, perceived the true character of imperialism and its antithetical relationship to black nationalism—one sought the elevation of blacks, and the other was premised on a racial ideology aimed at the subjugation and exploitation of the "darker race." Realizing the futility and illogicality of collaboration with Europeans, the new Pan-Africanists assumed a militant anticolonial posture and challenged Eurocentric assaults on blacks and Africa. They acknowledged and sought to mobilize the revolutionary potentialities of indigenous Africa, in unity with their own intellectual and practical resources. In fact, they assumed strong anticolonial postures, criticized European policies, and tried to curb the expansion of colonialism. It should be acknowledged, however, that this new generation was equally the product of Western "enculturation" and, like its predecessor, imbibed Eurocentric values and biases. Yet the commitment of members of the new generation to Pan-Africanism and the defense of black and African interests was compelling. They refused to allow the myth of dark and primitive Africa to blunt or diminish the force with which they engaged European imperialism. Rather than vilify African societies, cultural values, and practices, Du Bois and all those who participated in the Pan-African Congress movement exalted Africa and declared a strong commitment to the articulation and defense of black/African interests.

One area of success was Liberia. Paradoxically, it was American intervention and involvement, a policy Turner and Crummell had persistently advocated, that ultimately saved Liberia from suffering the fate of other African countries. However, when the intervention finally occurred, both men had long exited Africa, and events were moving at an alarming pace—the European scramble was gathering momentum. A new generation of black American nationalists, journalists, educators, and missionaries, witnesses to the atrocities of colonialism, fought desperately to spare Liberia by persistently imploring the United States government to intervene. They depicted British, French, and German activities as threats to American interests in Liberia. According to Sylvia Jacobs, "By 1914 black American perspectives on European imperialism focused less on the humanitarian and religious aspects of the 'civilizing mission' and more on the exploitative elements that had kept blacks throughout Africa in an inferior position since the arrival of the Europeans on the continent."[42] This contrasted sharply with the tradition of previous black nationalists who harmonized their intellectual and practical resources with those of the Europeans against the cultural artifacts and material resources of Africans. The new nationalists and Pan-Africanists evinced a strong sense of affinity with Africans whom they perceived as partners. The strong conviction of shared racial, cultural, and historical experience inspired cooperation between the two. Black Americans, blacks from the Caribbean, and Africans joined to organize the Pan-African Congresses. It is this transatlantic cooperation which black American nationalists of the preceding epoch sacrificed on the altar of Anglo-American and Anglo-Saxon "enculturation."

The new twentieth-century Pan-African force, unlike its immediate predecessor, was premised not on cooperating with Europeans, recognized as the oppressor, but on mobilizing African and diasporan resources. In essence, the Pan-Africanism that developed in the early twentieth century was a corrective to— indeed, in terms of its functional imperatives, was antithetical to—the Pan-African ideology that shaped black American nationalism of the preceding generation. The new nationalists and Pan-Africanists developed and sustained an aggressive and contentious movement, aimed at uprooting an edifice that their predecessors had helped erect. Colonialism was responsible for this dramatic difference. Colonialism represented the triumph of Eurocentrism in all its ramifications, graphically underscoring the centrality of race, the powerlessness of blacks, the failures and inherent problems of late-nineteenth-century black American nationalism, the irrationality of collaboration, and, perhaps most significantly, the reality of the racial boundary that the preceding nationalists had once drawn and then erased. Du Bois's statement represented a strong affirmation of the imperative of racial solidarity, a condition that the ambivalence displayed by Delany, Crummell, and Turner definitely compromised.

In fact, the transformation of black nationalist consciousness, the adoption by black Americans of a much more positive and sustained consciousness of affinity with Africa, was evident in the nationalist ideas associated with the "New Negro" of the Harlem Renaissance. By the first decade of the twentieth century, the collapse of Booker T. Washington's dream of an integrated America was a foregone conclusion. The great migrations to northern cities, the strengthening of Jim Crow, the ghettoization, marginalization, and impoverishment of blacks—all combined, like colonialism in Africa, to underscore the preeminence of race and encourage a truly black nationalist and Pan-African consciousness in black Americans.

Nationalists of the Harlem Renaissance consequently exhibited a much more positive attitude toward Africa. Their expressions of identity with Africa were much stronger and more deeply rooted than that of their late-nineteenth-century predecessors. They seemed to understand that identity with Africa had to be total for it to have any significance. In "Apropos of Africa," Alain Locke characterized the "missionary condescension" of the past generations of black Americans toward Africa as a "pious but sad mistake." Emphasizing the importance of a reorientation, Locke declared, "We must realize that in some respects we need what Africa has to give us as much as, or even more than, Africa needs what we in turn have to give her; and that unless we approach Africa in the spirit of the finest reciprocity, our efforts will be ineffectual or harmful. *We need to be the first of all Westerners to rid ourselves of the insulting prejudice, the insufferable bias of the attitude of 'civilizing Africa'*—for she is not only our mother but in the light of most recent science is beginning to appear as the mother of civilization in general."[43]

Locke very well understood the potential limitations and the problematic history of the black American orientation toward Africa. "With notable exception," he acknowledged, "our interest in Africa has heretofore been sporadic, sentimental and unpractical." He called for a new departure, a new orientation that embodied a strong, deep-rooted and holistic appreciation of Africa, and a desire to embrace and identify with "all of the African peoples." He envisioned the evolution of a "constructive Pan-African thought and endeavor" that would sustain a genuine relationship for mutual uplift. If black Americans were truly interested in the development of Africa, as opposed to "merely the exploitations of . . . the continent and its varied peoples," then, Locke suggested, "it is rather against than with the wish of the interested governments, that the American Negro must reach out toward his rightful share in the solution of Africa's problems and the development of Africa's resources." Locke discerned a basic flaw in the prevailing black American conceptions of and approaches to Africa: they seemed self-serving and exploitative, and they often complemented and reinforced the schemes and agendas of the interested European governments.[44]

There is no evidence of a conscious move on the part of either Delany, Crummell, or Turner to approach Africa in the "spirit of the finest reciprocity," as Locke envisioned, or to mobilize black American and African resources and power against European/white oppression and hegemony, as implied in their theoretical formulations. The paradigm they developed rested on a triad of ostensible cooperation between Europeans, black Americans, and Africans. The real cooperation, however, was between Europeans and the black American elite and was designed to facilitate the exploitation of African resources and cheap African labor.

The failure of Delany, Crummell, and Turner to sustain a truly

Pan-African focus could also be attributed to their awareness of the character of the international political economy. An alliance built on ethnic and cultural consanguinity, however real and substantive, could not have withstood the force of the material and technological power of Europe. Consequently, though these nationalists theoretically understood the racial context of oppression, practically they had no choice but to relegate race to the background, given their lack of the economic power essential to the realization of a nationality. This economic weakness became even more problematic given the reluctance and failure of the black American middle class, to whose economic self-interest they appealed, to commit its resources to the pursuit of a black nationality outside of the United States.

A black nationality conceived "in the spirit of the finest reciprocity," however, was never the intention of the nationalists covered in this study. They came to "possess," "exploit," and "dominate." The fact that they were willing to appeal to the Europeans for aid in suppressing African polities betrayed the imperialist character of their mission. McAdoo argues persuasively that the ultimate goal of black Zionism was to replicate the Liberia model throughout Africa.[45] The story of the exploitative and imperialistic activities of black Americans in Liberia is well documented. According to a recent authority, the most troubling was "the disdain and condescension that the New World men and women [black Americans] exhibited toward indigenous people. These 'westerners' viewed indigenous Africans as primitives and savages whose cultural practices were 'uncivilized.' . . . [T]hey used their Christian religion, western dress and English language to set themselves apart from the native population."[46] With the help of the English and of American military power, black Americans subjected Liberians to precisely the same humiliating and dehumanizing experiences that they themselves had been subjected to by whites in North America. It is this ostensibly successful cooperation between black American colonists and the American Colonization Society in Liberia which Delany, Crummell, and Turner sought to replicate in other parts of the continent.

John H. Bracey identifies two key attributes of black nationalism: first, *racial solidarity,* the notion of black unity based on common color and condition of oppression, both constituting the basis for developing group strength for mutual advancement, and second, *cultural nationalism,* the belief that blacks in the United States and elsewhere share a culture, style of life, aesthetic standard, and worldview distinct from that of white Americans and Europeans.[47] These two principles nurtured the Pan-African orientation of black nationalism throughout history. Late-nineteenth-century black American nationalism derived its Pan-African ethos from a combination of the two values—a theoretical presumption of a monolithic black world unified by shared values, cultural experiences, and historical experiences. As has been demonstrated, this theoretical monolithism was negated by the very strategy designed for its propagation.

Analysis of a few other conceptions of black nationalism will further underscore the divergence between the profession of identity and monolithism, on the one hand, and a reality of differences and complexity, on the other. Essien-Udom's acclaimed definition, referred to at the beginning of this study, underlines the attributes of shared cultural heritage and nationality.[48] Eric Foner perceives black nationalism as expressive of a revolt against rejection, alienation, and domination and of an "affirmation of the unique traditions, values, and cultural heritage of black Americans."[49] Edwin Redkey identifies the essence of black nationalism as "protest against American hypocrisy and white nationalism" and advocacy of black solidarity to combat those factors.[50] These definitions all underscore the centrality of identity, solidarity, mutuality, and shared ethnic and cultural experiences. These same values were projected into Pan-Africanism to affirm a monolithic Africa–black diaspora experience. Black nationalism, in its Pan-African dimension, presumes the existence of an African/black Atlantic world unified by shared historical, cultural, and ethnic experiences. This view strongly affirms the authenticity of an experiential and cultural world that transcends or, more accurately, nullifies the divergences and complexities created by geographical, ecological, and historical factors. A pervasive historiographical tendency reflective of this paradigm similarly hides the complexity, contradictions, and ambivalence of the black American, African, and entire black diasporan experiences behind a facade of Pan-African identity. Studies of black nationalism and Pan-Africanism remain plagued by a romanticized consciousness of African and black diasporan history and experience.

Studies that seem critical of black nationalism often fail to deal critically and exhaustively with the phenomenon of romanticization and other inherent contradictions. In *The Golden Age of Black Na-*

tionalism, 1850-1925, Wilson J. Moses does an excellent job of unearthing perhaps the most critical of the contradictions—the Anglo-Saxon character of black nationalism. Knowledge of this contradiction is undoubtedly crucial to comprehending the ideological foundation of black American nationalism. There is, however, a need to probe the contradiction's broader ramifications. In essence, one needs to know its logical progression and development, especially in light of the fact that the larger Anglo-Saxon culture from whence it evolved was a dynamic force in European expansion overseas. It is imperative to explore in detail the imperialist dynamics of the Anglo-Saxon values in black American thought. The Anglo-Saxon nationalism and worldview that black American nationalists embraced legitimized Europe's global quest for empire. The Anglo-Saxon worldview justified British and European global hegemony. Given this reality, it seems pertinent to enquire as to how black American nationalists who embraced this orientation digested an ideology designed to dominate all blacks and negate their place in history. The fundamental question therefore is: How did black American nationalism, a phenomenon that evolved as critical of the exploitation and domination of blacks in the United States, and in opposition to racism, deal with the globally hegemonic trajectories of Eurocentrism?

Critical studies of black nationalism betray a reluctance to explore this intricate dimension. Perhaps, as Clarence Walker argues in *Deromanticizing Black History*, such an exposition would have weakened the dominant theoretical framework within which black nationalism, and indeed black history, has generally been assessed—the concept of the Community. The Community is a romantic construct that conjures the image of blacks as a monolithic people with shared experiences and values, beclouding the contradictions and ambiguities of the black and African experience. This community focus shaped discourse on black nationalism and Pan-Africanism throughout its history. It is, however, a historical fallacy to suggest that black Americans and Africans perceived themselves as a global community. It is the contention of this study that the transatlantic ethos of mutuality in black American nationalism was more rhetorical and propagandistic than real in the nineteenth century. The presumption of a monolithic black Atlantic and African experience flies in the face of the complexity not only of Africa but also of the black diaspora experience. It is only in the twentieth century that black American nationalism began to project a truly global Pan-African character. Black experiential linkages derived from colonialism, both foreign (in Africa) and domestic (in the United States), and from exploitation and racism, nurtured a truly Pan-African consciousness, aimed at effecting a unified movement for the elevation of blacks in Africa, the United States, the Caribbean, and Latin America, against problems that were deemed mutual—European colonialism and racism.

It seems more appropriate, therefore, to utilize the term *nationalism,* as this study does, when discussing the nationalist ideas and programs of United States blacks in the nineteenth century. What was often projected in global, Pan-African terms as "black nationalism," especially in the second half of that century, was infused with a strong dose of Anglo- and Euro-American values, consciousness, and aspirations, creating a contradiction between theory/principles and practice. Although leading black American nationalists expounded what seemed like a diaspora or "Pan" theory of nationalism, ostensibly to advance and defend the global interests of Africans and peoples of African descent, the schemes they proposed in support of this nationalism were localized and designed more to enhance the fortunes of the black American elite class whom they represented, and to whom they appealed, and the Europeans, at the expense of indigenous Africans. From its inception in slavery, black American nationalism was molded by one enduring aspiration: the search for a more rational American order, that is, the attainment of full citizenship rights and privileges. The "Pan-African" schemes proposed were directed toward the realization of this prime objective. The development and uplifting of continental Africans was indeed peripheral. This is certainly black American nationalism, not black nationalism in the broader Pan-African context. The concept "black nationalism" connotes a deeper global consciousness of affinity among blacks in Africa and the diaspora. This became a reality in the early twentieth century, when black nationalism assumed a truly anti-imperial and anti-European character, armed with a strong black- and African-centered agenda, aimed at the extrication of blacks in Africa, and in the diaspora, from the clutches of colonial exploitation and racism.

If black nationalism and Pan-Africanism, as they developed in the early twentieth century, sought the combined mobilization of Africans and peoples of African descent for a struggle for mutual benefits against a common threat or enemy, as many suggest, then what Delany, Crummell, and Turner defended earlier was definitely not Pan-African. It was certainly nationalistic, situated within the American context, but a truly Pan-African and black nationalist program is one propelled by conscious efforts to harmonize, theoretically and practically, blacks in the diaspora and in the African continent. Blacks in the diaspora had to approach Africans not only as a people with whom they shared certain experiences—an issue Delany, Crummell, and Turner acknowledged—but also as equals and partners, with whom they shared a common struggle for redemption. There had to be a demonstrable sincerity and commitment to the profession of affinity with Africa. This was not the case with the nationalists in this study. While they embraced Africans as partners in misery, with whom they shared certain negative experiences, they did not accept Africans as partners in struggle. Instead, they turned to the Europeans, the very people they accused of originating and perpetuating the negative experiences. It is not clear from their policies and thought, beyond conjecture, how the adoption of Eurocentric solutions would have elevated Africans and, at the same time, freed and elevated all blacks in the United States.

Wilson J. Moses's recent study fails to advance understanding of the nuances of black American nationalism. On the contrary, he seems to reaffirm the traditional Pan-African paradigm that his earlier writings had questioned. Underscoring the antiquity of Pan-African consciousness among black Americans, Moses writes,

> Black nationalism, from its earliest origins, has been closely associated with the doctrine of Pan-Africanism, the idea that Africans everywhere should work together for their mutual benefit and for the uplift of the mother continent. The ideology of African emigrationism, as expressed by American black nationalists, has seldom attempted to justify itself purely in terms of African American interests. Black nationalist emigrants to Africa have recognized that their moral position would be ill-served if they were to adopt the ruthless expansionist principles of a settler-state. *Thus, American black nationalists have never openly advocated the displacement or oppression of indigenous African populations.* At least in their speeches and writings they have always made the claim of a commitment to the universal improvement of the African condition.[51]

A critical examination and analysis of the nationalist ideas and schemes of Delany, Crummell, and Turner does not sustain Moses's contention. Black American nationalists have indeed "openly advocated the displacement [and] oppression of indigenous African populations." Pan-Africanism, in and of itself, does not import the absence of hegemonic values. Black American nationalists did profess interest in, and concern for the plight of, Africans and did propose cooperation with Africans for mutual upliftment. Yet this "Pan-African" disposition did not deter them from asserting superiority over Africans and advocating cooperation with Europeans that eventuated in the destruction of the sovereignty of African peoples.

It is important, therefore, to stress how contrary to the spirit of Pan-Africanism black American nationalism was during the second half of the nineteenth century. A distinction is pertinent between the rhetoric of Pan-Africanism and black nationalism that Delany, Crummell, and Turner used and the essentially American and anti-Pan-African character of their idiosyncrasies. Despite a strong profession of identity with Africa, they divorced themselves culturally from indigenous Africa. They clothed their bourgeois or middle-class American aspirations in Pan-Negro robes. The study of black nationalism has historically been blurred by this mystique of "PAN." A comprehensive knowledge of the nuances of black nationalism has been clouded by the mystique of an African and black diasporan community of shared experience. The mystique obscures the complexity, diversity, and even the conflicts that informed the experiences of Africans and peoples of African descent in the diaspora.

The push, shape, and essence of colonialism are aptly represented in the alluring descriptions that Delany, Crummell, and Turner gave of the wealth and resources of Africa; in the promises they made to the Europeans about the benefits to be derived from exploiting those resources; in their vilifications of Africans and demeaning caricatures of African traditions, languages, and lifestyles; and in their advocacy of the use of force against Africans coupled with support for policies meant to alienate Africans from their cultural roots. In return for the exploitation and subordination that colonialism entailed, Africans were promised three things—commerce, Christianity, and civilization—"cruel euphemisms," John Oliver Killens insists, "for colonization, exploitation, genocide and slavery."[52] Of the three, only one was capable of yielding tangible material reward—commerce. Even then, the reward would go disproportionately to the Europeans and their black American partners. The impacts of the other two C's could only be ascertained in behavioral and idio-syncratic changes—that is, Africans would be transformed into "civi-lized beings," as conceived in the image formed by the Europeans. Civilizing Africans entailed alienating them from indigenous values and norms, and all three nationalists in this study endorsed this policy without considering the negative and long-term consequences of African cultural alienation. Commerce involved the draining of Afri-can resources and wealth to generate wealth for black Americans and their European partners. The by-product of the successful spread of commerce would, many believed, be the demise of slavery in the United States. Beyond the imposition of European traditions, man-nerisms, and languages, none of the nationalists clearly outlined what tangible benefits would accrue directly to Africans from the exploi-tation of their resources and labor. They all emphasized the tangible rewards that Europeans and black American entrepreneurs would derive. It is therefore plausible to suggest that colonial economic, political, cultural, social, and educational policies were predetermined long before the actual occupation of Africa, and black American na-tionalists, perhaps without quite realizing the full implication of collaboratory nationalism, played a key role in the process.

The ambivalence and contradictions evident in the nationalist ideas and schemes of Delany, Crummell, and Turner suggest a po-tent and complex dimension to the cultural transformation and alien-ation that shaped the black American experience in the New World. Having accepted European notions of progress and civilization as normative, and having been acculturated to see themselves through the images of white society, black Americans had difficulty embrac-ing Africans. They acknowledged Europeans as the bearers of civili-zation, of universal and normative values that Africans should emu-late. Their proximity to Europe became a blessing that set them apart from "primitive" Africa. Consequently, the opportunism, "engage-ment," and imperialism that Clarence Walker discerns in Garveyism had their precedents in late-nineteenth-century black American na-tionalism. Clarence Walker, Valentin Mudimbe, and Anthony Appiah underscore the need to reconceptualize paradigms that have tradi-tionally shaped discourse on the black experience. Although Delany, Crummell, and Turner professed a commitment to the advancement of black/African interests, they connived not only with their own oppressors but also with the despoilers of African sovereignty. The character of black American nationalism, therefore, to echo Clarence Walker (in a different context), was "not one of transcendence but one of engagement" with the oppressors.[53]

Paul Gilroy's study situates the black Atlantic in a context that is at variance with the traditional paradigm of the diaspora experience that presupposes an artificial unity or monolith.[54] Critically analyzing the thoughts of Delany, Blyden, and Crummell, Gilroy underlines the Eurocentric, "Ameri-centric," and "Anglo-centric" values that are often deliberately submerged beneath the mystique of PAN. The complexity of the black Atlantic experience and reality explains the ambivalent reactions and contradictory values in black American nationalism. To expect of black American nationalists absolute and unswerving commitment to Africanism and Pan-Africanism is unrealistic. This expectation assumes a preparedness on their part to sacrifice an equally significant part of their consciousness—the "Ameri-centric" self and identity.

Nineteenth-century black American nationalism therefore entailed a balancing act between the components of a complex, multicultural experience, precipitated by a dialectical interaction between the African, Euro-American, and Anglo-American dimensions of the black experience in the diaspora. The triumph of the Euro- and Anglo-American dimensions, plus the fact that the experience of blacks in the diaspora was influenced by the way indigenous Africans were perceived and treated, created ambivalence in black American thought. While superficially contesting the validity and superiority of the Euro-American world, they sought greater ties with that world by distancing themselves from the traditionalism and "primitivism" of Africa. It seems plausible to argue that the Pan-African impulse of black American nationalism was conflicted by two desires—to realize the elusive American nationality and to effect a distance from the troubling implications of the African identity. The latter was supposed to facilitate the actualization of the former. Black American nationalists who spearheaded the call for an African/black nationality were consequently no less American than their integrationist opponents. Both very much cherished, above all else, the American identity and nationality.

Although Delany, Crummell, and Turner acknowledged their racial identity as blacks of African ancestry, they were less than forthright in asserting ethnic/cultural ties with Africa. On the latter issue, the Euro- and Anglo-American dimensions took precedence. In other words, on ethnicity and culture, they seemed more comfortable with what linked them to Europe and America. All three went to great lengths to underline their compatibility with European values and civilization. Africa seemed like an albatross. The claim of historical and racial identity with Africa was in fact an indirect and convenient means of externalizing and broadening the scope and basis of attempts to realize the American nationality.

Since racism and its concomitant ethnocentrism combined to justify the enslavement and dehumanization of blacks in the New World, race and ethnicity became critical to an understanding of the trajectories of black nationalism. Put differently, black nationalism evolved primarily because of the racially and ethnically conditioned experiences that blacks in general encountered. Blackness and African ethnicity were considerations central to the decision on whom to enslave and dehumanize. To be of African origin was considered primitive and backward. Blackness was, by definition, synonymous with primitivism and inferiority. In its reflective mode, black American nationalism combined race and ethnicity, projecting a strong African consciousness. In the praxis mode, however, it glorified only the Euro-American dimension of ethnicity. That is, the most crucial dynamic of the practical schemes proposed by the nationalists in this study was the construction of an "Anglo-centric" identity. They defined aspirations and goals that were conditioned essentially by their experiences and needs as blacks with European/American connections.

In a recent study, Stephen Burman explores the relationship between race and identity. He identifies two ways in which race creates identity. First, race generates a positive self-conception through the vilification of someone else. When engaged in by a socially powerful group, such a process becomes the basis for exploiting or abusing the group defined as inferior. The result of this process for the vilified group is the creation of a negative identity that is a mirror image of the oppressor's worldview. The second and less noted function is one in which race is self-constructed. Although this process invariably results from the experience of discrimination, it is not necessarily a negative phenomenon. Discrimination is capable of inducing group cultural commonality, and in this way it becomes the product of, and an aid to, political struggle. Cultural affinity becomes both a product of conflict and an inducement for solidarity, and thus generates positive consciousness in the oppressed.[55]

Although Burman's insight is plausible, he ignores an equally significant issue. Undoubtedly the black American experience demonstrates the propensity of discrimination to induce positive identity, cultural affinity, and political engagement. Black nationalism generally has been analyzed in terms of the consciousness of identity and affinity among the members of an oppressed group. While this is true of the domestic black American context, the cultural affinity that evolves is not necessarily exclusive, that is, confined to the oppressed in-group, as defined in racial and ethnic terms (blacks and Africans only). That is, the awareness created by discrimination does not necessarily involve total alienation from the culture of the oppressor class. This is evident in the ideas and schemes of Delany, Crummell, and Turner and in the larger historical debate between separatist and integrative forces among black Americans. Although both were tormented and victimized by slavery and racism, integrationists and separatists responded differently, but neither was willing to give up completely on America. As alienated and angry as black American emigrationists felt, few cherished the idea of a complete break with America. It is, however, in the international or Pan-African context of nineteenth-century black American nationalism that the radicalizing or empowering character of discrimination reveals a curious dilemma. Although the negative experience of slavery and racism induced alienation and protest consciousness, it also produced a corresponding integrative consciousness, reflected in assertions of cultural identity with the oppressor—another kind of cultural affinity! The resulting sense of supracultural authority is then externalized (that is, Europeans and Euro-Americans in alliance with black Americans as a socially and culturally powerful group), and it becomes the basis for exploiting and abusing a subordinate group conceived as inferior (indigenous Africans). Paradoxically, the positive self-construction of race, as a potent weapon against white domination, is accomplished by counterpoising a negative construction that sanctions the denigration of another group.

The contradictions inherent in black American nationalism in the second half of the nineteenth century included both epistemological and existential dimensions. Black American perceptions of Africa derived from Eurocentric cultural lenses. The black American self-perception and sense of identity and heritage betrayed unease with the African connection, a validation of Du Bois's articulation of the problematic of black identity. The critical theoretical postulations of black American nationalism included a set of contradictions—a strong profession of commitment to the defense of Africa, coupled with a reluctance to identify too closely with Africa; a critique and rejection of Eurocentrism, and a frenzied determination to identify with Europeans. The solidarity that Delany, Crummell, and Turner proposed was between black Americans and Europeans. Their nationalist ideas negated the spirit of Pan-Africanism as it later developed, which emphasizes, *a priori*, solidarity between Africa and peoples of African descent in the diaspora. It seems reasonable to characterize late-nineteenth-century black American nationalism as an expression of the worldview and aspirations of a marginalized and alienated elite, anxious to gain the respect, confidence, camaraderie, and acceptance of whites and Europeans by assuming an ambivalent posture of identification with—and alienation from—both Africa and Euro-America.

History certainly has a curious way of repeating itself. One reality of the Atlantic slave trade that both Africans and black Americans are in agreement on is the fact that few Europeans, if any, ventured into the interior of Africa to enslave Africans. African middlemen enslaved their own for sale to the Europeans. However, there is another reality that most Africans and black Americans have difficulty coming to grips with—the fact that the descendants of Africans enslaved in the Atlantic trade became implicated in the second enslavement of Africans—colonialism. The half-century period (1850-1900) of gestation of colonial values preceding the conquest and occupation of Africa was indeed the nadir of black American imperialism, as leading nationalists of the epoch connived with Europeans and stressed the benefits that would accrue from the possession of Africa. That these nationalists may have been dead, or out of the African scene, on the eve of European occupation does not absolve them of complicity in the epochal events that followed.

The most critical and substantive character of late- nineteenth-century black American nationalism, therefore, was not so much its Anglo-Saxon or Anglo-American adaptations, reflected in its assertion of superiority over indigenous Africa, but the extent to which these adaptations implicated black American nationalists in the subversion of Africa's independence. To capture the full essence of nineteenth-century black American nationalism, scholars must advance beyond merely acknowledging its Anglo-Saxon connections. It should not surprise anyone that black Americans, whether nationalists or integrationists, imbibed Anglo-Saxon and Anglo-American cultural traits and values. Their socialization and maturation occurred within a Western cultural milieu. It is, however, their extrapolation of the values derived from this socialization, and the utilization of such values as the basis of redefining their relationship with Africa, that is problematic. The contradictions in black American understanding and interpretation of African societies and values compelled some black Americans to identify with the schemes that ultimately destroyed African sovereignty.

Notes

Note: For full bibliographical information, see the bibliography.

Introduction: Black American Nationalism: Definition, Background, Concepts

1. Gellner, *Nations and Nationalism*, 1.
2. Hutchinson and Smith, eds., *Nationalism*, 4.
3. Essien-Udom, *Black Nationalism*, 6.
4. See Carmichael, *Stokely Speaks;* Carmichael and Vincent, *Black Power;* Lincoln, *Black Muslims;* Morrison, ed., *Writings of Huey P. Newton;* and Van Deburg, *New Day in Babylon*.
5. Pinckney, *Red, Black, and Green*, 1.
6. Blassingame, *Slave Community;* Rawick, *From Sundown to Sunup*.
7. Rabinowitz, ed., *Southern Black Leaders*.
8. See Blaut, *Colonizer's Model;* Lauren, *Power and Prejudice;* Pieterse, *White on Black;* Smedley, *Race in North America*.

Chapter 1. The Cultural Context of Black Nationalism: Racist Ideology and the Civilizing Mission

1. Pieterse, *White on Black*, 34-35.
2. Blaut, *Colonizer's Model*, 21-26, 5.
3. Bolt, "Race and the Victorians," 146.
4. Pieterse, *White on Black*, 45.
5. Quoted in ibid., 40.
6. Smedley, *Race in North America*, 239-41.
7. Quoted in Pieterse, *White on Black*, 46.
8. Ibid., chap. 2. See also Curtin, *Image of Africa*, chap. 15; and Smedley, *Race in North America*, chap. 11.
9. Smedley, *Race in North America*, 166-67.
10. Ibid., 168-69.

11. Quoted in Pieterse, *White on Black*, 34; emphasis in first quotation added.

12. Quoted in Curtin, *The Image of Africa*, 42. See also Jordan, *White over Black*, 253; and Smedley, *Race in North America*, 184.

13. Edward Long, *History of Jamaica* (1774). Cited in Pieterse, *White on Black*, 41.

14. Arendt, *Origins of Totalitarianism*, chap. 6; See also Blaut, *Colonizer's Model;* Bolt, "Race and the Victorians"; Curtin, *Image of Africa;* Lauren, *Power and Prejudice;* Smedley, *Race in North America;* Snyder, ed., *Imperialism Reader*.

15. Arendt, *Origins of Totalitarianism*, 158-59.

16. Magubane, *Ties That Bind*, 52.

17. Liggio, "English Origins of Early American Racism," 1-36. Also see Smedley, *Race in North America*, 52-53.

18. Robinson and Gallagher, *Africa and the Victorians*, 3. See also Bartels, "*Othello* and Africa"; Blackburn, "European Colonial Slavery"; Vaughan and Vaughan, "Before *Othello*"; and Worsley, *Third World*.

19. Robinson and Gallagher, *Africa and the Victorians*, 3. See also Bolt, "Race and the Victorians"; Smedley, *Race in North America;* Curtin, *Image of Africa;* and Arendt, *Origins of Totalitarianism*.

20. Boahen, Ade Ajayi, and Tidy, *Topics in West African History*, 117-18.

21. Worsley, *Third World*, 26-30; Pieterse, *White on Black*, 35. See also Blaut, *Colonizer's Model;* Lauren, *Power and Prejudice;* Smedley, *Race in North America*.

22. Blaut, *Colonizer's Model*, 1, 14-17.

23. Lauren, *Power and Prejudice*, 38.

24. Quoted in Pieterse, *White on Black*, 65. See also Lloyd, ed., *Livingstone;* and Snyder, *Imperialism Reader*.

25. Hannah Arendt, *Origins of Totalitarianism*, 185, 190.

26. Fredrickson, *Black Image*. See also his *White Supremacy and Arrogance of Race;* Newby, *Segregationist Thought;* Cell, *White Supremacy;* and Williamson, *Crucible of Race*.

27. Lauren, *Power and Prejudice*, chaps. 1 and 2.

28. See, e.g., Appiah, *In My Father's House;* McAdoo, *Pre–Civil War Black Nationalism;* Magubane, *Ties That Bind;* Moses, *Golden Age;* Mudimbe, *Invention of Africa;* Rigsby, *Alexander Crummell;* Scruggs, "We the Children."

29. Moses, *Golden Age*, 25.

30. Mudimbe, *Invention of Africa*, 98-134.

31. Walker, *Deromanticizing Black History*, chap. 2.

32. Appiah, *In My Father's House*, 3-27.

33. See, e.g., Moses, *Golden Age;* Stuckey, *Ideological Origins;* Jacobs,

African Nexus; Franklin, *Williams and Africa;* and Williams, "John Henry Smith" and "Attitudes toward Africa."

34. Skinner, *African Americans and United States Policy,* 16.

35. Ibid., 516.

Chapter 2. The Historical Context of Black Nationalism: The Quest for American Nationality

1. McAdoo, "Pre–Civil War Black Nationalism," 1; see also his *Pre–Civil War Black Nationalism,* 1.

2. Moses, *Golden Age,* 16. For other discussions of black nationalism's roots in slavery, see Aptheker, "Consciousness of Negro Nationality to 1900," in his *Toward Negro Freedom,* and *"One Continual Cry";* Draper, *Rediscovery of Black Nationalism;* Loomis, "Paul Cuffe's Black Nationalism," 298-302; McCartney, *Black Power Ideologies;* Miller, "Father of Black Nationalism" and *Search for a Black Nationality;* Ofari, *"Let Your Motto be RESISTANCE";* Pease and Pease, "Black Power"; and Sterling, *Speak Out in Thunder Tones.* Stuckey, *Slave Culture* and *Ideological Origins.*

3. Aptheker, *American Negro Slave Revolts.*

4. Simmons, "Negro Antislavery Movement"; Litwack, *North of Slavery.*

5. Bell, *Survey of the Negro Convention Movement,* "Some Reform Interests of the Negro," and "Expressions of Negro Militancy"; Harding, *There Is a River;* Litwack, *North of Slavery;* Pease and Pease, "The Negro Convention Movement," in Huggins et al., eds., *Key Issues in the Afro-American Experience,* vol. 1, and *They Who Would Be Free;* Quarles, *Black Abolitionists.*

6. Walker, *David Walker's Appeal,* 55-56, 65.

7. Ibid., articles 1 and 2.

8. Aptheker, *"One Continual Cry,"* 54; Stuckey, *Slave Culture,* 123, 135.

9. Fisher, "Lott Cary"; Harris, *Paul Cuffe;* Sherwood, "Paul Cuffe."

10. Garnet, "Address to the Slaves," in Ofari, *"Let Your Motto Be RESISTANCE,"* 149, 152.

11. Brewer, "Henry H. Garnet"; Pease and Pease, *Bound with Them in Chains;* Quarles, *Black Abolitionists;* Schor, *Henry H. Garnet;* Stuckey, *Ideological Origins.* For an opposing view and revisionist critique of Garnet's "Address," see Reed, "Garnet's Address to the Slaves."

13. Garnet, "Speech Delivered at the Seventh Anniversary of the American Anti-Slavery Society, 1840," in Ofari, *"Let Your Motto Be RESISTANCE."*

14. Ofari, *"Let Your Motto Be RESISTANCE";* Schor, *Henry H. Garnet.*

15. Foner and Walker, eds., *Proceedings of the Black State Conventions,* vols. 1 and 2; Bell, *Proceedings of the National Negro Conventions.* See also Bell's *Survey of the Negro Convention Movement.*

16. Horton, *Free People of Color,* 158. The subsequent discussion is also informed by Reed, *Platform for Change,* and Curry, *The Free Black in Urban America.*

17. See, e.g., Delany to Frederick Douglass, 22 March 1853, *Frederick Douglass' Paper,* 11 April 1853. See also Delany's critique of the Fugitive Slave Law in his *Condition,* chap. 16. For detailed discussions of the emigrationist and assimilationist debate among blacks, see Kinshasa, *Emigration vs. Assimilation;* Dick, *Black Protest,* chaps. 1 and 5; and Mehlinger, "Attitude of the Free Negro."

18. See Fehrenbacher, *Slavery, Law, and Politics.*

19. See Delany, *Condition.* See also his "Political Destiny," in Rollin, *Life and Public Services;* Kinshasa, *Emigration vs. Assimilation;* Reed, *Platform for Change,* chap. 5.

20. McPherson, *Negro Civil War,* chaps. 1-5. See also his *Struggle for Equality;* Wesley and Romero, *From Slavery to Citizenship;* and Quarles, *The Negro in the Civil War* and *Lincoln and the Negro.*

21. See, e.g., Cox and Cox, eds., *Reconstruction;* Drago, *Black Politicians and Reconstruction;* Du Bois, *Black Reconstruction;* Franklin, *Reconstruction;* Holt, *Negro Political Leadership;* Rabinowitz, *Southern Black Leaders;* Simkins and Woody, *South Carolina during Reconstruction;* Taylor, *Negro in South Carolina;* Uya, *From Slavery to Public Service;* Wharton, *The Negro in Mississippi;* Williamson, *After Slavery.*

22. Cox and Cox, *Politics, Principle and Prejudice;* Gillette, *Retreat From Reconstruction;* Mandle, *Not Slave, Not Free;* Oubre, *Forty Acres and a Mule;* Perman, *Reunion without Compromise;* Woodward, *Reunion and Reaction.*

23. Woodward, *Strange Career of Jim Crow.* See also Frederickson, *Black Image;* Newby, ed., *Segregationist Thought;* Rable, *No Peace;* and Williamson, *Crucible of Race.*

24. Berry and Blassingame, *Long Memory;* Cohen, *At Freedom's Edge;* Franklin and Moss, *From Slavery to Freedom;* Nieman, *Promises to Keep,* chaps. 1-4.

25. Painter, *Exodusters.* See also Athearn, *In Search of Canaan;* Cohen, *At Freedom's Edge;* Hamilton, *Black Towns and Profit;* Marks, *Farewell We're Good and Gone;* Pease and Pease, *Black Utopia.*

26. Meier, "Emergence of Negro Nationalism," 96.

27. Bell, "Negro Nationalism: A Factor in Emigration" and "Negro Nationalism in the 1850s"; Griffith, *The African Dream,* 15-57; Schor, *Henry H. Garnet,* 150-70. See also Blackett, "Martin R. Delany and Robert Campbell"; Schor, "Frederick Douglass and Henry Highland Garnet." The proceedings of the black state and national conventions of the 1850s clearly establish that emigration was a minority movement. See Foner and Walker, eds., *Proceedings of the Black State Conventions.*

28. Amin, *Class and Nation,* 3.

29. Brown, *Black Man and Negro in the American Rebellion;* Delany, *Condition,* chaps. 6-12; Garnet, "Destiny of the Colored Race," in Ofari, *"Let Your Motto Be RESISTANCE;* Nell, *Services of the Colored Americans;* Walker, *David Walker's Appeal;* Williams, *History of the Negro Race.*

30. Article in *Putnam's Monthly,* summer 1856, quoted in Robinson, *Black Marxism,* 98, emphasis added.

31. Robinson, *Black Marxism,* 99, 105.

32. Perhaps the most vocal critic of the perceived Anglo-Saxon and Anglo-American conspiracy against blacks was Martin Delany. See his "Political Destiny" and "International Policy of the World," in Rollin, *Life and Public Services.* See also Delany to Prof. M.H. Freeman of Avery College, *Weekly Anglo-African,* 1 February 1862.

Chapter 3. Martin Robison Delany: The Economic and Cultural Contexts of Imperialism

1. Draper, "Father of Black American Nationalism"; Ullman, *Delany;* Stuckey, *Ideological Origins;* Fauset, "Rank Imposes Obligations."

2. *Douglass' Monthly,* August 1862, 695.

3. Rollin, *Life and Public Services,* 40.

4. Ullman, *Delany;* Rollin, *Life and Public Services;* Sterling, *Making of an Afro-American.*

5. McCormick, "William Whipper"; Bell, "Moral Reform Society." See also Bell, "National Negro Conventions."

6. Letter in the *North Star,* 15 December 1848. See also his letters and reports to the *North Star,* 3 March, 7 and 14 April, 26 May, 9 and 16 June, and 15 August 1848; and 16 February, 6 and 15 June 1849.

7. "Minutes of the State Convention of the Colored Citizens of Pennsylvania," in Foner and Walker, eds., *Proceedings of the Black State Conventions,* vol. 1, 124.

8. Delany, *Condition,* 154-55, 209.

9. Delany, "Political Destiny," 329. See also Delany's "Appendix," in *Condition;* "Important Movement" (letter to Dr. James McCune Smith), in *Chatham Provincial Freeman,* 29 May 1856; and "Official Report," in Bell, ed., *Search for a Place,* 108-12.

10. Delany to Prof. M.H. Freeman of Avery College, *Weekly Anglo-African,* 1 February 1862.

11. Delany, "Political Aspect of the Colored People of the United States," presidential address to the first annual meeting of the National Board of Commissioners, Pittsburgh, 24 August 1855, *Chatham Provincial Freeman,* 13 October 1855.

12. Delany, *Condition,* 156.

13. Delany, "Political Destiny," 335.

14. Ibid., 332-35. See also Delany, "Important Movement" and *Condition*, chap. 16.

15. Delany, "Important Movement."

16. Bell, *Survey of the Negro Convention Movement.*

17. "Proceedings of the First Convention of the Colored Citizens of the State of Illinois, Chicago, Oct. 6-8, 1853," in Foner and Walker, eds., *Proceedings of the Black State Conventions,* vol. 2, 60. For Delany's response, see "Illinois Convention," *Frederick Douglass' Paper,* 18 November 1853, 1.

18. Delany, "Important Movement."

19. The discussion in this and the following paragraph is drawn from Delany, "Political Events," *Chatham Provincial Freeman,* 5 July 1856.

20. See also Delany's "Political Destiny," and "Appendix," in his *Condition*. Delany reaffirmed the centrality of Africa to the future elevation and economic solvency of a black nationality in his fictional work, *Blake; or the Huts of America,* serialized in *Anglo-Africa Magazine,* January-July 1859, and in *Weekly Anglo-Africa Magazine,* November 1861–April 1862; the work was compiled and published in 1970 by Floyd J. Miller.

21. Delany, *Condition* and "Political Destiny." See also his "Important Movement," "Political Events," and "Political Aspect." Equally important is Delany's response to Frederick Douglass's solicitation of assistance from a white woman, Harriet Beecher Stowe, author of *Uncle Tom's Cabin.* See Delany's letter to Frederick Douglass of 22 March 1853, in *Frederick Douglass' Paper,* 11 April 1853. For a fictional advocacy of emigration, see Delany's *Blake*.

22. Delany, *Condition,* 53, and "Political Destiny," 316-17. See also Delany's "International Policy" and *The Origin of Races and Color.*

23. Delany, "International Policy," 317.

24. Ibid., 326.

25. "Call for a National Emigration Convention," *Chatham Provincial Freeman,* 25 March 1854.

26. Delany, "Official Report." See also Kirk-Greene, "America in the Niger Valley."

27. Eric Williams, *Capitalism and Slavery;* Robinson and Gallagher, *Africa and the Victorians,* chaps. 1 and 2.

28. Delany, "Official Report," 36-38. See also Blackett, "Delany and Campbell."

29. Delany, "Political Destiny," 327-38. See also Delany, "Political Aspect," "Important Movement," and "Official Report," 43.

30. Delany to Prof. M. H. Freeman of Avery College, *Weekly Anglo-African,* 1 February 1862

31. Delany, *Condition,* 172-73, 193, 208; and chaps. 17 and 21, passim. See also his "Political Destiny," 337, 353.

32. Delany, "Domestic Economy," *North Star,* 16 and 23 March, 13 April 1849. See also his *Condition,* chaps. 4 and 5, and "Political Destiny," 353.

33. Delany, *Condition,* 214.

34. Blackett, *Building an Anti-Slavery Wall,* 176-77. See also his "Delany and Campbell," 1-4, 13-15, and "Return to the Motherland."

35. Delany, "Official Report," 43-63; "Martin R. Delany in Liberia," *Weekly Anglo-African,* 1 October 1859.

36. Delany, "Official Report," 64-87, 116-22. See also Kirk-Greene, "America in the Niger Valley," 235-36; and Robert Campbell, "Pilgrimage to My Motherland," 181-201.

37. Delany, "Official Report," 102-6, 109-11

38. Horton, "Double Consciousness," 146-64.

39. Asante, *Afrocentricity.* See also Asante, *Kemet, Afrocentricity, and Knowledge; The Afrocentric Idea;* "The Afrocentric Idea in Education"; and "Racism, Consciousness, and Afrocentricity"; Ziegler, *Molefi Asante and Afrocentricity;* and Keto, *Vision, Identity and Time.* Perhaps one of the most forceful, definitive, and provocative assertions of African identity for black Americans is by Dona Marimba Richards, in her *Let the Circle Be Unbroken.*

40. Lewis and Bryan, eds., *Garvey;* Clarke, ed., *Marcus Garvey;* Rodney, *The Groundings with My Brothers;* Hill, ed., *Walter Rodney Speaks;* Thomas, "Rodney and the Caribbean Revolution."

41. Delany, "Appendix," in *Condition,* 212.

42. Delany, "Official Report," 122-48; Blackett, *Building an Anti-Slavery Wall,* chap. 5, and "Delany and Campbell."

43. Blackett, *Building an Anti-Slavery Wall,* chap. 5, and "Delany and Campbell."

44. Delany, "Official Report," 133-34.

45. Delany, "Official Report," 137-42.

46. Moleah, *South Africa,* chaps. 4 and 5.

47. Delany, "Official Report," 136-37.

48. Davidson, *Search for Africa;* Rodney, *How Europe Underdeveloped Africa.*

49. Martin R. Delany, "Political Economy," *North Star,* March 16, 1849; "Domestic Economy," *North Star,* 23 March, 13 and 20 April 1849. See also his "Prospect of the Freedmen on Hilton Head," in Rollin, *Life and Public Services,* 230-41.

50. Delany, "Moral and Social Aspects of Africa," *Liberator,* 1 May 1863.

51. Rollin, *Life and Public Services,* chaps. 14-19; Ullman, *Martin R. Delany,* chaps. 13 and 14; Sterling, *Making of an Afro-American,* chap. 20.

52. Delany, *Trial and Conviction,* 4.

53. *Charleston News and Courier,* 16 April 1878; Delany to H.R. Latrobe, president, American Colonization Society, 8 July 1878; and Delany to William Coppinger, Charleston, S.C., 18 August 1880, both in Delany file, Cross Cultural Learner's Center, London, Ontario.

Chapter 4. Alexander Crummell: Religious, Moral, and Cultural Legitimation of Imperialism

1. Rigsby, *Alexander Crummell: Pioneer in Nineteenth-Century Pan-African Thought,* 13. Further references to this biography will be cited parenthetically in the text. On Crummell's life, see Du Bois, "Of Alexander Crummell," in *Souls of Black Folk; Moses, Alexander Crummell: A Study and Golden Age;* Scruggs, "We the Children"; and Wahle, "Alexander Crummell: Black Evangelist."

2. See also Stockton, "Integration of Cambridge."

3. Blackett, *Building an Anti-Slavery Wall,* 163-64, 170-72, 188-90; Franklin, *Living Our Stories,* 23-58; Moses, *Alexander Crummell: A Study,* 52-88; Rigsby, *Alexander Crummell: Pioneer,* 54-70.

4. Crummell, "Relations and Duties," 215-84. See also Uya, ed., *Black Brotherhood.*

5. Crummell, "Relations and Duties." See also his "Regeneration of Africa" and "Address to the British and Foreign Anti-Slavery Society," 87-89.

6. Crummell, "Relations and Duties." See also Rigsby, *Alexander Crummell: Pioneer,* and Akpan, "Crummell and His African Race Work."

7. Crummell, "The Duty of a Rising Christian State."

8. Crummell, "Emigration," 405-30; see also his "Regeneration of Africa," 431-54.

9. Crummell, "The Duty of a Rising Christian State," 71-72.

10. Crummell, "Relations and Duties," 219-20.

11. Crummell, "The Duty of a Rising Christian State," 87.

12. Crummell, "Progress of Civilization," 107.

13. Crummell, "Relations and Duties," 222.

14. Crummell, "Our National Mistakes," 167-80.

15. Crummell, "Relations and Duties," 231; emphasis added.

16. Ibid., 244.

17. Crummell, "Progress of Civilization," 107. See also "Relations and Duties," 220.

18. Crummell, "Progress of Civilization," 109-29. See also Crummell, "Address before the American Geographical Society."

19. Crummell, "Progress of Civilization," 107-8.

20. Crummell, "English Language in Liberia," 31.

21. Crummell, "The Progress of Civilization," 107.

22. Crummell, "The Destined Superiority," 46.

23. Crummell, "Address before the American Geographical Society." 316-23.

24. Ibid., 311.

25. July, *History of the African People*, 384-91.

26. Crummell, "Emigration," 415.

27. Crummell, "Regeneration of Africa," 439-40.

28. Scruggs, "We the Children," 21-22.

29. Crummell, "Regeneration of Africa," 435.

30. Ibid., 433-53.

31. Crummell, "Our National Mistakes."

32. Afigbo, "Establishment of Colonial Rule"; Boahen, *Topics in West African History,* chap. 16; Hargreaves, "Partition of West Africa"; Oloruntimehin, "Western Sudan"; Uzoigwe, "European Partition and Conquest of Africa."

33. Crummell, "Our National Mistakes," 181-87; Crummell, "Address before the American Geographical Society," 314-16.

34. Scruggs, "We the Children," 13.

35. Crummell, "Address before the American Geographical Society," 311.

36. Crummell, "English Language in Liberia," 18-21.

37. Curtin, *Image of Africa,* 394.

38. Moses, *Alexander Crummell: A Study,* 295.

39. Du Bois, *Souls of Black Folk,* 3-4.

40. Cesaire, *Discourse on Colonialism;* Fanon, *Black Skin, White Masks;* Gendzier, *Frantz Fanon;* Jinadu, *Fanon;* Memmi, *Colonizer and the Colonized;* Rodney, *How Europe Underdeveloped Africa;* Zahar, *Colonialism and Alienation.*

41. Mazama, "Relevance of Ngugi Wa Thiong'o," 211-12.

Chapter 5. Henry McNeal Turner:
The Cultural Imperative of Imperialism

1. On Turner's life see Ponton, *Life and Times of Henry McNeal Turner;* and Redkey, "Bishop Turner's African Dream."

2. Coulter, "Henry M. Turner"; Angell, *Bishop Henry McNeal Turner.*

3. Coulter, "Henry M. Turner."

4. Ibid., 384-85, 400-406. Also Du Bois, *Black Reconstruction,* 502.

5. Trimiew, *Voices of the Silenced,* 21-35; Turner, "Emigration Convention," 156; Delany, *On National Polity,* 6.

6. Turner, "American Negro and His Fatherland," 167-71.

7. Turner, "American Colonization Society," 43.

8. Ibid., 44.

9. Turner, "Critique of the Atlanta Compromise," 165-66.

10. Turner, "American Colonization Society." See also his "Emigration to Africa," 52-59.

11. Turner, "Planning a Trip to Africa," 83.

12. Turner, "Missionaries to Africa," 50-51. See also "American Colonization Society," 42.

13. Turner, "Eleventh Letter," 120.

14. Turner, "American Colonization Society." See also his "Afro-American Future," 188-91; "Barbarous Decision," 60-69; "Race Mixture and Emigration," 143-44; "American Negro and His Fatherland," 168-71; and "African Emigration Excitement," 135-38.

15. Turner, "Barbarous Decision," 62.

16. Turner, "American Colonization Society," 42.

17. Ibid., 44, emphasis added.

18. Records of the black state and national conventions clearly underscore the unpopularity of colonization and emigration among blacks. See, e.g., Foner and Walker, eds., *Proceedings of the Black State Conventions*, vols. 1 and 2; Litwack, *North of Slavery*, 20-27, 252-62, 272-78; Mehlinger, "Attitude of the Free Negro," 276-301; and McCartney, *Black Power Ideologies*, chap. 2.

19. Turner, "American Colonization Society."

20. Turner, "Missionaries to Africa," 50-51.

21. Turner, "Emigration Convention" and "American Colonization Society."

22. Turner, "Emigration to Africa," 55.

23. Turner, "American Negro and His Fatherland," 167-71; "Emigration to Africa," 52-59; and "Emigration Convention," 145-59. See also Williams, *Role of the Christian Recorder;* Redkey, "Flowering of Black Nationalism," 107-24.

24. Turner, "American Colonization Society," 44.

25. Turner, "Emigration to Africa," 55; see also his "Question of Race," 75.

26. Turner, "Emigration to Africa," 55.

27. Turner, "An Emigration Convention," 147.

28. Turner, "Question of Race," 74. See also Turner, "American Negro and his Fatherland."

29. Turner, "Question of Race," 73; W.E.B. Du Bois, "Back to Africa," in Clarke, ed., *Marcus Garvey*, 117-19; Cyril Briggs, "Decline of the Garvey Movement," in Clarke, ed. *Marcus Garvey*, 176-77.

30. Moses, introduction to *Classical Black Nationalism*, 2-3.

31. Douglass Turner Ward proclaimed himself a slavocentrist, and forcefully defended the slavocentric perspective in his keynote address to the annual meeting of the Southern Conference on Afro-American Studies in Baton Rouge, Louisiana, in February 1995. Stanley Crouch's views are well

articulated in his most recent book, *The All-American Skin Game; or, the Decoy of Race, the Long and the Short of It, 1990-1994* (New York: Pantheon, 1995). Whoopi Goldberg has on many occasions publicly declared her rejection of the African linkage.

32. Richburg, *Out of America*, xiii.

33. Redkey, "Flowering of Black Nationalism."

34. Turner, "Third Letter," in Redkey, *Respect Black*, 93-96.

35. Ibid. See also his "Fourth Letter" and "Fifth Letter," in Redkey, *Respect Black*, 96-105.

36. Turner, "Eleventh Letter," in Redkey, *Respect Black*, 120.

37. Turner, "Afro-American Future," 189-90.

38. Turner, "Eleventh Letter," 120.

39. Turner, "American Negro and His Fatherland," 167.

40. See Redkey, *Respect Black*, 116-33.

41. Turner, "Thirteenth Letter," in Redkey, *Respect Black*, 129-30.

42. Trimiew, *Voices of the Silenced*, 31.

43. Freire, *Pedagogy of the Oppressed*, chap. 2.

44. Turner, "My Trip to South Africa," 178-81, quotation on 179.

Chapter 6. Black American Nationalism and Africa: Ambivalence and Paradoxes

1. Blackett, *Building an Anti-Slavery Wall;* chap. 5.

2. Moses, *Alexander Crummell: A Study;* Oldfield, ed., *Civilization and Black Progress;* Rigsby, *Alexander Crummell: Pioneer.*

3. Moses, *Alexander Crummell: A Study*, 295.

4. Delany, *Condition*, 203, emphasis added.

5. Delany to William Coppinger, Charleston, S.C., 18 August 1880, Delany file, Cross Cultural Learner's Center, London, Ontario.

6. Lauren, *Power and Prejudice;* chaps. 1 and 2; Feuer, *Imperialism and the Anti-Imperialist Mind.*

7. Nabudere, *Political Economy of Imperialism,* chaps. 1, 2, and 3.

8. Magubane, *Ties That Bind,* 26.

9. Worsley, *Third World*, 30.

10. Magubane, *Ties That Bind,* 27.

11. Crummell, "Civilization as a Collateral," 119-24.

12. Turner, "Afro-American Future," 188-89.

13. Crummell, "A Defense of the Negro Race," 87-88.

14. Crummell, "Emigration," 413-14.

15. Du Bois, "Africa, Abused Continent: The Roots of War and Imperialism," in Giosetti, ed., *On Prejudice,* 26-37; Nabudere, *Political Economy of Imperialism;* Offiong, *Imperialism and Dependency;* Rodney, *How Europe Underdeveloped Africa;* Williams, *Destruction of Black Civilization.*

16. For a summary of the contentions of some of the leading scholars of the modernization school, see Offiong, *Imperialism and Dependency,* chap. 2.

17. Curtin, *Image of Africa,* 47.

18. Quoted in Curtin, *Image of Africa,* 241.

19. Ibid., 386.

20. Boahen, ed., *Africa under Colonial Domination;* Crowder, *West Africa under Colonial Rule;* Davidson, *Modern Africa;* Freund, *Making of Contemporary Africa.*

21. Ajayi and Crowder, eds., *History of West Africa,* vol.2; Barkindo, Omolewa, and Maduakor, *Africa and the Wider World;* Ikime, ed., *Groundwork of Nigerian History;* Isichei, *History of West Africa.*

22. Davidson, *Modern Africa;* Freund, *Making of Contemporary Africa;* Isichei, *History of West Africa.*

23. Davidson, *Search for Africa,* 257, emphasis added.

24. Freire, *Pedagogy of the Oppressed,* chaps. 2 and 3.

25. Ibid., 75-118.

26. Williams, "Black American Attitudes toward Africa," 190.

27. Robinson, *Black Marxism,* 257.

28. Semmes, *Cultural Hegemony,* chap. 1.

29. Marx, "The Eighteenth Brumaire of Louis Bonaparte," 398.

30. See, e.g., Williamson, *Crucible of Race;* Fredrickson, *Arrogance of Race;* Smedley, *Race in North America;* and Lauren, *Power and Prejudice.*

31. Williams, "Attitudes toward Africa," 190.

32. Draper, "Father of Black American Nationalism." Also see his *Rediscovery.*

33. McAdoo, *Pre–Civil War Black Nationalism,* 23-46.

34. Fierce, *Pan-African Idea,* 16.

35. Blackett, *Building an Anti-Slavery Wall,* chap. 5.

36. Robinson, *Black Marxism,* 259-60.

37. Jacobs, *African Nexus.*

38. Appiah, *In My Father's House,* chap. 1.

39. Esedebe, *Pan-Africanism: The Idea;* Legum, *Pan-Africanism: A Short Political Guide.*

40. Campbell, "Pan-Africanism and African Liberation," 288, emphasis added.

41. Esedebe, *Pan-Africanism: The Idea,* 45.

42. Jacobs, *African Nexus,* 227.

43. Locke, "Apropos of Africa," 413, emphasis added.

44. Ibid., 412.

45. McAdoo, *Pre–Civil War Black Nationalism,* 23-34.

46. Franklin, *Living Our Stories,* 39. See also Akpan, "Black Imperial-

ism," "African Policy of the Liberian Settlers," and "Liberia and the Origins of the Scramble for West Africa"; Beyan, *American Colonization Society;* Foster, "Colonization of Free Negroes in Liberia"; Rigsby, *Alexander Crummell: Pioneer;* and Shick, *Behold the Promised Land.*

47. Bracey, "Black Nationalism Since Garvey." See also Bracey, Meier, and Rudwick, eds., *Black Nationalism in America,* xxvi-xxvii.

48. Essien-Udom, *Black Nationalism,* 20.

49. Foner, "In Search of Black History," 11.

50. Redkey, *Black Exodus,* 304.

51. Moses, *Classical Black Nationalism,* 11, emphasis added.

52. Killens, *Black Man's Burden,* 11-12.

53. Walker, *Deromanticizing Black History,* 34-55, quotation on 49.

54. Gilroy, *Black Atlantic,* chap. 1.

55. Burman, *Black Progress,* chap. 5.

BIBLIOGRAPHY

Afigbo, A.E. "The Establishment of Colonial Rule, 1900-1918." In *History of West Africa*, vol. 2, ed. J.F. Ade Ajayi and Michael Crowder, 424-83. London: Longman, 1974.

Ajayi, J.F. Ade, and Michael Crowder, eds. *History of West Africa*. Vol. 2. London: Longman, 1974.

Akpan, Monday B. "The African Policy of the Liberian Settlers, 1841-1932: A Case Study of the 'Native' Policy of a Non-Colonial Power in Africa." Ph.D. diss., University of Ibadan, 1968.

———. "Alexander Crummell and His African Race Work: An Assessment of His Contributions in Liberia to Africa's Redemption." *Historical Magazine of the Protestant Episcopal Church* 45 (June 1976).

———. "Black Imperialism: Americo-Liberian Rule over the African Peoples of Liberia, 1822-1964." *Canadian Journal of African Studies* 7, no. 2 (1973).

———. "Liberia and the Origins of the Scramble for West Africa." *Calabar Historical Journal* 1, no. 2 (1976).

Alpers, Edward A., and Pierre-Michel Fontaine, eds. *Walter Rodney, Revolutionary and Scholar: A Tribute*. Los Angeles: Center for Afro-American Studies, 1982.

Amin, Samir. *Class and Nation: Historically and in the Current Crisis*. New York: Monthly Review, 1980.

Angell, Stephen Ward. *Bishop Henry McNeal Turner and the African-American Religion in the South*. Knoxville: University of Tennessee Press, 1992.

Appiah, Anthony K. *In My Father's House: Africa in the Philosophy of Culture*. New York: Oxford University Press, 1992.

Aptheker, Herbert. *American Negro Slave Revolts*. New York: International, 1952.

———. *"One Continual Cry": David Walker's Appeal to the Colored Citizens of the World*. New York: Humanities, 1965.

————. *Toward Negro Freedom: Historic Highlights in the Life and Struggles of the American Negro People from Colonial Days to the Present.* New York: New Century, 1956.

Arendt, Hannah. *The Origins of Totalitarianism.* New ed. New York: Harcourt, Brace, and World, 1966.

Asante, Molefi K. *The Afrocentric Idea.* Philadelphia: Temple University Press, 1987.

————. *Afrocentricity.* Trenton, N.J.: Africa World Press, 1988.

————. *Kemet, Afrocentricity, and Knowledge.* Trenton, N.J.: Africa World Press, 1990.

————. "The Afrocentric Idea in Education." *Journal of Negro Education* 60, no. 2 (1991).

————. "Racism, Consciousness, and Afrocentricity." In *Lure and Loathing: Essays on Race, Identity, and the Ambivalence of Assimilation,* ed. Gerald Early, 127-43. New York: Penguin, 1993.

Athearn, Robert G. *In Search of Canaan: Black Migration to Kansas, 1879-1880.* Lawrence: Regent Press of Kansas, 1978.

Barkindo, Bawuro, Michael Omolewa, and E.N. Maduakor. *Africa and the Wider World.* Lagos, Nigeria: Longman, 1989.

Bartels, Emily C. "*Othello* and Africa: Postcolonialism Reconsidered." *William and Mary Quarterly,* 3d ser., vol. 54, no. 1 (1997).

Bell, Howard H., ed. *Minutes of the Proceedings of the National Negro Conventions, 1830-1864.* New York: Arno Press and the *New York Times,* 1969.

————. *Search for a Place: Black Separatism and Africa.* Ann Arbor: University of Michigan Press, 1971.

————. *A Survey of the Negro Convention Movement.* New York: Arno Press and the *New York Times,* 1969.

————. "The American Moral Reform Society, 1836-1841." *Journal of Negro Education* 27, no. 1 (1958).

————. "Expressions of Negro Militancy in the North, 1840-1860." *Journal of Negro History* 45 (January 1960).

————. "National Negro Conventions in the Middle 1840s: Moral Suasion vs. Political Action." *Journal of Negro History* 42 (October 1957).

————. "Negro Nationalism: A Factor in Emigration Projects, 1858-1969." *Journal of Negro History* 47 (January 1962).

————. "Negro Nationalism in the 1850s." *Journal of Negro Education* 35, no. 1 (1966).

————. "Some Reform Interests of the Negro during the 1850s as Reflected in State Conventions." *Phylon* 21 (summer 1960).

Berry, Mary F., and John Blassingame. *Long Memory: The Black Experience in America.* New York: Oxford University Press, 1982.

Beyan, Amos J. *The American Colonization Society and the Creation of the Liberian State: A Historical Perspective, 1822-1900*. Lanham, Md.: University Press of America, 1991.

Blackburn, Robin. "The Old World Background to European Colonial Slavery." *William and Mary Quarterly*, 3d ser., vol. 54, no. 1 (1997).

Blackett, Richard J.M. *Building an Anti-Slavery Wall: Black Americans in the Atlantic Abolitionist Movement, 1830-1860*. Baton Rouge: Louisiana State University Press, 1983.

————. "Martin R. Delany and Robert Campbell: Black Americans in Search of an African Colony." *Journal of Negro History* 62, no. 1 (1977).

————. "Return to the Motherland: Robert Campbell, a Jamaican in Early Colonial Lagos." *Phylon* 40, no. 4 (1979).

Blassingame, John. *The Slave Community: Plantation Life in the Antebellum South*. Rev. ed. New York: Oxford University Press, 1979.

Blaut, J.M. *The Colonizer's Model of the World: Geographical Diffusionism and Eurocentric History*. New York: Guilford Press, 1993.

Boahen, Adu, ed. *Africa under Colonial Domination, 1880-1935*. UNESCO General History of Africa, vol. 7. Paris: Heinemann, 1985.

Boahen, Adu, Jacob F. Ade Ajayi, and Michael Tiddy. *Topics in West African History*. London: Longman, 1986.

Bolt, Christine. "Race and the Victorians." In *British Imperialism in the Nineteenth Century*, ed. C.C. Eldridge. New York: St. Martin's Press, 1984.

Bracey, John H. "Black Nationalism since Garvey." in *Key Issues in the Afro-American Experience*, vol. 1, ed. Nathan I. Huggins. New York: Harcourt Brace Jovanovich, 1971.

Bracey, John H., August Meier, and Elliott Rudwick, eds. *Black Nationalism in America*. New York: Bobbs-Merrill, 1970.

Brewer, William M. "Henry H. Garnet." *Journal of Negro History* 13 (January 1928).

Briggs, Cyril. "The Decline of the Garvey Movement." In *Marcus Garvey and the Vision of Africa*, ed. John H. Clarke. New York: Vintage, 1974.

Brown, William W. *The Black Man: His Antecedents, His Genius, and His Achievements*. New York, 1853.

————. *The Negro in the American Rebellion: His Heroism and Fidelity*. Boston: Lee Shepard, 1867.

Burman, Stephen. *The Black Progress Question: Explaining the African-American Predicament*. Thousands Oaks, Calif.: Sage, 1995.

Campbell, Horace. "Pan-Africanism and African Liberation." In *Imagining Home: Class, Culture, and Nationalism in the African Diaspora*, ed. Sidney J. Lemell and Robin D.G. Kelley. New York: Verso, 1994.

Campbell, Robert. "A Pilgrimage to My Motherland." In *Search for a Place:*

Black Separatism and Africa, ed. Howard H. Bell, 149-250. Ann Arbor: University of Michigan Press, 1971.

Carmichael, Stokely. *Stokely Speaks: Black Power Back to Pan-Africanism.* New York: Vintage, 1971.

Carmichael, Stokely, and Charles V. Hamilton. *Black Power: The Politics of Liberation in America.* New York: Vintage, 1967.

Cell, John W. *The Highest Stage of White Supremacy: The Origins of Segregation in South Africa and the American South.* Cambridge: Cambridge University Press, 1982.

Cesaire, Aime. *Discourse on Colonialism.* New York: Monthly Review, 1972.

Clarke, John Henry, ed. *Marcus Garvey and the Vision of Africa.* New York: Vintage, 1974.

Cohen, William. *At Freedom's Edge: Black Mobility and the Southern White Quest for Racial Control, 1861-1915.* Baton Rouge: Louisiana State University Press, 1991.

Coulter, E. Merton. "Henry M. Turner: Georgia Negro Preacher-Politician during the Reconstruction Era." *Georgia Historical Quarterly* 48, no. 4 (1964).

Cox, Lawanda, and John Cox, eds. *Politics, Principle, and Prejudice, 1865-1866: The Dilemma of Reconstruction America.* New York: Athenaeum, 1976.

———. *Race, the Negro, and the New South.* Columbia: University of South Carolina Press, 1973.

Crowder, Michael. *West Africa under Colonial Rule.* London: Hutchinson, 1968.

Crummell, Alexander. *Addresses and Proceedings of the Congress on Africa Held under the Auspices of the Stewart Missionary Foundation for Africa.* Atlanta: Gammon Theological Seminary, 1896.

———. *Africa and America: Addresses and Discourses.* 1891. Reprint, New York: Negro University Press, 1969.

———. *The Future of Africa: Being Addresses, Sermons, Delivered in the Republic of Liberia.* New York: Charles Scribner, 1862.

———. *The Greatness of Christ and Other Sermons.* New York: Thomas Whittaker, 1882.

———. "Address before the American Geographical Society." In *Africa and America: Addresses and Discourses,* 307-23. 1891. Reprint, New York: Negro University Press, 1969.

———. "Address to the British and Foreign Anti-Slavery Society." *Anti-Slavery Reporter* 2 (June 1851): 87-89.

———. "Civilization as a Collateral and Indispensable Instrumentality in Planting the Christian Church in Africa." In *Addresses and Proceedings of the Congress on Africa Held under the Auspices of the Stewart*

Missionary Foundation for Africa. Atlanta: Gammon Theological Seminary, 1896.

———. "A Defense of the Negro Race in America from the Assaults and Charges of Rev. J.L. Tucker, D.D., of Jackson, Miss." In *Africa and America: Addresses and Discourses*, 85-125. 1891. Reprint, New York: Negro University Press, 1969.

———. "The Destined Superiority of the Negro." In *Civilization and Black Progress: Selected Writings of Alexander Crummell on the South*, ed. J.R. Oldfield, 43-53. Charlottesville: University of Virginia Press, 1995.

———. "The Duty of a Rising Christian State to Contribute to the World's Well-being and Civilization." In *The Future of Africa: Being Addresses, Sermons, Delivered in the Republic of Liberia*, 57-102. New York: Charles Scribner, 1862.

———. "Emigration, an Aid to the Civilization of Africa." In *Africa and America: Addresses and Discourses*, 409-29. 1891. Reprint, New York: Negro University Press, 1969.

———. "The English Language in Liberia." In *The Future of Africa: Being Addresses, Sermons, Delivered in the Republic of Liberia*, 9-54. New York: Charles Scribner, 1862.

———. "Our National Mistakes and the Remedy for Them." In *Africa and America: Addresses and Discourses*, 167-98. 1891. Reprint, New York: Negro University Press, 1969.

———. "The Progress of Civilization along the West Coast of Africa." In *The Future of Africa: Being Addresses, Sermons, Delivered in the Republic of Liberia*, 105-29. New York: Charles Scribner, 1862.

———. "The Regeneration of Africa." In *Africa and America: Addresses and Discourses*, 431-54. 1891. Reprint, New York: Negro University Press, 1969.

———. "The Relations and Duty of Free Colored Men in America to Africa." In *The Future of Africa: Being Addresses, Sermons, Delivered in the Republic of Liberia*, 215-81. New York: Charles Scribner, 1862.

Curry, Leonard P. *The Free Black in Urban America, 1800-1850: The Shadow of the Dream*. Chicago: University of Chicago Press, 1981.

Curtin, Philip D. *The Image of Africa: British Ideas and Action, 1780-1850*. Madison: University of Wisconsin Press, 1964.

Davidson, Basil. *Modern Africa: A Social and Political History*. 3d ed. London: Longman, 1994.

———. *The Search for Africa: History, Culture, and Politics*. London: Random House, 1994.

Delany, Martin R. *Blake; or, The Huts of America*. 1859.

———. *The Condition, Elevation, Emigration, and Destiny of the Colored People of the United States*. Philadelphia, 1852.

————. *On National Polity*. Charleston, S.C.: Republican Book and Job Office, 1870.

————. *The Origin of Races and Color*. 1879, as *Principia of Ethnology*. Reprint, Baltimore: Black Classic Press, 1991.

————. *Trial and Conviction*. Charleston, S.C., 1876.

————. "The International Policy of the World towards the African Race." In *Life and Public Services of Martin R. Delany*, ed. Frank A. Rollin, 313-27. Boston: Lee and Shepard, 1868.

————. "Official Report of the Niger Valley Exploring Party, 1861." In *Search for a Place: Black Separatism and Africa*, ed. Howard H. Bell, 27-148. Ann Arbor: University of Michigan Press, 1971.

————. "Political Aspect of the Colored People of the United States." Presidential address to the first annual meeting of the National Board of Commissioners, Pittsburgh. *Chatham Provincial Freeman*, 13 October 1855.

————. "Political Destiny of the Colored Race on the American Continent." In *Life and Public Services of Martin R. Delany*, ed. Frank A. Rollin, 327-67. Boston: Lee and Shepard, 1868.

————. "Prospect of the Freedmen on Hilton Head." In *Life and Public Services of Martin R. Delany*, ed. Frank A. Rollin, 230-41. Boston: Lee and Shepard, 1868.

Dick, Robert C. *Black Protest: Issues and Tactics*. Westport, Conn.: Greenwood Press, 1974.

Drago, Edmond. *Black Politicians and Reconstruction in Georgia: A Splendid Failure*. Baton Rouge: Louisiana State University Press, 1982.

Draper, Theodore. *The Rediscovery of Black Nationalism*. New York: Viking, 1970.

————. "The Father of Black American Nationalism." *New York Times Review of Books*, 12 March 1970.

Du Bois, W.E.B. *Black Reconstruction: An Essay toward a History of the Part Which Black Folk Played in the Attempt to Reconstruct Democracy in America*. New York: Russell and Russell, 1935.

————. *The Souls of Black Folk: Essays and Sketches*. Chicago: A.C. McClurg, 1903.

————. "Back to Africa." In *Marcus Garvey and the Vision of Africa*, ed. John H. Clarke. New York: Vintage, 1974.

Early, Gerald, ed. *Lure and Loathing: Essays on Race, Identity, and the Ambivalence of Assimilation*. New York: Penguin, 1993.

Esedebe, Olisawunche. *Pan-Africanism: The Idea and Movement, 1776-1991*. 2d ed. Washington, D.C.: Howard University Press, 1994.

Essien-Udom, E.U. *Black Nationalism: A Search for an Identity in America*. New York: Dell, 1964.

Fanon, Frantz. *Black Skin, White Masks*. New York: Grove, 1965.

Fauset, Jessie. "Rank Imposes Obligations." *Crisis* (November 1926).

Fehrenbacher, Don E. *Slavery, Law, and Politics: The Dred Scot Case in Historical Perspective*. New York: Oxford University Press, 1981.

Feuer, Lewis S. *Imperialism and the Anti-Imperialist Mind*. London: Transaction, 1989.

Fierce, Mildred C. *The Pan-African Idea in the United States, 1900-1919: African-American Interest in Africa and Interaction with West Africa*. New York: Garland, 1993.

Fisher, Miles Mark. "Lott Cary, the Colonizing Missionary." *Journal of Negro History* 7 (October 1922).

Foner, Eric. "In Search of Black History." *New York Review of Books*, 22 October 1970.

Foner, Philip S., and George E. Walker, eds. *Proceedings of the Black State Conventions, 1840-1865*. Vols. 1 and 2. Philadelphia: Temple University Press, 1979.

Foster, William I. "The Colonization of Free Negroes in Liberia, 1816-1835." *Journal of Negro History* 48 (1953).

Franklin, John H. *George Washington Williams and Africa*. Washington, D.C.: Howard University Press, 1971.

———. *Reconstruction: After the Civil War*. Chicago: University of Chicago Press, 1961.

Franklin, John H., and Alfred A. Moss. *From Slavery to Freedom: A History of Negro America*. 7th ed. New York: McGraw-Hill, 1994.

Franklin, V.P. *Living Our Stories, Telling Our Truths: Autobiography and the Making of the African American Intellectual Tradition*. New York: Scribner, 1995.

Fredrickson, George. *The Arrogance of Race: Historical Perspectives on Slavery, Racism, and Social Inequality*. Middletown, Conn.: Wesleyan University Press, 1988.

———. *The Black Image in the White Mind: The Debate on Afro-American Character and Destiny, 1817-1914*. New York: Harper and Row, 1971.

———. *White Supremacy: A Comparative Study in American and South African History*. New York: Oxford University Press, 1981.

Freire, Paulo. *Pedagogy of the Oppressed*. New York: Continuum, 1992.

Freund, Bill. *The Making of Contemporary Africa: The Development of African Society since 1800*. Bloomington: Indiana University Press, 1984.

Gellner, Ernest. *Nations and Nationalism*. Ithaca, N.Y.: Cornell University Press, 1983.

Gendzier, Irene L. *Frantz Fanon: A Critical Study*. New York: Vintage, 1974.

Gillette, William. *Retreat from Reconstruction, 1869-1879*. Baton Rouge: Louisiana State University Press, 1978.

Gilroy, Paul. *The Black Atlantic: Modernity and Double Consciousness*. Cambridge, Mass.: Harvard University Press, 1993.

Giosetti, Daniela, ed. *On Prejudice: A Global Perspective*. New York: Doubleday, 1993.

Griffith, Cyril E. *The African Dream: Martin R. Delany and the Emergence of Pan-African Thought*. University Park: Pennsylvania State University Press, 1975.

Hamilton, Kenneth. *Black Towns and Profit: Promotion and Development in the Trans-Appalachian West, 1877-1915*. Urbana: University of Illinois Press, 1991.

Harding, Vincent. *There Is a River: The Black Struggle For Freedom in America*. New York: Vintage, 1983.

Hargreaves, J.D. "The European Partition of West Africa." In *History of West Africa*, vol. 2, ed. J.F. Ade Ajayi and Michael Crowder. London: Longman, 1974.

Harris, Sheldon H. *Paul Cuffe: Black America and the African Return*. New York: Simon and Schuster, 1972.

Hill, Robert, ed. *Walter Rodney Speaks: The Making of an African Intellectual*. Trenton, N.J.: Africa World Press, 1990.

Holt, Thomas. *Black over White: Negro Political Leadership in South Carolina during Reconstruction*. Urbana: University of Illinois Press, 1977.

Horton, James Oliver. *Free People of Color: Inside the African-American Community*. Washington, D.C.: Smithsonian Institution Press, 1993.

Huggins, Nathan I., et al., eds. *Key Issues in the Afro-American Experience*. Vol. 1. New York: Harcourt Brace Jovanovich, 1971.

Hutchinson, John, and Anthony D. Smith, eds. *Nationalism*. New York: Oxford University Press, 1994.

Ikime, Obaro, ed. *Groundwork of Nigerian History*. Ibadan, Nigeria: Heinemann, 1980.

Isichei, Elizabeth. *History of West Africa since 1800*. London: Macmillan, 1977.

Jacobs, Sylvia M. *The African Nexus: Black American Perspectives on the European Partitioning of Africa, 1880-1920*. Westport, Conn.: Greenwood Press, 1981.

Jinadu, L. Adele. *Fanon: In Search of the African Revolution*. Enugu, Nigeria: Fourth Dimension, 1980.

Jordan, Winthrop D. *White over Black: American Attitudes toward the Negro, 1550-1812*. Baltimore: Penguin, 1968.

July, Robert W. *A History of the African People*. 4th ed. Prospect Heights, Ill.: Waveland, 1992.

Keto, C. Tsehloane. *Vision, Identity, and Time: The Afrocentric Paradigm and the Study of the Past*. Dubuque, Iowa: Kendall/Hunt, 1995.

Killens, John Oliver. *Black Man's Burden*. New York: Simon and Schuster, 1970.

Kinshasa, Kwando M. *Emigration vs. Assimilation: The Debate in the African American Press, 1827-1861*. Jefferson, N.C.: McFarland, 1988.

Kirk-Greene, A.H.M. "America in the Niger Valley: A Colonization Centenary." *Phylon* 22, no. 4 (1962).

Lauren, Paul Gordon. *Power and Prejudice: The Politics and Diplomacy of Racial Discrimination*. Boulder, Colo.: Westview, 1988.

Legum, Colin. *Pan-Africanism: A Short Political Guide*. Westport, Conn.: Greenwood Press, 1976.

Lewis, Rupert, and Patrick Bryan, eds. *Garvey: His Work and Impact*. Trenton, N.J.: Africa World Press, 1991.

Liggio, Leonard P. "English Origins of Early American Racism." *Radical History* 3, no. 1 (1976).

Lincoln, C. Eric. *The Black Muslims of America*. Rev. ed. New York: Kayode, 1973.

Litwack, Leon. *North of Slavery: The Negro in the Free States, 1790-1860*. Chicago: University of Chicago Press, 1961.

Lloyd, B.W., ed. *Livingstone, 1873-1973*. Cape Town: C. Struik, 1973.

Locke, Alain. "Apropos of Africa." In *Apropos of Africa: Afro-American Leaders and the Romance of Africa*, ed. Martin Kilson and Adelaide Hill. Garden City, N.Y.: Doubleday, 1971.

Loomis, Sally. "The Evolution of Paul Cuffe's Black Nationalism." *Negro History Bulletin* 36 (October/November 1974).

McAdoo, Bill. *Pre–Civil War Black Nationalism*. New York: David Walker, 1983.

———. "Pre-Civil War Black Nationalism." *Progressive Labor* (June/July 1966).

McCartney, John T. *Black Power Ideologies: An Essay on African-American Political Thought*. Philadelphia: Temple University Press, 1992.

McCormick, Richard P. "William Whipper: Moral Reformer." *Pennsylvania History* 43 (January 1976).

McPherson, James. *The Negro's Civil War*. New York: Alfred A. Knopf, 1969.

———. *The Struggle for Equality: Abolitionists and the Negro in the Civil War and Reconstruction*. Princeton, N.J.: Princeton University Press, 1964.

Magubane, Bernard M. *The Ties That Bind: African-American Consciousness of Africa*. Trenton, N.J.: Africa World Press, 1987.

Mandle, Jay. *Not Slave, Not Free: The African-American Economic Experience since the Civil War*. Durham, N.C.: Duke University Press, 1992.

Marks, Carole. *Farewell We're Good and Gone: The Great Black Migration*. Bloomington: Indiana University Press, 1989.

Marx, Karl. "The Eighteenth Brumaire of Louis Bonaparte." In *Karl Marx and Friedrich Engels: Selected Works*, vol. 1. Moscow: Progress, 1976.

Mazama, Ama. "The Relevance of Ngugi Wa Thiong'o for the Afrocentric Quest." *Western Journal of Black Studies* 18, no. 4 (1994).

Mehlinger, Louis R. "The Attitude of the Free Negro toward African Colonization." *Journal of Negro History* 1 (July 1916).

Meier, August. "The Emergence of Negro Nationalism," pt. 1. *Midwest Journal* 4 (winter 1951).

Memmi, Albert. *The Colonizer and the Colonized*. Boston: Beacon Press, 1967.

Miller, Floyd J. *The Search for a Black Nationality: Black Emigration and Colonization*. Urbana: University of Illinois Press, 1975.

———. "The Father of Black Nationalism: Another Contender." *Civil War History* 17, no. 4 (1971).

Moleah, Alfred T. *South Africa: Colonialism, Apartheid, and African Dispossession*. Wilmington, Del.: Disa, 1993.

Morrison, Toni, ed. *To Die for the People: The Writings of Huey P. Newton*. New York: Writers and Readers, 1973.

Moses. Wilson J. *Alexander Crummell: A Study of Civilization and Discontent*. New York: Oxford University Press, 1989.

———. *Classical Black Nationalism: From the American Revolution to Marcus Garvey*. New York: New York University Press, 1996.

———. *The Golden Age of Black Nationalism, 1850-1925*. New York: Oxford University Press, 1978.

Mudimbe, Valentin. *The Invention of Africa*. Bloomington: Indiana University Press, 1988.

Nabudere, Dan. *The Political Economy of Imperialism: Its Theoretical and Polemical Treatment from Mercantilist to Multilateral Imperialism*. London: Zed, 1978.

Nell, William C. *Services of the Colored Americans in the Wars of 1776 and 1812*. Boston: Prentiss and Sawyer, 1855.

Newby, Idus. *The Development of Segregationist Thought*. Homewood, Ill.: Dorsey, 1968.

Nieman, Donald G. *Promises to Keep: African Americans and the Constitutional Order, 1776 to the Present*. New York: Oxford University Press, 1991.

Ofari, Earl. *"Let Your Motto Be RESISTANCE": The Life and Thought of Henry H. Garnet*. Boston: Beacon Press, 1972.

Offiong, Daniel A. *Imperialism and Dependency*. Enugu, Nigeria: Fourth Dimension, 1982.

Oldfield, J.R., ed. *Civilization and Black Progress: Selected Writings of Alexander Crummell on the South*. Charlottesville, Va.: University of Virginia Press, 1995.

Oloruntimehin, B.O. "The Western Sudan and the Coming of the French, 1800-1893." In *History of West Africa*, vol. 2, ed. J.F. Ade Ajayi and Michael Crowder. London: Longman, 1974.

Oubre, Claude F. *Forty Acres and a Mule: The Freedmen's Bureau and Black Land Ownership*. Baton Rouge: Louisiana State University Press, 1978.

Painter, Neil I. *Exodusters: Black Migrations to Kansas after Reconstruction*. Lawrence: University of Kansas Press, 1976.

Pease, Jane H., and William H. "Black Power: The Debate in 1840." *Phylon* 29, no. 1 (1968).

————. "The Negro Convention Movement." In *Key Issues in the Afro-American Experience*, vol. 1, ed. Nathan I. Huggins. New York: Harcourt Brace Jovanovich, 1971.

Pease, William, and Jane Pease. *Black Utopia: Negro Communal Experiments in America*. Madison: University of Wisconsin Press, 1963.

————. *Bound with Them in Chains: A Biographical History of the Anti-Slavery Movement*. Westport, Conn.: Greenwood Press, 1972.

————. *They Who Would Be Free: Blacks' Search for Freedom, 1830-1861*. Urbana: University of Illinois Press, 1990.

Perman, Michael. *Reunion without Compromise: The South and Reconstruction, 1865-1868*. Cambridge: Cambridge University Press, 1973.

Pieterse, Jan Nederveen. *White on Black: Images of Africa in Western Popular Culture*. New Haven: Yale University Press, 1992.

Pinkney, Alphonso. *Red, Black, and Green: Black Nationalism in the United States*. London: Cambridge University Press, 1976.

Ponton, Mungo M. *Life and Times of Henry McNeal Turner*. New York: Negro University Press, 1970.

Quarles, Benjamin. *Black Abolitionists*. New York: Oxford University Press, 1969.

————. *Lincoln and the Negro*. New York: Oxford University Press, 1962.

————. *The Negro in the Civil War*. Boston: Little, Brown, 1953.

Rabinowitz, Howard. *Southern Black Leaders of the Reconstruction Era*. Urbana: University of Illinois Press, 1982.

Rable, George C. *But There Was No Peace: The Role of Violence in the Politics of Reconstruction*. Athens: University of Georgia Press, 1984.

Rawick, George P. *From Sundown to Sunup: The Making of the Black Community*. Westport, Conn.: Greenwood Press, 1972.

Redkey, Edwin S. *Black Exodus: Black Nationalists and Back-to-Africa Movements, 1890-1910*. New Haven: Yale University Press, 1969.

————. "Bishop Turner's African Dream." In *Black Brotherhood: Afro-Americans and Africa,* ed. Okon Uya. Lexington, Mass.: D.C. Heath, 1971.

————. "The Flowering of Black Nationalism: Henry M. Turner and Marcus Garvey." In *Key Issues in the Afro-American Experience,* vol. 1, ed. Nathan I. Huggins. New York: Harcourt Brace Jovanovich, 1971.

————, ed. *Respect Black: The Writings and Speeches of Henry McNeal Turner.* New York: Arno Press, 1971.

Reed, Harry. *Platform for Change: The Foundations of Northern Free Black Community, 1775-1865.* East Lansing: Michigan State University Press, 1994.

————. "Henry Highland Garnet's *Address* to the Slaves of the United States of America Reconsidered." *Western Journal of Black Studies* 6 (winter 1982).

Richards, Dona Marimba. *Let the Circle Be Unbroken: The Implications of African Spirituality in the Diaspora.* Trenton, N.J.: Red Sea, 1980.

Richburg, Keith B. *Out of America: A Black Man Confronts Africa.* New York: Basic Books, 1997.

Rigsby, Gregory. *Alexander Crummell: Pioneer in Nineteenth-Century Pan-African Thought.* Westport, Conn.: Greenwood Press, 1987.

Robinson, Cedric J. *Black Marxism: The Making of the Black Radical Tradition.* London: Zed, 1983.

Robinson, Ronald, and John Gallagher. *Africa and the Victorians: The Official Mind of Imperialism.* London: Macmillan, 1961.

Rodney, Walter. *The Groundings with My Brothers.* London: Bogle L'Ouverture, 1969.

————. *How Europe Underdeveloped Africa.* London: Bogle L'Ouverture, 1972.

Rollin, Frank, ed. *Life and Public Services of Martin R. Delany.* Boston: Lee and Shepard, 1868.

Schor, Joel. *Henry H. Garnet: A Voice of Black Radicalism in the Nineteenth Century.* Westport, Conn.: Greenwood Press, 1977.

————. "The Rivalry between Frederick Douglass and Henry H. Garnet." *Journal of Negro History* 44 (January 1979).

Scruggs, Ottey M. "We the Children of Africa in This Land: Alexander Crummell." In *Africa and the Afro-American Experience,* ed. Lorraine A. Williams. Washington, D.C.: Howard University Press, 1977.

Semmes, Clovis E. *Cultural Hegemony and African-American Development.* Westport, Conn.: Praeger, 1992.

Sherwood, Henry Noble. "Paul Cuffe and His Contribution to the American Colonization Society." *Proceedings of the Mississippi Valley Historical Association,* 1912-1913, vol. 6 (1913).

————. "Paul Cuffe." *Journal of Negro History* 8 (April 1923).

Shick, Tom W. *Behold the Promised Land: A History of Afro-American Settler Society in Nineteenth-Century Liberia.* Baltimore: Johns Hopkins University Press, 1980.

Simkins, Francis B., and Robert H. Woody. *South Carolina during Reconstruction.* Gloucester, Mass.: Peter Smith, 1966.

Simmons, Adam D. "Ideologies and Programs of the Negro Anti-Slavery Movement, 1830-1861." Ph.D. diss., Northwestern University, 1983.

Skinner, Elliott P. *African Americans and United States Policy toward Africa, 1850-1924: In Defense of a Black Nationality.* Washington, D.C.: Howard University Press, 1992.

Smedley, Audrey. *Race in North America: The Origin and Evolution of a Worldview.* Boulder, Colo.: Westview, 1993.

Snyder, Louis L. *The Imperialism Reader: Documents and Readings on Modern Expansionism.* New York: D. Van Nostrand, 1962.

Sterling, Dorothy. *The Making of an Afro-American: Martin R. Delany, 1812-1885.* New York: Doubleday, 1971.

————. *Speak Out in Thunder Tones: Letters and Other Writings by Black Northerners, 1787-1865.* Garden City, N.Y.: Doubleday, 1973.

Stockton, C.R. "The Integration of Cambridge: Alexander Crummell as Undergraduate, 1849-1853." *Integrated Education* 86 (March/April 1977).

Stuckey, Sterling. *Ideological Origins of Black Nationalism.* Boston: Beacon Press, 1972.

————. *Slave Culture: Nationalist Theory and the Foundations of Black American Nationalism.* New York: Oxford University Press, 1987.

Taylor, Alrutheus A. *The Negro in South Carolina during the Reconstruction.* Washington, D.C.: ASALH, 1924.

Thomas, Clive Y. "Walter Rodney and the Caribbean Revolution." In *Walter Rodney; Revolutionary and Scholar: A Tribute,* ed. Edward A. Alpers and Pierre-Michel Fontaine. Los Angeles: Center for Afro-American Studies, 1982.

Thornton, A.P. *Doctrines of Imperialism.* New York: Wiley and Sons, 1965.

Trimiew, Darryl. *Voices of the Silenced: The Responsible Self in a Marginalized Community.* Cleveland: Pilgrim, 1993.

Turner, Henry McNeal. "African Emigration Excitement." In *Respect Black: The Writings and Speeches of Henry McNeal Turner,* ed. Edwin S. Redkey, 135-38. New York: Arno Press, 1971.

————. "The Afro-American Future." In *Respect Black: The Writings and Speeches of Henry McNeal Turner,* ed. Edwin S. Redkey, 188-91. New York: Arno Press, 1971.

————. "The American Colonization Society." In *Respect Black: The Writ-*

ings and Speeches of Henry McNeal Turner, ed. Edwin S. Redkey, 42-44. New York: Arno Press, 1971.

———. "The American Negro and His Fatherland." In *Respect Black: The Writings and Speeches of Henry McNeal Turner,* ed. Edwin S. Redkey, 167-71. New York: Arno Press, 1971.

———. "The Barbarous Decision of the Supreme Court." In *Respect Black: The Writings and Speeches of Henry McNeal Turner,* ed. Edwin S. Redkey, 60-69. New York: Arno Press, 1971.

———. "An Emigration Convention." In *Respect Black: The Writings and Speeches of Henry McNeal Turner,* ed. Edwin S. Redkey, 145-60. New York: Arno Press, 1971.

———. "Emigration to Africa." In *Respect Black: The Writings and Speeches of Henry McNeal Turner,* ed. Edwin S. Redkey, 52-59. New York: Arno Press, 1971.

———. "Missionaries to Africa." In *Respect Black: The Writings and Speeches of Henry McNeal Turner,* ed. Edwin S. Redkey, 50-51. New York: Arno Press, 1971.

———. "My Trip to South Africa." In *Respect Black: The Writings and Speeches of Henry McNeal Turner,* ed. Edwin S. Redkey, 178-81. New York: Arno Press, 1971.

———. "Planning a Trip to Africa." In *Respect Black: The Writings and Speeches of Henry McNeal Turner,* ed. Edwin S. Redkey, 83-84. New York: Arno Press, 1971.

———. "The Question of Race." In *Respect Black: The Writings and Speeches of Henry McNeal Turner,* ed. Edwin S. Redkey, 73-75. New York: Arno Press, 1971.

———. "Race Mixture and Emigration." In *Respect Black: The Writings and Speeches of Henry McNeal Turner,* ed. Edwin S. Redkey, 143-44. New York: Arno Press, 1971.

Ullman, Victor. *Martin R. Delany: The Beginnings of Black Nationalism.* Boston: Beacon Press, 1971.

Uya, Okon E., ed. *Black Brotherhood: Afro-Americans and Africa.* Lexington, Mass.: D.C. Heath, 1971.

———. *From Slavery to Public Service: Robert Smalls, 1839-1915.* New York: Oxford University Press, 1971.

Uzoigwe, G.N. "European Partition and Conquest of Africa: An Overview." In *Africa under Colonial Domination, 1800-1935,* ed. Adu Boahen. UNESCO General History of Africa, vol. 7. Paris: Heinemann, 1985.

Van Deburg, William L. *New Day in Babylon: The Black Power Movement and American Culture, 1965-1975.* Chicago: University of Chicago Press, 1992.

Vaughan, Alden T., and Virginia Mason Vaughan. "Before *Othello:* Elizabethan Representations of Sub-Saharan Africa." *William and Mary Quarterly,* 3d ser., vol. 54, no. 1 (1997).

Wahle, Kathleen O'Mara. "Alexander Crummell: Black Evangelist and Pan-Negro Nationalist." *Phylon* 29, no. 1 (1968).

Walker, Clarence E. *Deromanticizing Black History: Critical Essays and Reappraisals.* Knoxville: University of Tennessee Press, 1991.

Walker, David. *David Walker's Appeal to the Colored Citizens of the United States of America,* ed. Charles M. Wiltse. New York: Hill and Wang, 1961.

Weisbord, Robert. "Black America and the Italian-Ethiopian Crisis: An Episode in Pan-Negroism." *Historian* 34 (1972).

Wesley, Charles H., and Patricia Romero. *Afro-Americans in the Civil War: From Slavery to Citizenship.* 2d ed. Cornwells Heights, Pa.: Publishers' Agency, 1976.

Wharton, Vernon L. *The Negro in Mississippi, 1865-1890.* Chapel Hill: University of North Carolina Press, 1947.

Williams, Chancellor. *The Destruction of Black Civilization: Great Issues of a Race from 4500 B.C. to 2000 A.D.* Chicago: Third World Press, 1976.

Williams, Eric. *Capitalism and Slavery.* Andre Deutsch, 1964.

Williams, George Washington. *A History of the Negro Race in America, 1619-1880,* 2 vols. New York, 1882.

Williams, Gilbert A. "The Role of the *Christian Recorder* in the African Emigration Movement, 1854-1902." *Journalism Monograph,* no. 111 (April 1989).

Williams, Lorraine A., ed. *Africa and the Afro-American Experience.* Washington, D.C.: Howard University Press, 1977.

Williams, Walter L. "Black American Attitudes toward Africa, 1877-1900." *Pan-African Journal* 4, no. 2 (1971).

———. "Nineteenth-Century Pan-Africanist: John Henry Smith, United States Minister to Liberia, 1878-1885." *Journal of Negro History* 63 (January 1978).

Williamson, Joel. *After Slavery: The Negro in South Carolina during Reconstruction, 1861-1877.* Chapel Hill: University of North Carolina Press, 1965.

———. *The Crucible of Race: Black-White Relations in the American South since Emancipation.* New York: Oxford University Press, 1984.

Woodward, C. Vann. *Reunion and Reaction: The Compromise of 1877 and the End of Reconstruction.* Boston: Little, Brown, 1951.

———. *The Strange Career of Jim Crow.* New York: Oxford University Press, 1974.

Worsley, Peter. *The Third World.* 2d ed. Chicago: University of Chicago Press, 1970.

Zahar, Renate. *Colonialism and Alienation: Political Thought of Frantz Fanon*. Benin City, Nigeria: Ethiope, 1974.

Ziegler, Dhyana. *Molefi Asante and Afrocentricity: In Praise and Criticism*. Nashville: James C. Winston, 1995.

Newspapers and Periodicals Cited

Anti-Slavery Reporter
The Crisis
Douglass' Monthly
The Frederick Douglass' Paper
The Liberator
Charleston (S.C.) *News and Courier*
New York Times Review of Books
The North Star
Progressive Labor
Chatham Provincial Freeman
Putnam's Monthly
Weekly Anglo-African

INDEX

AAS (African Aid Society), 63
Abeokuta: British interest in
    cotton cultivation in, 62;
    Delany's treaty with, 58, 61
abolitionism, black, 3, 7, 41;
    Crummell on, 74
abolitionism, British, 57, 62, 74
abolitionism, white: Crummell
    and, 82; Delany on, 48
accommodationism, 3, 95–96
acculturation, of black Americans,
    and black Nationalist imperial-
    ism, 79. *See also* double identity
    (African and American)
Africa and Africans, depiction of:
    ambivalence/contradictions in,
    116–17, 118–19; by Crummell,
    76, 77–78, 79, 84, 87–88, 118,
    127; by Delany, 53, 58–59, 67,
    117, 118, 127; by explorers and
    missionaries, 22–25, 58–59; by
    Turner, 96, 99–100, 105–6,
    107–8, 117, 118, 127; by
    twentieth-century Pan-African
    Congress movement, 138
Africa and Africans, identification
    with, 37–38, 39–41, 42, 127–28;
    Delany and, 52–53; individual
    attitude toward America and,
    130; as temporary substitute for

American identity, 113–14; by
    Turner, 96; by twentieth-
    century black nationalists, 136,
    139–40. *See also* double identity
    (African and American);
    emigrationism; Pan-Africanism
African Aid Society (AAS), 63
African languages, 87–89, 90, 91
African Methodist Episcopal
    Church (AMEC), 92, 99, 105,
    109
African Mission, 75
"African Pan-Africanists," 136
Afrocentricity, 60, 130–31. *See also*
    Africa and Africans, identifica-
    tion with
Age of Reason, 15
Ajayi, Jacob F. Ade, 20
American Colonization Society, 57,
    69, 98–99, 141
American identity, 113–14. *See
    also* double identity (African
    and American)
American Revolution, 41
Amin, Samir, 38
Anglo-American and Anglo-Saxon
    conspiracy. *See* global con-
    spiracy
Anthropological Institute of Great
    Britain, 17